"Phil Moore's new commentaries are outstanding: biblical and passionate, clear and well-illustrated, simple and profound. God's Word comes to life as you read them, and the wonder of God shines through every page."

– Andrew Wilson, Author of Incomparable and If God Then What?

"Want to understand the Bible better? Don't have the time or energy to read complicated commentaries? The book you have in your hand could be the answer. Allow Phil Moore to explain and then apply God's message to your life. Think of this book as the Bible's message distilled for everyone."

– Adrian Warnock, Christian blogger

"Phil Moore presents Scripture in a dynamic, accessible and relevant way. The bite-size chunks – set in context and grounded in contemporary life – really make the Word become flesh and dwell among us."

– Dr David Landrum, The Bible Society

"Through a relevant, very readable, up-to-date storying approach, Phil Moore sets the big picture, relates God's Word to today and gives us fresh insights to increase our vision, deepen our worship, know our identity and fire our imagination. Highly recommended!"

– Geoff Knott, former CEO of Wycliffe Bible Translators UK

"What an exciting project Phil has embarked upon! These accessible and insightful books will ignite the hearts of believers, inspire the minds of preachers and help shape a new generation of men and women who are seeking to learn from God's Word."

– David Stroud, Leader of ChristChurch London and author of Planting Churches, Changing Communities

For more information about the Straight to the Heart series, please go to **www.philmoorebooks.com**.
You can also receive daily messages from Phil Moore on Twitter by following **@PhilMooreLondon**.

STRAIGHT TO
THE HEART OF

Peter, John
and
Jude

60 BITE-SIZED INSIGHTS

Phil Moore

MONARCH
BOOKS

Oxford, UK & Grand Rapids, Michigan, USA

Published by Monarch Books
an imprint of
Lion Hudson plc
Wilkinson House, Jordan Hill Road,
Oxford OX2 8DR, England
Email: monarch@lionhudson.com
www.lionhudson.com/monarch

ISBN 978 0 85721 756 1
e-ISBN 978 0 85721 757 8

First edition 2016

Acknowledgments
Unless otherwise marked, scripture
quotations are taken from the *Holy
Bible, New International Version*
Anglicised. Copyright © 1979, 1984,
2011 Biblica, formerly International
Bible Society. Used by permission of
Hodder & Stoughton Ltd, an Hachette
UK company. All rights reserved. "NIV"
is a registered trademark of Biblica.
UK trademark number 1448790. Both
1984 and 2011 versions are quoted in
this commentary.
Scripture quotations marked "King
James Version" taken from The
Authorized (King James) Version.
Rights in the Authorized Version are
vested in the Crown. Reproduced by
permission of the Crown's patentee,
Cambridge University Press.

p. 11: Extract from "2067: The End of
British Christianity" in *The Spectator*
magazine, copyright © The Spectator
magazine, 2015. Used by permission
of *The Spectator* magazine.
p. 48: Extract from *The Pleasures
of God* by John Piper, copyright
© Desiring God Ministries, 1991.
Used by permission of Desiring God
Ministries.
pp. 49–50: Extract from *The Inner Ring*
by C. S. Lewis, copyright © C.S. Lewis
Pte. Ltd. 1949. Extracts reprinted by
permission.
p. 106: Extract from 'Have We
Misread the Bible?' by Steve Chalke
in *Christianity Magazine*, copyright ©
Christianity Magazine, 2014. Used by
permission of Christianity Magazine.
p. 107: Extract from video debate
with Steve Chalke and Andrew Wilson
copyright © Premier Christianity,
2014. Used by permission of Premier
Christianity.
p. 128: Extract from *Surprised by Hope*
by Tom Wright, copyright © Tom
Wright, 2008. Used by permission of
SPCK Publishing.
pp. 147–49: Extract from *Center
Church* by Tim Keller © Tim Keller,
2012. Used by permission of
Zondervan.
pp. 154–55: Extract from *Chasing the
Dragon* by Jackie Pullinger, copyright
© Jackie Pullinger, 1980. Used by
permission of Hodder & Stoughton
religious.
pp. 217–18: Extract from *The Problem
of Pain* by C. S. Lewis, copyright ©
C.S. Lewis Pte. Ltd. 1949. Extracts
reprinted by permission.
pp. 254–56: Extract from sermon
preached by John Piper, 2008. Used by
permission of Desiring God Ministries.

A catalogue record for this book is
available from the British Library.

Printed and bound in the UK, May
2016, LH26

This book is for the leaders of Everyday Church.
Together we are seeing that the Gospel triumphs in the end.

CONTENTS

PART FIVE: TRUE LOVE (2 JOHN AND 3 JOHN)

About the *"Straight to the Heart"* Series

On his eightieth birthday, Sir Winston Churchill dismissed the compliment that he was the "lion" who had defeated Nazi Germany in World War Two. He told the Houses of Parliament that *"It was a nation and race dwelling all around the globe that had the lion's heart. I had the luck to be called upon to give the roar."*

I hope that God speaks to you very powerfully through the "roar" of the books in the *Straight to the Heart* series. I hope they help you to understand the books of the Bible and the message which the Holy Spirit inspired their authors to write. I hope that they help you to hear God's voice challenging you, and that they provide you with a springboard for further journeys into each book of Scripture for yourself.

But when you hear my "roar", I want you to know that it comes from the heart of a much bigger "lion" than me. I have been shaped by a whole host of great Christian thinkers and preachers from around the world, and I want to give due credit to at least some of them here:

Terry Virgo, Dave Holden, Guy Miller, John Hosier, Adrian Holloway, Greg Haslam, Lex Loizides and all those who lead the Newfrontiers family of churches. Friends and encouragers, such as Stef Liston, Joel Virgo, Stuart Gibbs, Scott Taylor, Nick Sharp, Nick Derbridge, Phil Whittall and Kevin and Sarah Aires. Tony Collins, Margaret Milton, Jenny Ward, Jessica Scott and Simon Cox at Monarch books. Malcolm Kayes and all the elders of The

Coign Church, Woking. My fellow elders and church members here at Everyday Church in London. My great friend Andrew Wilson – without your friendship, encouragement and example, this series would never have happened.

I would like to thank my parents, my brother Jonathan and my in-laws, Clive and Sue Jackson. Dad – your example birthed in my heart the passion which brought this series into being. I didn't listen to all you said when I was a child, but I couldn't ignore the way you got up at five o' clock every morning to pray, read the Bible and worship, because of your radical love for God and for his Word. I'd like to thank my children – Isaac, Noah, Esther and Ethan – for keeping me sane when publishing deadlines were looming. But most of all, I'm grateful to my incredible wife, Ruth – my friend, encourager, corrector and helper.

You all have the lion's heart, and you have all developed the lion's heart in me. I count it an enormous privilege to be the one who was chosen to sound the lion's roar.

So welcome to the *Straight to the Heart* series. My prayer is that you will let this roar grip your own heart too – for the glory of the great Lion of the Tribe of Judah, the Lord Jesus Christ!

Introduction: The Gospel Triumphs in the End

I felt compelled to write and urge you to contend for the faith that was once for all entrusted to God's holy people.

(Jude 3)

In June 2015, *The Spectator* magazine ran a feature on the haemorrhaging of the Church across the Western world. Taking the UK as a primary example, it observed that

> *It's often said that Britain's church congregations are shrinking, but that doesn't come close to expressing the scale of the disaster now facing Christianity in this country. Every ten years the census spells out the situation in detail: between 2001 and 2011 the number of Christians in Britain fell by 5.3 million – about 10,000 a week. If that rate of decline continues, the mission of St Augustine to the English, together with that of the Irish saints to the Scots, will come to an end in 2067. That is the year in which the Christians who have inherited the faith of their British ancestors will become statistically invisible... [They are] one generation away from extinction.*[1]

Shifting its gaze further afield, the article notes that the American Church is on a similar trajectory of decline too.

---

[1] Published on 13th June 2015, this article was entitled "2067: The End of British Christianity".

Christianity is in tatters right across the Western world and the article concludes that the Church's day in the developed world may well be done. *The Spectator* is by no means a Christian publication, and yet it urges people to wake up to two forces at work behind the catastrophic failure of Western Christianity. The first is external: an aggressive secularism which hates the Church and is determined to eradicate its historic creed. The second is internal: weak church leaders who are far too willing to dilute the Christian message in order to cling onto their places of influence in an increasingly secular world. *"They're led by middle-managers who are frightened of their own shadows. They run up the white flag long before the enemy comes down from the hills,"* the article concludes. *"It can't be stressed too often that the secularisation that happens inside churches is as important as the sort that happens outside them."*

If there is any truth in this article – and, let's face it, the Church is haemorrhaging across the Western world – then it means we are in desperate need of the six letters written by Peter, John and Jude.[2] Almost all the New Testament letters to the first generation of Christians were written by Paul.[3] He was a tentmaker and he knew how the first generation of believers ought to construct the Church on strong foundations in its early days. By way of contrast, almost all of the New Testament letters to the second generation of Christians were written by Peter, John and Jude.[4] Peter and John were fishermen who knew how to mend nets broken through long periods of fishing. Jude was the son of a carpenter and knew how to fix a wobbly table leg before the whole table fell over. God used these three men to

[2] John technically wrote four letters, not three, if we include Revelation. John tells us that he merely acted as scribe to Jesus in that fourth letter, so I have given it a separate volume in this commentary series.

[3] The only exception is James, written in c.48 AD. Paul wrote his last letter to a church in 61 AD. Thereafter he only wrote to train up Titus and Timothy as leaders for the second generation.

[4] The only exception is the anonymous letter to the Hebrews, written in c.68 AD.

mend the broken Church at a moment when everybody expected it to roll over and die.

Peter, John and Jude may sound a bit like a teenage boy band, but they were a trio of old men who had learned the hard way how to follow Jesus throughout life's ups and downs. God used their personal frailties and failures to teach the second generation of believers how the Gospel triumphs in the end if we remain faithful to his Word.

Peter had been a coward. He talked big but he had run away from danger and denied knowing Jesus on the eve of his crucifixion. When hostility against the Christians began to intensify, he was therefore the perfect man to write **1 Peter** to assure the persecuted believers that they had a **Living Hope** which no amount of suffering could extinguish.

Peter's lessons in cowardice and restoration also made him the perfect man to write **2 Peter** from death row in 65 AD to combat false teachers, who were offering a way to make life easier by accommodating the Gospel to Greek thinking and Greek morals. Peter reminded them that their **Precious Faith** was not theirs to change. The Gospel would triumph over their enemies and their false friends, but only if they refused to exchange the crown jewels of the Gospel for the bric-a-brac imitations of the world.

Jude was one of Peter's teammates. While Peter wrote to the Gentile believers across the world, it appears that Jude wrote a similar message to the Jewish Christians. Since he was the son of Mary and Joseph, who had once mocked the idea of believing that his older half-brother was the Messiah, he was the perfect man to write **Jude** and to urge them to hold on to their **Holy Faith**.[5] They of all people needed to remain faithful to the hope of Israel as it had come to them in Jesus.

By the time John wrote his three letters, between 85 and 93 AD, he was the final survivor of the twelve disciples.

---

[5] Mark 3:21; 6:3; John 7:3–5.

He was therefore the perfect man to write **1 John** and to help the believers keep hold of the **True Knowledge** that God had given them. Even though the Roman persecution was now so systematic and so violent that many of them were dying, and even though the false teachers at work within the Church were becoming more and more determined, if they held onto the truth as they had received it from Jesus then the Gospel would triumph in the end.

He was also the perfect man to write **2 John** and **3 John** to explain what **True Love** meant for the Church. It meant opening wide the door to godly teachers and it meant slamming the door hard on false teachers – even on those who were friends. John is the last writer of the New Testament, so he assures them that, if they hold on to the truth, the Gospel will triumph in the end.

In today's world, where Christian believers are facing increased levels of persecution, we need to understand why Peter calls the Gospel the *"living hope"* that overcomes. In today's world, where false teaching is often accepted and encouraged, we need to understand why Jude *"felt compelled to write and urge you to contend for the faith that was once for all entrusted to God's holy people"*. In today's world, where the commentators seem to agree that the Church will soon succumb to its enemies, we need to understand what made John so sure that the Church would *"overcome them, because the one who is in you is greater than the one who is in the world"*.[6]

These letters could not be more relevant to our generation. Their message could not be more urgent. So let's study them together. Let's allow them to teach us how the Church can survive and thrive in our own day. Faced with enemies on the outside and false friends on the inside, let's not panic. Let's discover how the Gospel triumphs in the end.

---

[6] 1 Peter 1:3; 1 John 4:4; Jude 3.

Part One:

Living Hope

(1 Peter)

God's Doorman (1:1)

*Peter, an apostle of Jesus Christ, to God's elect,
exiles scattered throughout the provinces of Pontus,
Galatia, Cappadocia, Asia and Bithynia.*

(1 Peter 1:1)

The Jewish leaders were very good at slamming doors. In 30 AD, they forced the Roman governor in Jerusalem to drag Jesus out of the city gates and to crucify him outside the city walls. We need to hear the Jewish leaders slamming the door on Jesus if we want to understand Peter's ministry and his letters. God had appointed Peter to be his doorman.

There's a reason Peter is normally pictured holding a bunch of keys in religious iconography. Jesus had singled him out in Matthew 16:16–19, promising to use his confession that *"You are the Messiah, the Son of the living God"* as the solid ground on which to build his Church and as the key with which to open locked doors to the Gospel:

> *Blessed are you, Simon son of Jonah, for this was not revealed to you by flesh and blood, but by my Father in heaven. And I tell you that you are Peter, and on this rock I will build my church, and the gates of Hades will not overcome it. I will give you the keys of the kingdom of heaven; whatever you bind on earth will be bound in heaven, and whatever you loose on earth will be loosed in heaven.*

Seven weeks after the Jewish leaders slammed the door on Jesus, Peter stood up on the Day of Pentecost and pleaded with the crowds to *"Save yourselves from this corrupt nation."* Although most English translations of Acts 2:40 take the Greek word *genea* to mean *generation*, it is often used in the New Testament to refer to the Jewish nation.[1] Peter was deliberately opening a door for Jews to identify with the true Israel of God. That's why he commanded his 3,000 Jewish converts to be baptized in water, a ceremony reserved for Gentile converts to Judaism, as a confession that their Jewish birth had no power to save them. He urged them to confess that their only hope lay in the death and resurrection of the Jewish Messiah.[2]

Three years later, the Jewish leaders slammed the door on Jesus yet again. They stoned Stephen to death and launched such a violent wave of persecution against the Church that the believers were forced to flee Jerusalem. While at the port of Joppa, Peter received a vision from God that convinced him it was time to open the door of salvation to the Gentiles. He confessed freely to a group of Romans in Acts 10–11 that *"It is against our law for a Jew to associate with or visit a Gentile"* but that God had instructed him to preach the Gospel to them all the same. He later told his horrified Jewish friends that *"As I began to speak, the Holy Spirit came on them as he had come on us at the beginning."* Peter's preaching opened the door on the Day of Pentecost for the pagans, proving that *"God does not show favouritism but accepts from every nation the one who fears him and does what is right."*

This was too much for the Jewish leaders. It made them hate the Christian message even more. In 57 AD, they slammed the door on Jesus for a third time. Acts 21:30 tells us that *"seizing*

---

[1] The word *genea* must mean the Jewish *nation* in Matthew 11:16, Mark 13:30, and Luke 17:25 and 21:32.

[2] Peter became an "apostle to the Jews" by opening this door (Galatians 2:8). Paul and John explain more about "true Jews" and "false Jews" in Romans 9:6–9, Galatians 3:16–29 and Revelation 2:9 and 3:9.

Paul, they dragged him from the temple, and immediately the gates were shut." Peter's ministry had already changed significantly from the days when Paul was able to describe him as "an apostle to the Jews". But now we can tell from the opening verses of his first letter that this slammed door made him open the door of salvation even wider to the people of the non-Jewish world.[3]

First, Peter introduces himself as *"an apostle of Jesus Christ".*[4] This does not mean that he has now disowned his role as "an apostle to the Jews". He still opened the door of salvation to any who would listen. It simply means that he has also become far more than this. He has learned to be God's doorman for the Gentiles too.

Second, Peter does not address his letter to a group of Jews. He writes it to Gentile believers in the five Roman provinces in the north of Asia Minor (the first-century name for modern-day Turkey). Pontus, Galatia, Cappadocia, Asia and Bithynia had smaller Jewish populations than the two southern provinces of Lycia and Cilicia, and Peter makes it clear that his readers used to live in pagan ignorance, pagan immorality and a thoroughly pagan lifestyle. Nevertheless, he assures them that they are now the children of Abraham and Sarah: *"Once you were not a people, but now you are the people of God."*[5] Make sure you don't miss this. It is massive. Peter is telling us that, despite the Jewish rejection of the Gospel, it was still marching on.

Third, Peter uses three Greek words that include these Gentile believers in the Jewish story. The word *eklektos* means *chosen* or *elect.* Peter says that God has chosen these Gentiles in

---

[3] Although Paul described Peter this way in 49 AD in Galatians 2:8, he tells us only six years later in 1 Corinthians 1:12 and 9:5 that Peter soon began to open the door of salvation to the Gentiles too.

[4] None of the leaders of the early Church ever disputed Peter's authorship of 1 Peter. It takes 2,000 years of distance to do that. It was quoted as early as 95 AD, in 1 Clement.

[5] For some clear examples, see 1 Peter 1:14, 1:18, 2:9–12, 3:6 and 4:3. Nevertheless, Peter describes these Gentile believers as "the people of God" in contrast to the pagans around them.

the same way that he chose Isaac over Ishmael, Jacob over Esau and the Jewish nation over the pagans. The word *parepidēmos* means a *resident alien* or a *sojourner*. Peter says that God has made these Gentiles citizens of heaven and foreigners on earth, like the patriarchs in Canaan, like the Hebrews in Egypt and like the Jews in Babylon.[6] The word *diaspora* was a technical term for the *scattered Jews* who lived across the Roman Empire. Peter tells these Gentile believers that they have been scattered as God's people all across the world in order to preach the Gospel.[7]

This perspective matters, especially if you live in a Western nation and are tempted to think that the declining Church means that the Gospel has lost its power. Philip Jenkins reminds us that this is not the case in the developing world:

> *Until recently, the overwhelming majority of Christians have lived in white nations, allowing some to speak of "European Christian" civilization... Over the last century, however, the centre of gravity in the Christian world has shifted inexorably away from Europe, southward, to Africa and Latin America, and eastward, toward Asia... By 2050, only about one-fifth of the world's 3.2 billion Christians will be non-Hispanic whites. Soon, the phrase "a white Christian" may sound like a curious oxymoron, as mildly surprising as "a Swedish Buddhist." Such people can exist, but a slight eccentricity is implied.[8]*

GOD'S DOORMAN (1:1)

19

---

[6] Genesis 23:4; 28:4; Exodus 2:22; 23:9; Psalm 39:12; 137:4; Hebrews 11:13.

[7] Jews outside the land of Israel were known as *Diaspora Jews*, based on the Greek word used in the Septuagint translation of Deuteronomy 28:25 and Psalm 147:2. It is used to describe them in James 1:1.

[8] Philip Jenkins in *The Next Christendom: The Coming Age of Global Christianity* (second edition, 2011).

Peter is God's doorman and he says that, whenever people slam the door on Jesus, God always opens up other Gospel doors all around the world.

Peter has barely started his letter. He hasn't even finished his opening greetings. But he has already reminded us that he is God's doorman and that he serves the one who says in Revelation 3:7: *"These are the words of him who is holy and true, who holds the key of David. What he opens no one can shut, and what he shuts no one can open."* Peter's first verse shouts above the sound of many slamming doors that the Gospel always triumphs in the end.

Triangulation (1:2)

... chosen according to the foreknowledge of God the Father, through the sanctifying work of the Spirit, to be obedient to Jesus Christ and sprinkled with his blood.

(1 Peter 1:2)

It's easy to tell where you are in the world if you possess a smartphone. By establishing the position of nearby transmitter masts, a modern phone can work out its own position through triangulation. As long as it determines the location of two or three fixed points, no matter how dark or foggy it may be, it can calculate its own position from them.

Peter wrote this letter in around 62 AD, at a time when the Church was disorientated and reeling.[1] The Jewish high priest had just broken Roman law by callously murdering the leader of the church in Jerusalem. He had taken James to the top of the Temple and, when he refused to deny Jesus, he had thrown him down to his death below. When James survived the fall, his enemies had encircled him and crushed his skull with heavy stones. James was one of Peter's closest friends, so this must have hit him hard, but what hit him harder was the way that many Christians were panicking at the news.[2] That's why he starts his letter with some urgent triangulation. Peter gives us

---

[1] Since it talks about fierce persecution but does not mention slaughter, it must have been written between the execution of James in 62 AD and the launch of Nero's persecution in 64 AD.

[2] James is named as the leader of the church in Jerusalem in Acts 12:17 and 21:18. His murder is described by Josephus in *Antiquities of the Jews* (20.9.1) and Eusebius in *Church History* (2.23.1–25).

three fixed bearings to reassure us that, no matter what, the Gospel always triumphs in the end.

First, Peter tells the believers that they *"have been chosen according to the foreknowledge of God the Father"*. They must not panic at the news that James has been killed, since their God knows the events of history long before each one of them comes to pass. They must not feel isolated and vulnerable, because this same all-knowing God has told them to call him Father. They must not doubt his love for them because, unlike a human father who only meets his newborn baby for the first time at its birth, the Lord has known them since before the dawn of time. He chose to love them and to make them part of his earthly family. They must not panic as a thick cloud of persecution descends on the churches of Asia Minor. Even in their darkest hour, their position never changes. They can still address the Lord God Almighty as their Dad.

Second, Peter reassures the believers that they have been saved *"through the sanctifying work of the Spirit"*. The Greek word here for sanctification is *hagiasmos*, which means *being set apart as holy*. God has therefore chosen to make them his very own people in the midst of a rebellious world. He has demonstrated this by sending his Holy Spirit down from heaven to fill them and to turn them into his earthly home. If they feel weak and fearful, the Spirit will strengthen them with God's own power and make them brave. If they are arrested for their faith, the Spirit will tell them what their Father wishes them to say. If their possessions are confiscated, the Spirit will give them a joy that can never be taken away. If they feel like throwing in the towel on their faith altogether, the Spirit will encourage them by giving them a fresh glimpse of God's glory. He will remind them of their own place in his plans. He will ensure that they can never lose.[3]

---

[3] Matthew 10:19–20; Luke 10:21; John 14:26; Acts 1:8; 4:31; 7:55; 9:31; 13:52; 1 Thessalonians 1:6.

Third, Peter tells the believers that God has chosen them *"to be obedient to Jesus Christ and sprinkled with his blood"*. This Greek word *rhantismos* and its sister words are only ever used in the New Testament to refer to high priests sprinkling sacrificial blood on Temple worshippers to purify and consecrate them to the Lord.[4] Peter is therefore telling his readers that their lives are of incredible importance to world history. They are the ones for whom the Son of God shed his precious blood. They are the ones who have been declared pure and sinless in God's sight, consecrated as holy and obedient work tools in the Messiah's hands.

Like a smartphone determining its position on the earth's surface by triangulating with nearby phone masts, these three factors show us our true position in the world. When we know where we are in relation to God the Father, God the Son and God the Spirit, it tells us where we are in relation to everything else too. This verse is one of the earliest declarations of the Trinity, ranking alongside the command of Jesus in Matthew 28:19 to *"Go and make disciples of all nations, baptising them in the name of the Father and of the Son and of the Holy Spirit,"* but Peter sees it as far more than a statement of theology. He also sees it as a statement of geography. If we have been chosen by the Father, saved through the Son and filled with the Spirit, our position in the world is guaranteed.

You particularly need to hear this if you are a Christian living in the West. It is all very well for Philip Jenkins to remind us in the previous chapter that the Gospel is triumphing in Africa and Asia and Latin America, but what about Europe and North America? I'm sure that Philip Yancey is correct in his remark that *"As I travel, I have observed a pattern, a strange historical phenomenon of God 'moving' geographically from the Middle East to Europe, to North America, to the developing world. My theory is this: God goes where He's wanted"* – but I'm also

---

[4] See Hebrews 9:13, 19, 21; 10:22; 12:24.

pretty sure that he is wrong.[5] Is God any less my Father if I am a European? Is Jesus any less my Saviour if I am Canadian? Is the Holy Spirit any less available to me if I am German? If the answer to these three questions is "no" then Peter wants us to see that our fundamental position hasn't changed. God has not "moved on" from our nations. We simply need to tell him that we want him and that our churches want him too. We simply need to triangulate our position correctly and to cry out for the Gospel to triumph in Western nations too.

That's why I love the opening greeting in both of Peter's letters. It is similar to the one used by Paul and yet it is subtly different. It literally translates *"May grace and peace be multiplied to you."*[6] It reminds us that God does not need ration books to dole out his diminishing reserves of blessing. He is not the God of meagre rationing but the God of lavish multiplying! He can work more in Asia, Africa and Latin America without needing to work any less in Europe and North America. So away with foolish ideas about God having "moved on"! Our position in his purposes remains the same.

If you are going through a difficult season personally, like Peter when he lost his close friend James, then let the Father, Son and Spirit help you triangulate your true position. If you are going through a difficult season in your church, like Peter's friends in Asia Minor, let the Father, Son and Spirit help you triangulate your church's position too. Let the three Persons of the Trinity open your eyes to your place in their perfect plan. Let them multiply the grace and peace of God to you today.

1 PETER: LIVING HOPE

---

[5] The Christian author said this in an interview with *Christianity Today* magazine (5th February 2001).

[6] Paul normally begins his letters, *"Grace and peace to you from God our Father and from our Lord Jesus Christ."*

Alive and Kicking (1:3–12)

In his great mercy he has given us new birth into a living hope through the resurrection of Jesus Christ from the dead.

(1 Peter 1:3)

When most people think of the word "hope", they tend to think of optimism, the cheery self-assurance that life has to get better. We hope that it won't rain on a Bank Holiday Monday. We hope that our team will win the trophy this year. We hope that things will not turn out as all our past experience leads us to expect.

That's not at all what Peter means by hope. When he assures us that the Gospel will triumph, it isn't wishful thinking. He is not a fisherman putting a brave face on a storm he knows his small boat cannot handle.[1] When he talks about hope in his opening greeting, it is so tangible that it stirs him into ten verses of excited worship. Peter's hope in the Gospel is based on real facts in real history. He tells us that the Christian hope is very much alive and kicking.

In 1:3–4, Peter tells us that the Christian hope is based on the resurrection of Jesus from the dead. The Greek poet Theocritus claimed that *"For the living there is hope, but for the dead there is none."*[2] Peter tells us that this claim has been demolished through the Gospel. It is *"a living hope"* because it is the message that God has triumphed over the grave. Peter was an eyewitness to the death and resurrection of Jesus, even if the

---

[1] Hebrews 6:19 uses this metaphor, assuring us *"We have this hope as an anchor for the soul, firm and secure."*

[2] Theocritus wrote this in c.270 BC in his Idylls (4.42).

second generation of believers that he was writing to were not. He had seen Jesus robbed of any earthly hope and reduced to a lifeless corpse inside a tomb. He had seen Jesus raised to life after three days, dealing death a mortal blow and overcoming every weapon in the Devil's arsenal. Peter assures us that the Christian hope is therefore not mere optimism. It is a certain trust that the one who has overcome death cannot be defeated by anything.

We are apt to forget this. All too often we treat Christianity as our own work for Jesus. Peter reminds us that it isn't about human reform or resolutions; it is about divine resurrection and rebirth.[3] It is God's announcement that *"in his great mercy he has given us new birth into a living hope through the resurrection of Jesus Christ from the dead, and into an inheritance that can never perish, spoil or fade."* Through faith we have been united with Jesus: we have been crucified with him, buried with him, raised to new life with him and exalted to heaven to reign with him. Our hope is alive and kicking because Jesus is.

In 1:4-5, Peter explains what this means for us in the present. Being permitted to call God our Father conveys more than intimacy. It also conveys inheritance. It means that God has adopted us in Jesus to be heirs to his Kingdom – just as Julius Caesar adopted Augustus, Augustus adopted Tiberius, Tiberius adopted Caligula and Claudius adopted Nero. The high priest who murdered James could not defeat the church in Jerusalem. He would be deposed by the Romans within the year. Nor could those who were persecuting the Christians in Asia Minor defeat the churches there. The fact that Jesus is alive acted as a living guarantee of their security. He guards our inheritance in heaven and he guards our churches on earth.[4] Anybody who attacks

---

[3] The Greek word *anagennaō*, meaning *to be born again*, is only used in the New Testament in 1:3 and 23. However, note how much this echoes the teaching of John 3:1–8. Peter and John were very good friends.

[4] The Greek word *tēreō* in 1:4 is used to describe Peter being *guarded* by Roman soldiers in Acts 12:5–6. The Greek word *phroureō* in 1:5 is used to

God's resurrection people will soon discover that they have picked a fight with the wrong foe.

In 1:5–9, Peter explains what this means for us in the future. Although persecution and trials are undeniably painful, the pain is nothing compared to the glory which will be ours when Jesus is revealed as Lord at the end of time.[5] On that day, we will thank God for the trials that forced us to rely on him and that made our faith even stronger, like a goldsmith subjecting precious metal to great heat in order to remove any last vestiges of dross in his refiner's fire.[6] Peter commends the believers in Asia Minor for responding to persecution with love, faith and great joy.[7] He reassures them that their trials are deepening God's work of salvation in their souls.[8]

In 1:10–12, Peter explains what this means for us with regards to the past. He tells us that the Old Testament prophets longed to know more about the living hope which is now our daily lifestyle. They experienced something of Jesus when they prophesied about the Messiah (note how Peter deliberately describes the third Person of the Trinity as *"the Spirit of Christ"*).[9] Nevertheless, men like Isaiah and Ezekiel knew that their great visions of God were simply warm-up acts for the far greater vision which would be ours when the Messiah finally came. They had to accept that they could only see from afar the living hope which would be enjoyed by a later generation. Peter tells

describe troops *guarding* the city of Damascus in 2 Corinthians 11:32.

[5] Our living hope gives us an eternal perspective that makes our trials, not just bearable, but a reason to rejoice. Peter practises what he preaches in Acts 5:40–41. See also 2 Corinthians 4:17 and Acts 16:23–25.

[6] Peter takes this metaphor right out of the Old Testament. See Psalm 66:10; Isaiah 48:10; Malachi 3:3.

[7] Note the echo of John 16:20–24, 20:24–29 and 21:15–19. As I said, Peter and John were great friends.

[8] Peter repeatedly tells us in this letter that on the one hand we have been saved and that on the other hand God still wants to work out his salvation fully in our lives. Our salvation is both now and not-yet.

[9] Peter will explain more about the inspiration of the Old Testament Scriptures in 2 Peter 1:20–21.

us that we are that generation. The living hope is ours. What Isaiah and Jeremiah and Ezekiel longed to experience is what should now be bread-and-butter Christianity.[10]

That would be amazing enough, but Peter then goes one step further. He says that even angels are unable to understand this living hope in the way we do. They have never sinned, so they can never know salvation. That's one of the reasons we never find them proclaiming the Gospel after the resurrection of Jesus. An angel breaks Peter out of prison and commands him to preach the Gospel to the Jews, but he does not join him. Another angel appears to Philip and tells him to preach the Gospel to an Ethiopian on the desert road, but he does not go along for the ride. An angel appears to Cornelius and tells him that he needs to hear the Gospel, but he does not preach it to him personally. Instead, he tells him where to find Peter because Gospel preaching isn't the privilege of angels. It is the privilege of the sinful humans God has chosen to save.[11]

Make no mistake about it: the Christian message isn't wishful thinking. It is a living hope based on concrete facts about the death and resurrection of God's Son. It is a hope that transforms our present and our future and our past. It declares that Jesus has triumphed over the grave and that he will triumph over every other enemy in the end.

---

[10] See Matthew 11:11, where Jesus says that the New Covenant grants the least of us a better experience of God than the greatest believer under the Old Covenant.

[11] Acts 5:18–20; 8:26; 10:1–6. Many Greek manuscripts do not contain the word *"your"* in the *"your souls"* of 1:9. If that is correct, then Peter is telling us in 1:9 that our faith ought to result in the salvation of many souls.

Going to Our Heads (1:13–2:3)

Therefore, with minds that are alert and fully sober,
set your hope on the grace to be brought to you when
Jesus Christ is revealed at his coming.

(1 Peter 1:13)

Peter wasn't a philosopher. He was a fisherman. He wasn't interested in academia but in action. That's why he stops after ten verses of general talk about the Christian hope and turns them into a springboard for practical Christian teaching. Peter starts 1:13 with the Greek word *dio*, which means *therefore*, because the Gospel cannot change us if it remains theological theory. It has to have a therefore. Like fine wine, it has to go to our heads.

In 1:13–16, Peter tells us that the Gospel has to transform the way we think. He commands us literally to *"Gird up the loins of your mind."* Men wore long tunics in the ancient world, so when they needed to run they would tuck the skirts of their tunic into their belts so that nothing would hinder their legs from moving fast. Peter says that we must do the same thing with our minds. A better paraphrase of his command is *"Get your mind ready for action."* In case we are unsure how to do this, he explains with four further commands: *"be sober"*, *"set your hope"*, *"do not conform"* and *"be holy".*[1]

The Gentile believers in Asia Minor had been brought up

---

[1] The word *nēphō*, meaning *to be sober*, is used only six times in the New Testament. Three of them are in 1 Peter 1:13, 4:7 and 5:8. Peter is determined to teach us to let the Gospel, rather than wine, go to our heads.

in ignorance, so they naturally pursued the evil longings that proceeded from their evil thoughts. Now Peter pointed out that their worldview has changed. They have more insight than any Old Testament prophet or any angel, and their insight needs to transform their daily lives. Peter loves action but he is not an activist. He does not believe that people are changed by what they do. He believes that godly living always flows out of godly thinking. He quotes from the book of Leviticus to help the Gentile believers understand that they are now living in the Jewish story. Six times the Lord told the Israelites at Mount Sinai to *"Be holy, because I am holy."*[2] They failed to obey because they failed to grasp the living hope that was prophesied to them. If we let our death and resurrection with Jesus go to our heads, it will make us live each day as the obedient children God now says we have become.

In 1:17–21, Peter tells us that when the Gospel goes to our heads it transforms the way we view the world. His readers had been taught to see the empty lifestyle of their pagan parents as normal. Their faith in Jesus ought to make it now feel very strange and foreign. Peter says they are *"resident aliens"* or *"sojourners"* in a pagan land, like the Hebrew patriarchs in Canaan, like the Hebrew slaves in Egypt and like the Hebrew fugitive Moses in Midian.[3] If they see themselves as having been united with Jesus in his death, resurrection and ascension, they will see everything else differently too. They will see this world as Egypt. They will see Jesus as the Passover Lamb whose blood redeems them. They will see their life on earth as an Exodus from Egypt to the Promised Land.

This is revolutionary. It is only 62 AD. The Temple is still standing in Jerusalem. Gentile believers are still made to feel subtly inferior to Jewish ones. Peter therefore repeats the

---

[2] Leviticus 11:44, 45; 19:2; 20:7, 26; 21:8.

[3] The Greek word *paroikia* in 1:17 and its sister words are used to describe people *sojourning* in 1 Peter 2:11, Acts 7:6, 7:29 and 13:17, and Hebrews 11:9. It is not the same word as *parepidēmoi* in 1:1.

message that he preached to Cornelius and his Roman friends in Acts 10:34. He assures the Gentile believers that God is *"no respecter of faces"*.[4] He is just as much their Father and they are just as much part of the people of God as the Jewish believers. Until Jesus returns, he encourages them to *"live out your time as foreigners here in reverent fear."*[5]

In 1:22–2:3, Peter tells us that when the Gospel goes to our heads it transforms the way we feel. In some Greek manuscripts he commands us to *"love one another deeply from a pure heart."* In others he simply commands us to *"love one another deeply, from the heart."* Either way, it's clear that Peter expects our living hope to change our emotions. Having told us in 1:8 that the Gospel produces, not just nodding heads, but an inexpressible joy in our hearts, Peter also tells us that it produces an intense love for anyone else for whom Jesus died. If we claim to believe the Gospel but have no love for those around us, Peter warns us that we have not truly understood the Gospel at all.[6]

Only when the Gospel goes to our heads does Peter say our hearts will be changed. He echoes John's gospel when he tells us that our salvation originated with the Holy Spirit entering our hearts and bringing us to new birth, not with our own decision or human willpower. The same Holy Spirit who implanted the living embryo of Jesus in a virgin's womb has implanted the living Word of God into our hearts so that the likeness of Jesus will grow inside us.[7] Peter backs this up with a quotation from

---

[4] Although Peter is making a general point here about God's character (Matthew 22:16; Romans 2:11; Galatians 2:6; Ephesians 6:9; Colossians 3:25), he is also giving specific reassurance to Gentile believers.

[5] Peter reminds them that God appointed Jesus to be Saviour before the dawn of time (Revelation 13:8). Their faith in the Jewish Messiah who pre-dates Jewish history easily offsets their lack of Jewish ancestry.

[6] The Greek word *philadelphia* in 1:22 speaks specifically about love for our Christian brothers and sisters, but this will also naturally spill over into love for unbelievers.

[7] The Greek word *anagennaō*, meaning *to be born again*, is only ever used in the New Testament in 1 Peter 1:3 and 23. However, Peter's words are closely

Isaiah 40:6–8 that emphasizes the powerlessness of humans and the power of God's Word. He assures us that our hope in the living Word of God can never result in dead emotion. It will always change our hearts and create in us an active love for one another.

Peter describes this love in detail. He tells us that it leaves no room for wickedness, for deception, for playacting, for petty jealousies or for gossip and backbiting. If we have been united with Jesus in his death, resurrection and ascension, we do not need to fight over the things of this world. Everything is ours in Jesus. Peter quotes from Psalm 34:8 to encourage us that we have merely had a first taste of the Lord's goodness. It is meant to make us long for more. Love causes us to crave the pure milk of the Word of God, like newborn babies, so that we can experience our salvation fully.[8] The Gospel is not a package that we can acquire as a one-time spiritual transaction. It births us into a lifetime of experiencing the living hope of Jesus more and more every day.

All of this poses a question: Is the Gospel truly a living hope to you? Has it really changed the way you think, the way you view the world and the way you feel? Has it transformed your daily lifestyle or does it still remain an abstract concept to you? Peter urges us to get our minds ready for action. It's time to let the Gospel go to our heads.

---

linked to the teaching of John 1:12–13 and 3:1–8.

[8] The Greek word *logikos* in 2:2 is the adjective of the noun *logos*, meaning *word*. Peter isn't therefore talking about "pure spiritual milk" so much as the "pure milk of God's Word".

Partway Through the Story
(2:3–12)

> *You are a chosen people, a royal priesthood, a holy*
> *nation, God's special possession... Once you were*
> *not a people, but now you are the people of God.*
>
> (1 Peter 2:9–10)

Have you ever walked in on a group of friends who are partway through watching a movie and decided to join them? It isn't easy to follow everything that is going on. You need somebody to explain the story so far. The same is also true if we want to understand what Peter is saying in these verses.

The Gentile believers in Asia Minor already knew Peter's story.[1] They already knew the story of the Jewish nation in the Old Testament. They didn't make the mistake of thinking that God's plans revolved around them. We need to remember this ourselves, because Peter tells us in these verses that we are partway through a much bigger story.

First, Peter reminds us in 2:3–4 that we are stepping into his own story. When he first met Jesus, he was a profoundly unstable fisherman named Simon. One minute he hailed Jesus as Lord; the next he contradicted him and was rebuked as a messenger of Satan. One minute he nodded at the command to turn the other cheek to our enemies; the next he hacked off a man's ear with his sword. One minute he promised to stand by Jesus till the end; the next he ran away and denied that he even

---

[1] Peter wrote from Rome (5:13) but he lists the five provinces in the order they were visited by a traveller heading north from Israel because he preached there en route from Jerusalem to Corinth (1 Corinthians 9:5).

knew him. Nevertheless, Jesus had renamed him Peter, which means Rock, and had promised to turn him into the solid kind of person he could build with. He told him that *"I have prayed for you, Simon, that your faith may not fail. And when you have turned back, strengthen your brothers."*[2]

Peter is answering the prayer even as he writes these verses. The Gentile believers felt powerless in the face of persecution for their faith. They felt that they could never see the same Gospel breakthrough in their region as a man like Peter. They felt just like us when we lament that we live in a difficult time and place in Church history, or when we fantasize about what it would be like if we possessed the same power as Peter and his friends. Peter tells us that we do. He was not special. He was just as weak as you and I. He had to tell people to stop putting him on a pedestal, because *"I am only a man."* Peter tells us that his life was transformed when he discovered Jesus as *"the living Stone"*. That was the only reason he was able to become a rock with which Jesus could build, and it is why we are equally able to become *"living stones"* with which he can build too. Peter tells us that his story is our story. We simply need to live by the same faith as him.[3]

Second, Peter reminds us in 2:5–8 that we are stepping into the story of God's Temple. He quotes from Isaiah 28:16, Psalm 118:22 and Isaiah 8:14 in order to show us that Jesus is far greater than King Solomon and that he is building a far greater Temple.[4] The Old Testament prophesied that the Jewish nation would reject Jesus, the Living Stone, and that the Temple in Jerusalem would be destroyed, but it also prophesied that God would build himself a better Temple, with the Messiah as the cornerstone.[5]

---

[2] Matthew 5:39; 16:16–23; 26:33–35, 56, 69–75; Luke 22:31–32; John 18:10–11; 1 Peter 5:10.

[3] Acts 3:12; 4:13; 10:26; 14:15. See also 2 Corinthians 10:10; James 5:17.

[4] Luke 11:31. Peter chooses a selection of verses. He might just as easily have chosen Zechariah 4:7 and 10:4.

[5] Peter uses the Greek word *petra* when he refers to Jesus in 2:8 as a *rock* of offence to the Jewish nation. Even when people slam the door on Jesus, he

Peter tells us that God is therefore doing this through us. We are living stones in his new Temple.[6] Our churches are God's house, our church members are his holy priests and our church activities are his Temple sacrifices.[7] We need to remember this when unbelievers despise our churches and when believers start to give up on organized Christianity. Peter tells us that individualism is sin. God has called us to come together as the building that takes centre stage in history to bring him glory.

Third, Peter reminds us in 2:9–12 that we are stepping into the story of Israel. Unless you know the Old Testament, this is where the storyline gets confusing. Peter's words are a quotation from Exodus 19:5–6, where the Lord speaks a mission statement over Israel at the foot of Mount Sinai. These were two of the most important verses for the Jewish nation, but Peter tells us that they now belong to any follower of Jesus. We are now God's *chosen people*. We are now God's *royal priesthood*. We are now God's *holy nation*. We are now God's *special possession*. We are now *the people of God*. It isn't hard to see why Peter and his friends were persecuted by the leaders of the Jewish nation! Peter is not saying that the Church has replaced Israel in God's plans. He is saying that the story of Israel carries on, but that Jews can choose to step out of it by rejecting their Messiah and that Gentiles can choose to step into it by accepting him.

Each of these phrases from Exodus 19:5–6 requires some explanation. When Peter repeats three times that God has chosen us to be his holy people, he is telling us that our true citizenship is now in heaven. We are no longer Americans or Africans or Europeans who happen to be Christians. Our primary identity

---

reassures us that God is still completely in control.

[6] The Devil loves it when Christians give up on the Church. Paul says more about God's plan to unite us together into his Temple in 1 Corinthians 3:16–17, 2 Corinthians 6:16 and Ephesians 2:19–22.

[7] Peter warns us in 2:5 that no amount of activity can win our churches favour with God. Even our worship and obedience are only acceptable to God through the blood of Jesus. It is about grace from start to finish.

is that we are Christians and our ethnicity is secondary. As a result, Peter is able to tell the Gentile believers in Asia Minor that they are *"foreigners and exiles"* in their own homeland. He is able to say that their own relatives and countrymen have become *"pagans"* to them. They might have started out life as pagans but they have now stepped into Israel's story.[8]

When Peter tells us that we are a royal priesthood, he is saying we have been called to succeed where the Jewish nation failed. They were meant to be an army of Gospel preachers, acting as kings wielding God's power and as priests holding out God's forgiveness to the world. Instead, they left the roles of king and priest to professionals. They were better at slaughtering and rejecting Gentiles than they were at inviting them to step into Israel's story. Peter is warning us not to succumb to the same lazy self-centredness as ancient Israel. Each of us is God's king and priest to the unsaved world.

When Peter tells us that we are now God's special possession, he is using a technical Greek word which referred to the private treasure collections of ancient kings.[9] God spoke this word over Israel whenever he wanted to emphasize how much he loved them. We may not feel as if we have much value. We may be tempted to throw in the towel. But God assures that he delights in us far more than any miser delights in his gold.

This is the story that we are part of. This is the story that we have joined partway through. The more we understand what God has already done and said so far in the story, the more we will see what he wants us to do here and now. A proper understanding of our place in God's great story changes our perspective completely. With promises like these, it isn't hard to see why the Gospel always triumphs in the end.

---

[8] Peter is not directly quoting from Hosea 1:6–10 and 2:23, but he appears to have these verses in mind, just as Paul does when he quotes them in Romans 9:26.

[9] It translates the Hebrew word *segūllāh*, which is used in 1 Chronicles 29:3, Ecclesiastes 2:8, Exodus 19:5, Deuteronomy 7:6, 14:2 and 26:18, Psalm 135:4 and Malachi 3:17. See also Ephesians 1:14 and Titus 2:14.

Fishing Lessons (2:9–12)

Live such good lives among the pagans that, though they accuse you of doing wrong, they may see your good deeds and glorify God on the day he visits us.

(1 Peter 2:12)

Let's face it. We are in the midst of an evangelism disaster. We simply aren't seeing very many people saved. A recent British survey asked believers *"When did you make your first personal response to Christ?"* The answers make for sobering reading. Twenty-nine per cent of people were converted as children and a further 41 per cent were converted as teenagers. In other words, many of the children in Christian households are being saved but very few unbelieving adults are. Only 30 per cent of conversions are of people old enough to have left school.[1]

The British survey gets even bleaker when it looks at those adult conversions. Over half of them took place before the respondent had reached the age of twenty-five. Only 2 per cent of people said they were converted after the age of forty-five. However difficult the Gentile believers in Asia Minor found their persecution, they would have been flabbergasted at our evangelistic famine. In many ways we need Peter's words even more than they did.

Peter was a fisherman. When Jesus called him and his fishing partners to follow him, he used a fishing metaphor to promise in Mark 1:17: *"Come, follow me, and I will make you fishers of men."* Sure enough, Peter became one of the most

[1] This data comes from a survey by the UK Evangelical Alliance in 2014, entitled *Time for Discipleship?*

fruitful evangelists the world has ever seen. When he opened God's door of salvation for the Jews on the Day of Pentecost, he saw 3,000 converted by a single sermon. When he took a lead in the church in Jerusalem, *"the Lord added to their number daily those who were being saved."* When he travelled around Judea, *"many people believed in the Lord."* When he opened God's door of salvation for the Gentiles at the house of Cornelius, *"the Holy Spirit came on all who heard the message."*[2] I am pointing this out in case you need convincing that Peter is qualified to help us respond to our evangelism crisis. I want to help you see that Peter deserves your rapt attention for his fishing lessons in these verses.

First, Peter tells us that we need to *live good lives*. He addresses us as soldiers, telling us that our sinful desires make us our own worst enemy. They wage war against our soul, robbing us of our own daily experience of salvation and making the unbelievers around assume that they have no need of our message of salvation. Broken nets will catch no fish and half-hearted Christians will catch no converts. But listen to the wonderful promise in Peter's command to *"Live such good lives among the pagans that, though they accuse you of doing wrong, they may see your good deeds and glorify God on the day he visits us."* Peter promises us that, if we let the truth of the Gospel go to our heads, our godly way of life will overcome our persecutors. It will attract them to Jesus and ensure that they are saved with us when he returns from heaven on the Final Day.[3]

Let's take Peter seriously. Let's listen to Mahatma Gandhi when he rebuked a British missionary for lamenting that India had rejected Christ: *"I don't reject Christ. I love Christ. It's just that so many of you Christians are so unlike Christ. If Christians would really live according to the teachings of Christ, as found in the Bible, all of India would be Christian today."*

---

[2] Acts 2:41, 47; 4:4; 5:14; 6:7; 9:42; 10:44.

[3] *"The day of visitation"* in 2:12 is an Old Testament phrase referring to the Day of Judgment.

Second, Peter tells us that we need to live our good lives in the world. Good nets are useless unless they are thrown into the water, so we need to live *"good lives **among the pagans**"*. This is surely part of our problem. As Christians, we have become cocooned in our own church communities. We work with unbelievers, we live next door to unbelievers and we walk past unbelievers every day, but we have lost sight of the fact that we are called to live good lives among them. We see them as distractions, as irritants, even as enemies. We have forgotten that people come to know God as part of a process and that the first stage in the process is seeing God at work in his people. Jesus left heaven and came into the world to reach us. Now he calls us to leave our churches and to go into the world to save others.

Third, Peter tells us that we need to *proclaim the Gospel*. Ours is a generation which loves to quote Francis of Assisi: *"Preach the gospel; if necessary use words."* Quite apart from the fact that Francis of Assisi never said it (the quote was misattributed to him at some point in the 1990s), it is plainly ridiculous. The only reason that we have a living hope in Jesus is that somebody explained it to us. The only way that others will share that living hope is if we explain it to them too. That's why Peter tells us that God saved us for a reason: *"that you may declare the praises of him who called you out of darkness into his wonderful light"*.[4] It's what Peter means when he tells us God has appointed us to be his priests: we are to bring the needs of the world before him in urgent prayer and to bring the words of God before the world in urgent proclamation. We must not make the same mistake as ancient Israel by leaving this task to the professionals. God has called each one of us to pass on to others the living hope which is within us.

Peter knew that fishing is all about the moment of truth.

---

[4] The Greek word *aretai* in 2:9 means literally that we are to declare God's *virtues*. This refers to witnessing in our communities as well as to worshipping in our churches.

Ensuring that our nets are good and are thrown into deep water is only the prelude to real fishing. There comes a moment when we have to pull on the net to see whether we have caught anything. Unless we do this we aren't fishing, we are merely pleasure-boating. When did you last use words to share the living hope of Jesus with an unbeliever? We do this with our children. That's why the survey reveals that many of them are being saved. If we are less diligent outside the home, we cannot be surprised that people fail to respond to a message they have not heard.

Fourth, Peter tells us that we need to *demonstrate the Gospel*. We aren't just priests. We are *royal* priests. In other words, we have authority to assert God's Kingdom wherever we go. Peter modelled this for us by gaining an eager hearing for the Gospel in Jerusalem and Judea by healing the lame, the ill and the demonized. Before we complain that he was an apostle and we are not, he interrupts us: *"Why does this surprise you? Why do you stare at us as if by our own power or godliness we had made this man walk?"*[5] Our problem is not that we are not Peter. It's that we lack Peter's faith that Jesus is Lord.

Peter has given us a simple remedy for our evangelism crisis. If we live godly lives so that unbelievers can see them, proclaiming and demonstrating the living hope we have in Jesus, we will discover that God is still eager to save many unbelievers of all ages through us today. We will discover that this is how the Gospel has always triumphed throughout Church history. We will see it triumph in the same way through us today.

---

[5] Acts 3:11–16. See *Straight to the Heart of Acts* for more on how we can see people healed too.

Victims and Victors
(2:11–3:7)

It is God's will that by doing good you should silence the ignorant talk of foolish people.

(1 Peter 2:15)

We live in a world of phobias. Accusations fly around of homophobia, Islamophobia, transphobia or xenophobia. It is hardly surprising, therefore, that some followers of Jesus claim to be the victims of Christianophobia. Although it's nowhere near late-first-century levels, public hostility towards Christians is definitely on the rise and how to respond to it is one of the most testing questions facing the Church today. We need to listen very carefully to what Peter says about our choice to act as victims or as victors.

In 2:11–17, Peter speaks to those who are being persecuted by the government for their faith. Since the Roman authorities only began to execute Christians for their faith in the summer of 64 AD, Peter must be talking about subtler types of persecution, such as losing jobs or being fined or flogged or ostracized by society. The Roman historian Tacitus tells us that the Christians were *"a class hated for their abominations"*. He records an incident in 57 AD when a woman's life was ruined because of her conversion to *"foreign superstition"*.[1] Peter therefore teaches the believers in Asia Minor how to respond.

Peter's response is surprising. He tells the believers that they must not cast themselves in the role of victim. They are

[1] Tacitus in his *Annals of Imperial Rome* (13.32 and 15.44).

victors. They are to demonstrate their faith that Jesus is Lord by submitting to the Roman emperor and his governors as the officers that God himself has appointed.[2] They must not use their Christian freedom to defy the government or even to despise it behind closed doors. Peter commands them to *"Show proper respect to everyone, love the family of believers, fear God, honour the emperor."*[3] They are not to see themselves as victims and to start talking about rebellion. They are to see themselves as victors and to start trusting in the resurrection.

Peter tells the believers that their greatest enemy is not the Roman government but their old ways of thinking. These sinful desires wage war against their souls, making them act with open aggression as rebels or with passive aggression as embittered victims.[4] Neither of these two roads leads to anywhere good. Instead, Peter promises in 2:12 and 2:15 that if we gladly walk the path of suffering with Jesus, then we will triumph through his resurrection power. *"It is God's will that **by doing good**"* we should silence our accusers and turn our enemies into believers.[5] During one of the fiercest bouts of Roman persecution, Tertullian observed that Peter's words were true:

> *Your cruelties merely prove our innocence of the crimes you charge against us. That's why God allows us to suffer. When you recently chose to hand a Christian girl over*

---

[2] The Greek word *hēgemōn* in 2:14 means *procurator* or *governor*. This was the office held by Pontius Pilate and by the rulers of the Roman provinces of Asia Minor. These verses echo Romans 13:1-7.

[3] The call to respect *"the family of believers"* alongside national rulers might be to challenge those who had stopped attending church to escape persecution. We are not just to attend church. We are to *love* the church.

[4] The Greek word *sarkikos* refers to the desires *of the flesh* or *of the old nature* which died with Jesus on the cross. Paul talks about this in Galatians 2:20 and Colossians 3:3.

[5] Do you want to know God's will for your life? Be careful what you wish for. God answers you in 2:15.

to a brothel-keeper rather than to the lions, you showed you know we hate impurity more than punishment and death... The more you mow us down, the more we grow. The blood of the martyrs is the seed of the church... Who sees us die without enquiring why we do so? Who, after enquiry, does not embrace our teaching? And after embracing it, who does not desire to suffer with us?... For this reason, we would like to thank you for passing sentence on us... Whenever we are condemned by you, we are acquitted by the Most High.[6]

In 2:18–25, Peter speaks to slaves, who had more reason than anyone to feel that they were being victimized.[7] They were the legal property of their masters and were commonly mistreated. When they converted to Christ, their unbelieving masters often hated them for having ideas above their station. Nevertheless, Peter tells the Christian slaves that their fear of God should result in glad submission to their masters, even to the bad ones – especially to the bad ones. Jesus is not just our Saviour. He is also our example. *"To this you were called, because Christ suffered for you, leaving you an example, that you should follow in his steps."* Peter therefore quotes five times from the song of the Suffering Servant in Isaiah 53.[8] He tells the Christian slaves that if they gladly choose the way of suffering with Jesus, then they will experience his resurrection power. As they count themselves victors instead of victims, they will see the Gospel triumph in the end.

This teaching is far from easy, but it is essential. It is what Jesus means when he tells us to *"Love your enemies, do good to*

---

[6] Tertullian in c.197 AD in his *Apology* (chapter 50), having tested Peter's words for 135 years.

[7] The Greek word *oiketēs* in 2:18 refers to free domestic servants as well as to domestic slaves.

[8] Although he paraphrases in 2:22–25, Peter appears to quote from Isaiah 53:4, 5, 6, 7 and 9.

those who hate you, bless those who curse you, pray for those who ill-treat you. If someone slaps you on one cheek, turn to them the other also." It is also what Paul means when he tells us, "Do not be overcome by evil, but overcome evil with good."[9] Everything within us wants to fight back, but we cannot act as victims and victors at the same time. That's why Peter began this passage by warning us that the biggest battle lies within our hearts.[10] It takes great faith for us to walk the death-and-resurrection road.

In 3:1–7, Peter addresses Christian women who are married to unbelieving husbands. Married women had rights but, however hard it is to be married to an unbeliever today, it was incalculably more difficult in the first century. Peter's command is the same. Don't play the role of victim; be a victor. Walk the road of suffering with Jesus and believe that the Gospel will triumph in the end. He tells Christian women to submit to their unbelieving husbands (he clarifies in Acts 4:19 and 5:29 that they can say "no" if their husbands command them to sin). He tells them to make themselves attractive to look at and even more attractive to live with, trusting that their godly lifestyle will eventually convince the rest of their household that their living hope is real.

Nobody is saying this is easy. They are simply saying it is true. The nineteenth-century evangelist D. L. Moody observed the same thing as Tertullian and testified that

> *If the whole Church of God could live as the Lord would have them live, why Christianity would be the mightiest power this world has ever seen. It is the low standard of Christian life that is causing so much trouble... If we just live in our homes as the Lord would have us, an*

---

[9] Luke 6:27–29; Romans 12:21.

[10] Most failures in this battle stem from our refusal to take Peter seriously in 2:11. We fool ourselves that our sinful desires are fun and harmless, when they are like traitors on the day of battle within our city walls.

even Christian life day by day, we shall have a quiet and silent power proceeding from us that will constrain them to believe on the Lord Jesus Christ. But an uneven life, hot today and cold tomorrow, will only repel. Many are watching God's people.[11]

---

[11] D. L. Moody in his book *Secret Power* (1881). Paul also agrees with Peter in Titus 2:3–10.

How to Lose Friends and Influence People (3:1–7)

... like Sarah, who obeyed Abraham and called him her lord. You are her daughters if you do what is right and do not give way to fear.

(1 Peter 3:6)

There is no doubt about it. Peter really knows how to lose friends and influence people. In seven short verses he manages to offend just about everybody. We notice it more here than we did when he was talking about slaves and governors because he addresses more live issues for our culture, so let's stop for a moment and consider why he acts in such an overtly offensive way. Let's catalogue some of his most outrageous statements and then let's consider three big reasons why he makes them. As we do so, Peter wants to train us in how to influence people in a culture that is hostile towards Christianity.

Peter tells wives to submit to their husbands (3:1 and 5). He tells them to obey their husbands like Sarah when she addressed Abraham as her lord (3:6).[1] He tells husbands to be considerate towards their wives and to *"treat them with respect as the weaker partner"* (3:7).[2] This alone is enough to get many readers hot under the collar, but Peter refuses to backpedal. He says that men and women are equal in value (3:7) but that

---

[1] Peter must be referring to Genesis 18:12. At other times Sarah was not such a paragon of godly submission.

[2] Peter does not specify in what ways women are weaker than men, so the natural inference is physical strength. Since both are heirs of God's Kingdom, we may assume that their spiritual strength is equal.

equality does not mean that they are exactly the same.[3] In stark contrast to the military language which he uses when addressing men throughout his letter, he tells Christian women that God wants them to have *"a gentle and quiet spirit"* (3:4).[4] He says that Christian men must lead their households lovingly and that Christian women must submit gladly to their lead. Peter knows what he is doing. He does not pull his punches.

Just in case he has not thoroughly offended us already, he has another go. He says that women should not let themselves go physically after they get married. They must pursue beauty instead of bling. They must try to be gorgeous rather than simply glamorous.[5] Their correct response to a culture that is obsessed with outward beauty is not to be outwardly dowdy, but to make the most of their external looks while paying even greater attention to the importance of their internal character. Sarah was so beautiful that Abraham lied that she was his sister out of fear that men might murder him to marry her, yet Peter points out that her true beauty was on the inside. He tells us that this is the kind of beauty that God is primarily seeking. Peter might have given these instructions to the young men who showed off their lithe bodies on the sports fields of Asia Minor, but instead he challenges women about how they look. He models courage to us. He tells us that we have to be willing to lose friends to influence people.

Are you offended yet? I hope you are at least a little,

---

[3] Like Paul in Ephesians 5:22–23, Peter emphasizes that women are to submit to their own husbands and not to men in general. This is teaching about male leadership within marriage, not in general. 1 Peter 1:17 and Galatians 3:28 both emphasize that men and women are of equal value, despite their differing roles.

[4] The Greek word *praüs* means *meek* or *humble*. The word *hēsuchios* means *quiet* or *tranquil*.

[5] Peter is not forbidding certain hairstyles or clothes or items of jewellery. He is simply telling us not to be obsessed with them like the pagans. Our beauty is not to come from what we wear but from who we are. See also 1 Timothy 2:9–10.

because I certainly am. If the Bible does not offend us in places, then either we are perfect or we have closed our ears to what God wants to say. That's why I find it helpful that Peter urges us in 3:6 to *"do what is right and do not give way to fear"*. If we want to be spokespeople for God in an unbelieving world, we need to face up to our fear of saying things that those around us find offensive. I can see three big reasons why Peter says such offensive things here.

First, Peter wants to model for us how to respond when the culture around us becomes increasingly hostile towards Christianity. He teaches us not to allow the outrage of unbelievers to make us doctor the message God has given us to say. John Piper asks us,

> *Are there any significant biblical teachings that have not been controversial? I cannot think of even one, let alone the number we all need for the daily nurture of faith. If this is true, then we have no choice but to seek our food in the markets of controversy... We do not have the luxury of living in a world where the most nourishing truths are unopposed. If we think we can suspend judgment on all that is controversial and feed our souls only on what is left, we are living in a dreamworld. There is nothing left. The reason any of us thinks that we can stand alone on truths that are non-controversial is because we do not know our history or the diversity of the professing church. Besides that, would we really want to give the devil the right to determine our spiritual menu by refusing to eat any teaching over which he can cause controversy?*[6]

Second, Peter wants to warn us that persecution does not just come as the iron fist of physical threat. It also comes wearing

---

[6] John Piper says this in *The Pleasures of God* (1991).

the velvet glove of subtle peer pressure. C. S. Lewis highlights
this danger very helpfully:

> *The prophecy I make is this. To nine out of ten of you the*
> *choice which could lead to scoundrelism will come, when*
> *it does come, in no very dramatic colours. Obviously*
> *bad men, obviously threatening or bribing, will almost*
> *certainly not appear. Over a drink, or a cup of coffee,*
> *disguised as a triviality and sandwiched between two*
> *jokes, from the lips of a man, or woman, whom you have*
> *recently been getting to know rather better and whom*
> *you hope to know better still – just at the moment when*
> *you are most anxious not to appear crude, or naïf or a*
> *prig – the hint will come. It will be the hint of something*
> *which the public, the ignorant, romantic public, would*
> *never understand: something which even the outsiders*
> *in your own profession are apt to make a fuss about, but*
> *something, says your new friend, which "we" – and at*
> *the word "we" you try not to blush for mere pleasure –*
> *something "we always do."*
>
> *And you will be drawn in, if you are drawn in, not*
> *by desire for gain or ease, but simply because at that*
> *moment, when the cup was so near your lips, you cannot*
> *bear to be thrust back again into the cold outer world.*
> *It would be so terrible to see the other man's face – that*
> *genial, confidential, delightfully sophisticated face – turn*
> *suddenly cold and contemptuous, to know that you had*
> *been tried for the Inner Ring and rejected. And then, if*
> *you are drawn in, next week it will be something a little*
> *further from the rules, and next year something further*
> *still, but all in the jolliest, friendliest spirit... Of all the*
> *passions, the passion for the Inner Ring is most skilful in*

making a man who is not yet a very bad man do very bad things.[7]

Third, Peter wants to teach us that we have to be willing to lose friends if we truly want to influence people. He reminds us in 3:7 that the Gospel is *"the gracious **gift of life**"*. People only believe the Gospel when the Holy Spirit enters their heart and grants them the gift of rebirth, not when a clever Christian shows them that it isn't really all that bad and they should give it a try. When we speak, the primary listener is God, on the lookout for people who fear him more than the outraged faces of the world. He is looking for those who know that the Gospel will advance through his power or not at all. That's the kind of courage through which the Gospel triumphs in the end.

---

[7] This essay entitled "The Inner Ring" appears in his book *The Weight of Glory* (1949).

The Christian's Secret Weapon (3:7)

Husbands, in the same way be considerate as you live with your wives… so that nothing will hinder your prayers.

(1 Peter 3:7)

Anybody watching Babur on the morning of 21st April 1526 would have had to conclude that the man was an idiot. He had invaded India with only 15,000 men and his spies were telling him that the Sultan of Delhi had 150,000 men on the other side of the battlefield. He had brought no war elephants with him but his spies informed him that the Sultan had at least 300. What was more, he was leaving great gaps in the makeshift barricades which protected his tiny army. This was clearly a man who knew nothing about how to win a military victory.

The Sultan of Delhi commanded his troops to advance and break through the holes in Babur's barricades. His massed troops and his war elephants shook the ground like an earthquake, but the greatest tremor of the day was yet to come. Babur was not an idiot. He had a secret weapon which would overturn the odds that were stacked high against him. The strange gaps in his barricades were for twenty-four cannons, a new superweapon that the people of India had not yet seen. At the first sound of his guns, the elephants panicked and stampeded back over the Sultan's advancing soldiers. The army broke and fled, the Sultan was killed, the Battle of Panipat was over and the Mughal Empire had begun. Babur's secret weapon had changed everything for him.

If we are going to walk the path of death and resurrection with Jesus in the face of fierce persecution, we are going to need a secret weapon too. Peter tells us in 3:7 that we have one. That's why we do not need to charm our way to victory by making our message bland and inoffensive. We may look feeble, but Peter assures us that we are on the winning side, just as long as nothing hinders our secret weapon from opening fire.

Peter had used this weapon to devastating effect himself during the first few years of Church history. He led the believers in constant prayer and, as persecution intensified, he encouraged them to pray even more. His enemies were even more surprised than the Sultan of Delhi at the sight of Babur's cannons when they saw that the Christian Gospel was advancing instead of dying. They found no explanation other than the fact that *"these men had been with Jesus"*.[1] Peter is therefore not telling us to love our persecutors and to preach the Gospel in all its outrageous glory because he is naïvely oblivious to battlefield realities. He is an old veteran who wants to teach a new generation of believers to succeed in the same way that he did. He says that prayer is the Christian's secret weapon. It enables us to lay hold of the gunpowder of heaven.

But there is a condition. Gunpowder must be kept dry for it to make any difference on the battlefield. In the same way, Peter warns us in 3:7 that the way husbands live with their wives affects the efficacy of their prayers.[2] He repeats in 3:12 that God listens to the prayers of the righteous but not to the prayers of evildoers.[3] Peter's close friend James says the same thing in his letter: *"The prayer of* ***a righteous person*** *is powerful and effective. Elijah was a human being, even as we are. He prayed*

---

[1] Acts 1:14, 24; 3:1; 4:13, 24, 31; 6:4, 6; 9:40; 10:9; 11:15; 12:5, 12.

[2] Although Peter is making a more general point here, this verse should also encourage married couples to lay hold of the promise in Matthew 18:19 by praying together.

[3] Answered prayers are entirely a gift of grace, but to receive them we need to lay hold of the gift of grace!

earnestly that it would not rain, and it did not rain on the land for three and a half years. Again he prayed, and the heavens gave rain."[4] Peter says we need to keep the powder of our secret weapon dry.

Prayer lays hold of the living hope we have in Jesus and brings down the inheritance that God is guarding for us in heaven to meet our present needs on earth. Prayer unleashes God's resurrection power on our behalf, which is why our prayers are blunted if we refuse to walk the path of death with Jesus towards our fleshly desires. When we wrangle with one another over earthly things, God closes his ears to our requests for heavenly things.[5] When we defy his authority by the way we live, God refuses to back up our attempts to wield his authority over sickness and demons.[6] When we doctor the Gospel message for fear that it will make us unpopular, God shows his displeasure by refusing to answer our prayers for conversions. Can you see why Peter is so firm with us that we need to walk the path of death and resurrection in every aspect of our lives? Failure to do so is to exchange our cannons for a peashooter in the midst of a great battle.

Most of the stories of Gospel breakthrough in Church history have involved Christians rediscovering the secret weapon of prayer. In 1904, a Welsh coal miner named Evan Roberts did so:

For a long time I was much troubled in my soul and my heart by thinking over the failure of Christianity – oh! It seemed such a failure – such a failure and I prayed and

[4] James 5:16–18. This condition is repeated in 1 Timothy 2:8, Hebrews 5:7, Psalm 66:18, Isaiah 1:15, Zechariah 7:13, and Proverbs 15:8, 15:29, 21:13 and 28:9.

[5] 1 Peter 3:7 goes alongside James 3:9–12. How we use our mouths all day affects their potency in prayer.

[6] Peter uses the Greek word *iaomai* in 2:24 to remind us that Jesus' death and resurrection has brought us physical healing as well as forgiveness. That's why he sees healing as something he can dispense in Acts 3:6.

prayed, but nothing seemed to give me any relief. But one Friday night last spring after I had been in great distress praying about this, I was taken up to a great expanse – without time and space. It was communion with God. I found myself with unspeakable joy and awe in the very presence of Almighty God. I was privileged to speak face to face with him as a man speaks face to face with a friend... I saw things in a different light and I knew that God was going to work in the land, and not this land only but in all the world.[7]

A few weeks later, the Welsh revival began, bringing mass conversions, not just in Wales, but all over the world.

In 1916, a British missionary to China named James Fraser also rediscovered the Christian's secret weapon of prayer. He concluded that *"The outlook here in Tantsah at present seems less hopeful than at any time since I first set foot in the place,"* yet he determined that *"I am now setting my face like a flint: if the work seems to fail, then **pray**; if services, etc., fall flat, then **pray still more**; if months slip by with little or no result, then **pray still more and get others to help you**."*[8] A few weeks later he witnessed the Gospel breakthrough that historians often pinpoint as the start of the explosive growth of the Church in China.

There is nothing stopping you from discovering the Christian's secret weapon of prayer too. If you are willing to walk the path of suffering and death with Jesus, God promises to answer your cries for resurrection power. He is guarding your inheritance for you right now in heaven and he promises to let you experience it right now on the earth. All you have to do is keep your powder dry and lay hold of it in unhindered prayer.

---

[7] Recorded in W. T. Stead's account of *The Revival in the West* (1905).

[8] James Fraser wrote this in his journal on Saturday 5th February 1916.

Obscure and Clear (3:8–22)

This water symbolises baptism that now saves you…
It saves you by the resurrection of Jesus Christ.

(1 Peter 3:21)

Sometimes it's pretty difficult being a dad. Try as hard as you like, you can never win. Let me give you a recent example. My daughter was on her way out to a party so I told her she looked beautiful. I said how much I liked her hair, her headband, her new dress, her necklace and her cardigan. She looked at me for a moment, ignoring my compliments, and asked accusingly, *"So what don't you like about my shoes?"*

It isn't just dads and daughters who have this problem. There is something universally human about our latching on to the wrong things. Take these fifteen verses, for example. When most people read them they home in on the parts that are very obscure and they miss what Peter is trying to make abundantly clear.

A lot of readers fixate on 3:19–20, where Peter says that Jesus preached through the Holy Spirit to the spirits of those who disobeyed God in the days of Noah. They spend a lot of time wondering what this means. The third-century writer Origen suggested that Jesus must have descended into hell while his body lay in the tomb for three days in order to preach the Gospel to those who had died in a previous generation. His obscure suggestion became mainstream when the words *"he descended to the dead"* made their way into the Apostles' Creed.[1] Today

---

[1] Origen says this in *Against Celsus* (2.43). Theologians refer to his idea as "the harrowing of hell".

many people extrapolate on Origen by claiming that angels interbred with humans in the days of Noah, creating a race of giant-sized Nephilim, and that Jesus went down to hell between his death and resurrection in order to proclaim his victory to them. If that sounds obscure and far-fetched to you, that's because it is. John Calvin laments that *"That ancient figment, concerning the intercourse of angels with women, is abundantly refuted by its own absurdity. And it is surprising that learned men formerly should have been fascinated by ravings so gross and prodigious."*[2]

Confessing that these two verses are obscure is the first step towards understanding them. If Martin Luther was willing to confess in his commentary on 1 Peter that *"This passage is perhaps more obscure than any other in the New Testament; as a result, I do not know for certain precisely what Peter means,"* so should we be. It helps to know that what Peter actually says in Greek is that the Spirit who raised Jesus to life is the same Spirit through whom Jesus preached to the world during Noah's generation, but we must not allow even this to obscure the plain message of this passage.[3] Peter only talks about Noah and the Flood to teach us how the Gospel always triumphs in the end.

Other readers fixate on 3:21, where Peter tells us that water baptism saves us. This is the verse that makes many people believe that a christening ceremony is able to save a baby. The Roman Catholic ceremony, for example, celebrates *"the new birth in baptism"* which *"sets this baby free from original sin"*. Again, we need to be careful not to focus on what is obscure at the expense of what is clear. When Peter says that Noah's Flood symbolized Christian baptism, he is not saying that baptismal

---

[2] Calvin says this in his commentary on Genesis 6:1–4. "The sons of God" who married "the daughters of humans" cannot have been angels (Mark 12:25). For who they were, see *Straight to the Heart of Genesis*.

[3] 1 Peter 4:6 explains that 3:19 is talking about the Gospel preaching that took place during BC history. 2 Peter 2:5 says that Noah was one of these Gospel preachers, inspired as he spoke by the Spirit of Jesus.

waters save us: the floodwaters brought death, not life! He is telling us that Noah walked the death-and-resurrection road when he trusted in God's Word and built an ark. He is telling us why baptism has to be the first milestone on our own Christian journey. It communicates that we are committed to walking in the footsteps of Jesus as the one who was *"put to death in the body but made alive in the Spirit"*. It expresses our faith in *"the resurrection of Jesus Christ"*.[4]

With this in mind, let's focus on what is clear in these fifteen verses instead of on what is obscure. In 3:8–12, Peter commands us to walk the death-and-resurrection road by loving one another. He quotes from Psalm 34:12–16 to remind us to let the Gospel go to our heads. If we have truly died to this world, we will no longer pursue our own earthly agendas at the expense of one another. If we have truly been raised to new life by the power of God, we will return love to those who hate and despise us.[5] Peter reminds us that we are no longer pagans. We have become children of Abraham and have inherited his calling in Genesis 12:2–3: *"I will bless you... and you will be a blessing."*

In 3:13–17, Peter commands us to walk the death-and-resurrection road by doing good at every single opportunity. The context once again is persecution, so Peter reminds us that those who have already died need have no fear except for that of displeasing the one who raised them from the dead. He quotes from Isaiah 8:12–13 to command us literally, *"Do not fear what they fear and do not be troubled; instead consecrate Christ in your hearts as Lord."*[6] Those who truly know that they have

---

[4] Paul also says in Romans 6:1–14 that baptism is all about dying and being raised with Jesus through faith.

[5] The Greek word *philadelphos* in 3:8 means *loving brothers* or *loving Christians*. However, the reminder of Abraham's blessing shows that our love for one another ought to spill over to unbelievers too.

[6] This quotation comes from the same chapter that Peter quoted from in 2:8, just as the quotation in 3:10–12 comes from the chapter he quoted from in 2:3. Isaiah 8:12–13 shows us that we ought to translate *ton de phobon autōn mē phobēthēte* as *"do not fear what they fear"* rather than *"do not fear their threats"*,

died and been raised to new life with Jesus can say with Peter's contemporary, Seneca: *"The dead have nothing left to fear."*[7]

In 3:18–22, Peter commands us to walk the death-and-resurrection road by letting the Gospel change the entire way in which we view the world. He is not referring here to what Jesus did during his three days in the tomb: he is saying that our final triumph is guaranteed, just like the triumph of Noah over his own disobedient generation. Nor is Peter referring here to the christening of babies: he calls baptism an act of mature faith, *"the pledge of a clear conscience towards God"*. Instead, he is telling us to focus on the clear message of the Gospel. Jesus was righteous and yet he died the death of the unrighteous to atone for our sins and bring us back to God.[8] We must therefore let this living hope go to our heads. We must consider ourselves to have died with him, to have been raised to life with him and to have been exalted to heaven to sit with him at God's right hand.[9] Instead of fixating on obscure questions about whether or not Jesus preached to imprisoned demons 2,000 years ago, we need to focus on the plain truth that every angel and demon has been subjected to him both now and forever!

So don't miss the point in these fifteen verses. Don't fixate on what is obscure. Celebrate what is clear. Fix your eyes on Jesus and follow him on the death-and-resurrection road.

---

and that the command to *hagiazō*, or *sanctify*, Christ in our hearts as Lord is a command for us to fear God instead of man.

[7] Seneca wrote this in about the same year as 1 Peter in his *Moral Letters to Lucilius* (Letter 82).

[8] In 3:18, Peter says this substitutionary sacrifice was *hapax*, or *once for all*, a word used eight times in Hebrews.

[9] Peter uses the Greek word *paschō* to describe both our *suffering* (3:17) and the *suffering* of Jesus (3:18) in order to emphasize that we are to walk the same path as Jesus.

One Rock is Enough
(3:15-16)

Always be prepared to give an answer to everyone who asks you to give the reason for the hope that you have.

(1 Peter 3:15)

There is a reason why one of the biggest alternative rock bands is named the Manic Street Preachers. There are plenty of Christians who aren't sharing the Gospel at all, but there are also plenty who are going about sharing it in an unhelpful way. They are offending people for all the wrong reasons. That's why Peter feels the need to clarify what he said to us earlier about our being willing to outrage people. The Gospel is inevitably offensive, but Peter warns us that one rock of offence is enough.

When Peter refers to Jesus in 2:8 as the *petra skandalou*, or the *rock of offence*, he uses the same word that Jesus used to commission him as God's doorman. Jesus took Peter's confession that *"You are the Messiah, the Son of the living God"* and declared, *"I tell you that you are Peter, and on **this rock** I will build my church, and the gates of Hades will not overcome it."*[1] The Gospel proclaims that Jesus is the Son of God and that he has come to save us from our sins. That's the rock of offence, and one rock is enough. Whenever we offend people with anything other than Jesus, it isn't part of the Gospel. It is part of the problem.

First, Peter tells us in 3:15 that we offend people for the wrong reasons when we share the Gospel in an *unbelieving*

---

[1] Matthew 16:16–19. Peter implies in 2:8 that Jesus had Isaiah 8:14 in mind when he spoke these words.

manner. He says that we need to consecrate Christ in our hearts as Lord. Becoming shrill and unnecessarily forceful proclaims that we have forgotten this. It doesn't matter if people intimidate us, despise us or outmanoeuvre us, we must not panic. We need to remember that our hope is in the death-and-resurrection road and that people are saved by God's power and not by our own persuasion.

Consecrating Jesus as Lord in our hearts means believing that he is the prime mover in evangelism. I recently had to confront a woman about her sexual sin and I could see my attempts at persuasion were getting nowhere. Rather than give up, I suggested that we pray. As we closed our eyes, the Holy Spirit fell on us in the room and she started crying and repenting. That's what it means for Jesus to be Lord of all our conversations. Even as we are talking, we expect him to be moving. Successful evangelism believes that God will act powerfully in people's hearts in response to our prayers, even as we share.

Second, Peter tells us that we offend people for the wrong reasons when we share the Gospel in an *untimely* manner. He says we always need to be prepared to share. In other words, God chooses when the time is right and not us. Proverbs 27:14 tells us that *"If anyone loudly blesses their neighbour early in the morning, it will be taken as a curse."* Good news shared at a bad time never receives a good hearing. If Jesus himself had to accept that *"The Son can do nothing by himself; he can do only what he sees his Father doing,"* then we must accept it too.[2] When we open our eyes to see what God is doing around us and join in, we discover the better promise of Proverbs 15:23: *"A person finds joy in giving an apt reply – and how good is a timely word!"*

Third, Peter tells us that we offend people for the wrong reasons when we share the Gospel in an *unthinking* manner. A few chapters ago we looked at a quotation from Tertullian's

---

[2] John 5:19. Jesus adds in 7:6, *"My time is not yet here; for you any time will do."*

Apology, his long defence of Christianity to the Roman world. The title comes from the Greek word *apologia*, which Peter uses in 3:15 when he commands us to *"be prepared to give **an answer** to everyone who asks you to give the reason for the hope that you have."* We must not misunderstand what Peter is saying. He is not telling us that we need only share the Gospel reactively if people ask us questions. An apologia is a well-reasoned defence of the Christian faith that predicts the questions of a hostile world.[3]

The Bible is the inspired Word of God, but Peter tells us not to start there in sharing the Gospel. We only believe this because someone took the time to introduce us to Jesus and explain to us what he says about the Scriptures. Jesus is the only way to God, but Peter warns us not to start there either. We only believe this because someone took the time to teach us about his unique life and ministry. John Stott was therefore right to warn that *"We cannot pander to man's intellectual arrogance, but we must cater to man's intellectual integrity,"* as otherwise we are just offering people fresh reasons not to believe.

Peter models this for us in the book of Acts. He has the courage to tell a crowd of Jews on the Day of Pentecost that they crucified Jesus, but he does not start there. He begins with *"fellow Jews"* and *"fellow Israelites"*, introducing them to who Jesus is before he confronts them with what they have done to him. He has the courage to tell the Jewish leaders that Jesus is the only way they can be saved, but he does not start there either. He starts with *"the God of our fathers"* and *"his servant Jesus"* before ramming home the implications of his uniqueness. Peter is willing to offend people with Jesus any time, but he takes care never to offend them with anything else. One rock of offence is enough.

Fourth, Peter tells us that we offend people for the wrong

---

[3] People tend to repeat the same 15 questions. Obeying this verse may be as simple as reading the right book.

reasons when we share the Gospel in an *ungodly* manner. He warns us to share with gentleness and respect, because the way we share is just as important as the words we share. We can win the argument but lose the person's soul, just as we can lose the argument in a gracious way and win the soul. Blaise Pascal observed that evangelism is as much about giving people a desire to believe as it is about giving them reasons to believe: *"Men despise religion. They hate it and are afraid it may be true. The cure for this is to show that religion is not contrary to reason, but worthy of reverence and respect. Then we must make it lovable, to make good men hope it is true."*[4] This means being winsome in the way we argue, even when we appear to lose.

As part of this, Peter also reminds us to keep a good conscience towards God while we share. This may be a warning to tell the truth – not to pretend with people that following Jesus will bring them health, wealth and problem-free living. Alternatively, it may be a warning that the way we share affects how much our prayers are answered. Since people are only saved through a divine miracle, we need to make the Lord the primary audience in our evangelism. Let nothing hinder him from answering your prayers.

So let's share the Gospel in a confident, timely, thoughtful and godly manner. Let's offend people with Jesus but with nothing else. Peter says one rock is enough.

---

[4] This is Blaise Pascal's 187th thought in his *Pensées* (1670).

The Story of Your Life
(4:1–6)

For you have spent enough time in the past doing
what pagans choose to do.

(1 Peter 4:3)

The story of our life shapes our identity. A man like Peter knew that only too well. He had been told by the Romans that he was a dirty Jew. He had been told by the Judeans that he was a despised Galilean. He had been told by the Galileans that he was just an uneducated fisherman. Worst of all, he had told himself that he was a failure. After all, he had denied Jesus three times on the eve of his crucifixion.

When Jesus appeared to Peter after his resurrection from the dead, he rewrote his story. He met him on the shores of Lake Galilee to show him that he cared about despised Galileans and uneducated fishermen. He spoke words of hope to him over a charcoal fire like the one over which Peter had denied him, to convey that he knew the worst about Peter and yet still loved him.[1] Peter's life had been transformed by this rewriting of his story. It had made the living hope of the Gospel the story of his life.

It's as if Peter cannot decide at the start of this chapter whether to teach us Christian doctrine or instruct us in practical Christian living. In the end he decides to do both. He rewrites the story of our own lives by telling us that Jesus has called us to follow in his footsteps too. These verses ought to be read slowly

---

[1] John 21:1–25. The only other mention of a *charcoal fire* in the New Testament is during Peter's denials in John 18:18.

because they are life-transforming. They explain what Peter meant in 1:3 by our having been granted *"new birth into a living hope through the resurrection of Jesus Christ from the dead"*.

In 4:1, Peter says that God has called us to walk the path of death with Jesus. The Greek word *paschō*, which means *to suffer*, is only used thirty-two times in the New Testament and twelve of them are in this short letter. Peter uses it four times to describe the sufferings of Jesus for us and eight times to describe our sufferings for him. Peter echoes the words of 2:11 when he tells us here that the new story of our lives is an epic battle story. We need to arm ourselves with the mind of Christ, just as a soldier arms himself with weapons in a war.[2] Every time we choose to walk the path of suffering, we confess that the Gospel is our life story. We have died with Jesus in order to be raised with him.[3]

In 4:2–3, Peter says that this path of death is also the path of resurrection. If we have died with Jesus, we have been raised with him too. We have received the resurrection power which enables us to live, not for the lusts of man, but for the will of God. Peter describes the pagan lifestyle that used to come so naturally to the Gentile believers – the unbridled excesses, the wicked cravings, the drunkenness, the immoral late-night parties, the drinking competitions and the wicked pursuit of idols – then he tells them that this is no longer their story. They have turned their backs on such night-time carousing because they are now people of the daytime.[4] The Greek Old Testament used the word *ethnos* to refer to non-Jews, so Peter uses it here to assure the

---

[2] Greek foot soldiers were known as hoplites and the Greek verb that Peter uses in 4:1 is *hoplizō*. He is consciously referring us back to the military imagery he used to describe our daily battle for holiness in 2:11.

[3] Peter uses the Greek word *sarx* twice in 4:1 to echo 3:18. Our old sinful *flesh* has died with Jesus. Unless we walk this path of fleshly death and suffering, we are not on the path of resurrection power.

[4] Peter particularly chooses six areas of late-night sin in order to link back to 2:9, where he told us that God *"called you out of darkness into his wonderful light"*.

Gentile believers that they are no longer numbered among the pagans. They are the people of God. The world is now as foreign to them as the Gospel used to be. Their faith in Jesus has raised them to new life within the Jewish story.

In 4:4, Peter says that unbelievers will be astonished when they see us living out our new story. That's the irony when people hope to win converts to Christ by blending in with the crowd. Peter tells us that we can only influence people if we are willing to lose friends by sticking out like a sore thumb. People ought to be surprised by the way we work hard when the boss is not looking. People ought to be surprised by the way we say no to some of our sexual desires. People ought to be surprised that we spend our free time reading the Bible and sharing our lives with people who aren't like us. People ought to be surprised that we voluntarily lower our standard of living in order to be able to give large sums of money away. People ought to be surprised that we squander some of our precious vacation entitlement on mission trips and discipleship conferences. People ought to be surprised that we consider prayer to be the answer for everything and drunkenness to be the answer for nothing. People ought to be surprised that we are honest to our own disadvantage and that we offer kindness to those who can offer us nothing in return. In fact, if people do not find our lives surprising, Peter warns us that we may not be walking on the death-and-resurrection road at all.

In 4:4-6, Peter says that this is the true reason why Christians are persecuted. When people witness our good deeds it convicts them of their own sin. Peter told us in 2:12, 2:15, 3:1-2 and 3:16 that this conviction will cause some of them to embrace the Gospel, but now he tells us the flipside. This conviction of sin will make others want to get rid of our constant challenge to their lives. They will try to squeeze our voices out of public debate and out of civilized society. They may even resort to imprisonment and murder. That's because they are spiritually dead and so the living hope within us exposes them as the corpses. It reminds them that a Judgment Day is coming.

This is how the early Church advanced so rapidly during its first two centuries. Listen to one observer:

> *Christians are no different from other people in their country or language... yet they display a wonderful and undeniably surprising way of life. They dwell in their own countries as sojourners. They fully play their role as citizens and yet they endure every hardship as if foreigners. Every foreign country is a fatherland to them and every fatherland is a land of strangers... Their existence is on earth but their citizenship is in heaven. They obey the prescribed laws but they also surpass the laws in their own lives. They love all people yet are persecuted by all. They are ignored and yet condemned. They are put to death and yet clothed with life... Doing good they are punished as evildoers. When punished, they rejoice as if it somehow quickens them to life... Those who hate them cannot explain why they hate them so.* [5]

Peter is inviting you to make this the story of your own life too. He is calling you to embrace the death-and-resurrection pathway, trusting that the Gospel will always triumph in the end.

---

[5] An anonymous Christian from Alexandria in Egypt wrote this in c.200 AD in the *Letter to Diognetus*.

Sober Up (4:7–11)

The end of all things is near. Therefore be alert and of sober mind so that you may pray.

(1 Peter 4:7)

Peter knew how to catch fish but he also knew how not to drink like one. He was there at the wedding at Cana to drink the best wine. He was there at the Last Supper to drink the cup of blessing. But he was very aware that drunkenness has no place among God's people. He tells us to sober up. Jesus is coming.

You have probably noticed that the Bible often treats being drunk on alcohol and being filled with the Holy Spirit as polar opposites. The priests of Israel are told not to drink alcohol if they want to enter the Tabernacle. Samson's mother is told not to drink alcohol during her pregnancy so that her son can be filled with God's Spirit for his life's mission. An angel prophesies that John the Baptist *"is never to take wine or other fermented drink, and he will be filled with the Holy Spirit"*. Peter corrects people on the Day of Pentecost for thinking that he and his Spirit-filled friends are drunk on wine. Paul commands us explicitly, *"Do not get drunk on wine... Instead, be filled with the Spirit."*[1] I think you get the picture. None of this means that Christians have to be teetotal, but it certainly means that Christians ought to be on their guard.

Drunkenness is usually about escapism. It is about finding a momentary release from the problems facing us. Being filled with the Holy Spirit isn't about escapism. It is about rescue. It is

---

[1] Leviticus 10:8–9; Judges 13:12–14; Luke 1:15; Acts 2:13–15; Ephesians 5:18.

about bringing the power of heaven down to confront earth's problems head on. It is about letting our bodies become the Temple and throne room of God so that he can accomplish his agenda through our flesh and blood. That's why Peter continues his teaching about death-and-resurrection living by telling us to sober up. If Roman sentry guards were executed for getting drunk on duty, we need to take our duty as Christians just as seriously. We need to be sober as we arm ourselves for spiritual war.

In 4:7, Peter tells us that God's Spirit inside us will help us to pray. Four out of the six sins Peter lists in 4:3 refer to the abuse of alcohol, because unbelievers tend to find their fun in dulling their senses. Christians are to find their fun in tuning in their senses to what God is doing in the world around them. Jesus is coming back soon and the sinful human race is running out of time, so we need to ensure that our minds remain sober and unbefuddled. We need to keep our gunpowder dry if we want to be able to unleash the secret weapon of our vigilant prayer.

In 4:8, Peter tells us that God's Spirit inside us will help us to love one another. He is quoting from Proverbs 10:12 when he tells us that love covers over a multitude of sins. The same verse is quoted in James 5:20 because church unity is of paramount importance in our warfare. Walking the path of death means that we do not fight back when other people in the church let us down and treat us badly. Peter encourages us to allow nothing to hinder the world from seeing the love of Jesus pulsating through our church communities. Jesus has given us a promise: *"As I have loved you, so you must love one another. By this everyone will know that you are my disciples, if you love one another."*[2]

In 4:9, Peter tells us that God's Spirit inside us will help us to love outsiders. The Greek word *philoxenos* literally means

---

[2] John 13:34–35. In the context of persecution, Peter may be referring here to loving and receiving back any believer who denies their faith out of fear and then later repents, just as Jesus loved and received back Peter.

loving foreigners or *loving strangers*. Peter is therefore not telling us here to entertain our Christian friends in our homes. He is either telling us to offer lodgings to Christian strangers who arrive from out of town (as is implied by his command for us to offer this kind of love *"to one another"*), or else he is telling us to open up our homes to unbelievers (as is implied by his use of the mirror word *philadelphia* to refer to *loving believers* in 1:22 and 3:8). Either way, Peter tells us that we need to keep our wits about us in the spiritual battle by not treating outsiders as our enemies. It is through persevering love that the Gospel will triumph in the end.

In 4:10-11, Peter tells us that God's Spirit inside us will give us all the weapons we need in the battle. He does not simply impart to us divine character. He also imparts to us divine power through the gifts of the Spirit.[3] Peter makes it clear that we each have different gifts but that each gift is needed for us to succeed together. He tells us to be *"faithful stewards of God's grace in its various forms"*, seeing our God-given gifts as a way to serve one another instead of hoarding them away. Some of us will have high-profile gifts, such as public preaching or clear one-on-one communication of the Gospel – in which case we should cast off false humility and speak in a manner that leaves our hearers in no doubt that we are speaking the very words of God.[4] Others of us will have more inconspicuous gifts, such as serving others – in which case we should be diligent in our background role that brings such conspicuous glory to God.

In 4:11, Peter tells us that God's Spirit inside us will teach us to operate on heaven's power supply. That's why we dare not dull our senses with too much alcohol. We cannot be drunk

---

[3] Peter uses the Greek word *charisma* to refer to these gifts in 4:10, from which we get the English phrase *charismatic gifts*. Paul explains much more about them in 1 Corinthians 12.

[4] Peter calls our words literally the *"oracles of God"*. The same Spirit who inspired the Old Testament prophets to speak Scripture (1:12) now inspires us to speak the Gospel.

and operate the heavy machinery of God's Kingdom! This is a marvellous promise. Peter is not merely saying that God will help us rally our own tired strength for the fight. He is saying that the Spirit inside us will teach us to operate on God's power – the same power that raised Jesus from the dead. If we keep our wits about us, there can be no doubt that the Gospel will triumph in the end.

The Austrian army achieved the impossible on 17th September 1788. It managed to lose the Battle of Karánsebes without the enemy army even making it onto the battlefield. They grew tired of waiting for the Ottoman army and began to sample the local schnapps. Getting drunk, the various Austrian units mistook one another for the enemy and opened fire on one another. When the Ottoman army finally reached the battlefield, all it found was an encampment of 10,000 dead or wounded Austrians.

So let's not be as foolish as the Austrians at Karánsebes. The end of all things is near, so let's stay sober and level-headed. Let's take responsibility for the advance of the Church in our generation. Let's not get drunk on beer or wine. Let's ask the Lord to fill us with his Spirit and to help us to confront earth's needs with heaven's resurrection power.

No Surprises (4:12–19)

Dear friends, do not be surprised at the fiery
ordeal that has come on you to test you, as though
something strange were happening to you.

(1 Peter 4:12)

Fifty years after Peter sent this letter to the five northern provinces of Asia Minor, the governor of Bithynia and Pontus wrote a letter back to Rome. Pliny the Younger wanted some advice from the Emperor Trajan on how to deal with the Christians in his region:

This is the course I have taken with those who were brought before me as Christians: I asked them whether they were Christians. If they admitted it, I asked them a second and third time, threatening them with punishment. If they kept to it, I ordered that they be executed – for I held that whatever the nature of their beliefs, such stubbornness and inflexible obstinacy surely deserved to be punished. There were others... who upon examination denied that they were or ever had been Christians. They repeated after me an invocation to the gods and offered prayer with wine and incense before your statue, which I had ordered to be brought with those of the gods for this purpose, and they even cursed the name of Christ – things which it is said those who are truly Christians cannot be forced to do. I thought it right, therefore, to discharge them.

The Emperor Trajan wrote back promptly:

> *You have adopted the right course, my dear Pliny, in investigating the Christians who were brought before you. It is not possible to lay down any general rule for all such cases. Do not go out of your way to look for them. If they are brought before you, and the crime is proven, they must be punished, but with this reservation: where the person denies he is a Christian and proves that he is not by invoking our gods, let him be pardoned based on his own repentance, regardless of any former suspicion.*[1]

A full fifty years would pass before Pliny became governor of these provinces. Nevertheless, Peter could already see that they were heading towards brutal persecution. The believers were already reeling in shock at the increased hostility of Roman society towards them. I find this correspondence between Pliny and Trajan pretty shocking myself. Pliny was one of the good guys in Roman history. He wasn't a wife beater or a traitor. He was a celebrated lawyer, a loving husband, a gifted poet and a devoted politician. Despite these virtues, he seems to think it very normal, even an act of public duty, to kill people for no crime other than being a Christian. I am sure that you find it shocking too. I can't be the only one.

But Peter disagrees with us. He says in 4:12, *"Dear friends, do not be surprised at the fiery ordeal that has come on you to test you, as though something strange were happening to you."* He tells them that this is simply part of the deal for a Christian. It is part and parcel of what it means for us to walk the death-and-resurrection road. If a cat and a budgie are put together inside the same cage, things rarely go well for the budgie. If the citizens of heaven dwell in a world in rebellion against God, things tend not to go well for them either. Persecution is neither strange nor

---

[1] This correspondence took place in 112 AD. It is recorded in Pliny's *Letters* (10.96–97).

unusual. We ought to find the absence of persecution a greater surprise. Paul tells us in 2 Timothy 3:12 to expect that *"Everyone who wants to live a godly life in Christ Jesus will be persecuted."*[2]

In 4:13–16, Peter warns us that persecution is generally far subtler than the iron fist of Pliny. Here it is quite helpful for us that the Romans only began executing Christians in 64 AD. It means that Peter is talking less here about the few times and places in history when Christians have been killed for their faith than he is about the subtle intimidations that have marked every time and place in history. Our participation in the suffering of Christ might only involve being misunderstood by our friends and neighbours. It might only mean being laughed at and called names. It might only mean rejection by a friend, missing out on a promotion or staying single because we want to marry a believer and there just don't seem to be enough single believers of the opposite sex to go around. Of course it may include beatings and death. Peter's point is simply that it doesn't have to. *"Rejoice **inasmuch** as you participate in the sufferings of Christ,"* whether your participation in them is very large or very small.

It is also quite helpful for us that when Peter wrote this letter almost none of the persecution against the believers in Asia Minor was state-sponsored. We tend to think of persecution as the product of totalitarian regimes, so we forget about the far subtler persecution of prevailing public opinion. In Western democracies, the media wields more power than the politicians and it can be more totalitarian than any dictator. We are not to be defensive and to start acting like victims when the media promotes wickedness as a virtue and condemns our godliness as a crime. We are to see this simply as the democratic expression of a nation's rebellion against God's commands.[3]

---

[2] The same Greek word *xenizō* describes our surprise over persecution in 4:12 and the world's surprise over our lifestyle in 4:4. The Church and the world ought to be poles apart. Conflict is entirely normal.

[3] Peter says in 4:17 that the Gospel is not merely something to be believed. It is also something to be obeyed.

In 4:18–19, Peter gives us three reasons to rejoice in the midst of persecution. First, he quotes from Proverbs 11:31 to promise us that God uses persecution to refine his children's faith.[4] The more we share in the sufferings of Jesus now, the more we will be able to share in his glory when he finally returns. Second, Peter promises us that persecution is God's will, that God is faithful and that he will empower us to continue to do good. You do not simply attract persecution because *"the Spirit of glory and of God rests on you,"* you also receive more of that Spirit as you walk further and further down the death-and-resurrection road. Third, Peter assures us that the Final Day of Judgment is approaching, when we will be vindicated and will see the Gospel triumph in the end.[5]

Pliny ends his letter to the Emperor Trajan with confidence that the Church will roll over and die in Asia Minor. *"The contagion of this superstition has spread not only to the cities but also to the villages and farms – yet it seems possible to check and cure it... It is easy to imagine what numbers might be reclaimed."* Not quite, Pliny. Think again. The year after Pliny wrote these words, he suddenly died. His province went on to become one of the greatest centres of Christian mission, since it became home to the city of Constantinople. The other great centre of mission was the Emperor Trajan's own capital city of Rome.

So don't be surprised when you are persecuted for being a Christian. Do not be afraid. Two thousand years of Church history have proven that Peter's promises are true. Whenever people are willing to suffer for Jesus, the Gospel always triumphs in the end.

---

[4] This echoes what Peter said in 1:6–7. Watch him practise what he preaches in Acts 5:40–42.

[5] The Greek word *telos* in 4:17 refers to the *outcome* of judgment, but in 4:7 it refers to Judgment Day itself.

I Am a Christian (4:16)

If you suffer as a Christian, do not be ashamed, but praise God that you bear that name.

(1 Peter 4:16)

I once made a serious faux pas in South Africa. I don't speak Afrikaans but I know enough Dutch to fool myself I do. Joining in a conversation, I repeated a word I had heard an Afrikaner say in a news interview. I could immediately tell from the shocked faces that it wasn't the innocuous word I thought it was. It was an offensive racial slur.

I was foolish not to check a foreign word before using it, but we are just as foolish if we speed past 4:16 without absorbing the full force of what Peter is trying to say. You see, the word *"Christian"* is never used by believers to describe themselves in the pages of the New Testament. It was a word that was only ever used by the enemies of Christians to insult them. It was the first-century equivalent of my forbidden Afrikaner word, so the fact that Peter uses it ought to make us sit up and listen carefully.

The word *"Christian"* is only ever used in two other places in the New Testament. The first time is in Acts 11:26, where the people of Antioch invent the word out of anger that far too many of their pagan neighbours are turning to the God of Israel. They hope that insulting the new believers will intimidate them into silence, rather like a right-wing newspaper labelling striking factory workers as Trotskyites or a left-wing newspaper labelling those who break up the strike as Thatcherites.

The second time the word is used in the New Testament is

in Acts 26:28. Paul senses that King Agrippa believes the Gospel, so he encourages him to follow through on his conviction. The horrified ruler replies that it would be social suicide. He cannot bear the shame: *"Do you think that in such a short time you can persuade me to be a Christian?"*

Understanding what the word Christian meant when Peter wrote this letter helps us to grasp what he means when he urges his readers, *"Do not be ashamed, but praise God that you bear that name."* Peter wants us to see people's insults as compliments in disguise. He wants us to consider it our glad privilege to suffer for bearing the name of Christian.

First, when people label us it means they recognize that we have a living hope in Jesus and that we no longer belong to their own dying world. People have always invented names to insult strong faith in Gospel. It happened to the first *Christians* (too much like Christ). It happened to the *Lollards* (meaning babblers, because they were too eager to evangelize). It happened to the *Puritans* (too concerned about sin). It happened to the *Quakers* (too likely to shake under the power of the Holy Spirit). It happened to the *Baptists* (too convinced that baptism was the pledge of a good conscience towards God rather than a magical salvation ceremony for babies). It happened to the *Methodists* (too self-disciplined in their pursuit of God). The list goes on and on. We should feel privileged if people include us in it. Being labelled as an outsider means that people have noticed how much we are now *"foreigners and exiles"* in the world.[1]

Second, when people label us it means they recognize that we are carrying on the ministry of Jesus in the world. The word Christ is the Greek equivalent of the Hebrew word Messiah. Both of those two words are used to describe Jesus as the *"Anointed One"*. In the Old Testament the words messiah and christ, with a small "m" and a small "c", were only ever used for people

---

[1] It proves that we are living as Peter commanded us in 1:1, 1:17 and 2:11.

whose lives strongly prefigured the future ministry of Jesus.[2] Peter tells the believers in Asia Minor that when people call them Christians it means that they have spotted the same Spirit who empowered Jesus of Nazareth now at work to empower them. What they mean as an insult is in fact an amazing piece of feedback. It means that people can see that *"the Spirit of glory and of God rests on you."*

Third, when people label us it means they recognize that we bear Christ's name. A literal translation of 4:14 is *"If you are insulted **in the name of Christ**, you are blessed."* When people insult us, it means they can tell that the story of our life has changed. We are walking with Jesus along the path of death and resurrection now. We are fulfilling the command of Hebrews 13:12–14: *"Jesus suffered outside the city gate to make the people holy through his own blood. Let us, then, go to him outside the camp, bearing the disgrace he bore. For here we do not have an enduring city, but we are looking for the city that is to come."* If our lives are so firmly bound up in Christ's name that our own countrymen disown us on earth, we can be sure that our prayers in Jesus' name will be answered in heaven.

Ptolemaeus was a church leader in Rome about a century after Peter wrote this letter. When he led a noblewoman to salvation, her unbelieving husband was furious. He sent a centurion to knock on his door with a very simple question: *"Are you a Christian?"* Ptolemaeus confessed freely, *"Yes, I am a Christian."*

Ptolemaeus was arrested, imprisoned and tortured for his faith in Jesus. When he was brought to trial, the woman's husband tried to goad him into saying something that would cost him his life. In front of a crowded gallery of witnesses he asked him again, *"Are you a Christian?"* Ptolemaeus gave the same reply: *"Yes, I am a Christian."*

---

[2] David in 2 Samuel 19:21. Abraham and the patriarchs in 1 Chronicles 16:22 and Psalm 105:15.

Such willingness to be insulted and persecuted because we bear the name of Christ gets a strong reaction. It makes people either glad or mad. The judge was furious and commanded that Ptolemaeus be led away for immediate execution. One of the spectators in the gallery was captivated, however.[3] A man named Lucius leapt to his feet and began shouting at the judge, *"What is the basis for this judgment? Why have you punished this man – not as an adulterer or fornicator or murderer or thief or robber or any other kind of convicted criminal, but only for confessing that he is called by the name of Christian?"* The judge called for order in his courtroom: *"You also seem to me to be a Christian."* Lucius answered defiantly: *"I most certainly am."* The judge ordered that the soldiers take him out for execution too. Even as he was hauled out of the gallery, a third man stood up and protested, *"Then take me also. I too am a Christian."*[4]

That is how the Gospel spread during the early years of the Church. It is still how the Gospel spreads today. When people gladly bear rejection for the name of Christ, the words of Revelation 12:11 are fulfilled: *"They triumphed over him by the blood of the Lamb and by the word of their testimony; they did not love their lives so much as to shrink from death."*

---

[3] Jesus tells us in Mark 13:9–13 and Luke 10:2–3 that persecution is the fertile soil in which the Gospel spreads. The Church does not advance in spite of persecution, but through it.

[4] Justin Martyr recorded this event in c.160 AD in his *Second Apology* (chapter 2).

The Old and the Young
(5:1–7)

To the elders among you, I appeal as a fellow elder and a witness of Christ's sufferings.

(1 Peter 5:1)

Peter was an old man by first-century standards when he wrote this letter. He was probably only in his sixties, but Jesus says in John 21:18–19 that this made him quite old for his day. The believers in Asia Minor saw him as a first-generation veteran. They looked to him for clear instruction in how to carry on the Church's story in the next generation. He therefore teaches them about the old and the young. He says our ages are not incidental to God's purposes for our lives. God has different roles for us to play.

In 5:1–4, Peter addresses the older men within the church. The Greek word *presbuteros* has three possible meanings. It can mean an *old man*, a church *elder* or a government *ambassador*, since such roles were usually held in the ancient world by men of grey-haired stature. It is quite obvious that Peter uses the word here to mean church elders, since he calls them *"shepherds of God's flock"* and reminds them that Jesus is *"the Chief Shepherd"*.[1] It is also pretty obvious that Peter expects these elders to be old. He contrasts them with the young men and assumes that they are seasoned in their faith, just like him.

Please don't misunderstand me. I have no personal axe to

---

[1] Peter describes their work in 5:2 using the Greek words *poimainō (to shepherd* or *to pastor)* and *episkopeō (to oversee)*. Acts 20:28 uses those same two words to describe the work of church leaders.

grind here about the fact that elders should be old. I became a church leader in my thirties and there are more elders in the church I lead in London under the age of forty than there are over it. I have grown up in a culture which prizes youth and despises age, even within the Church, and I am quite comfortable with it. My problem is that Peter tells me firmly that I shouldn't be.

If Peter merely used *old man* as shorthand for church leader, I could explain it away. After all, the Hebrew text of 2 Samuel 19:17 refers to a servant in his sixties as a *boy*. However, Peter does more than that. He clearly sees this as more than a job title. He expects church leaders to be men with a track record of godly living and enough life experience to be able to watch over people like a shepherd stopping sheep from stumbling, eating poisonous plants and playing into the jaws of wolves.[2] You don't have to have been a Christian for years to be able to spot false teaching and human folly, but it certainly helps. Peter also clearly expects these men to have a good track record of handling money, serving gladly in the background and releasing the gifting of others instead of making church life all about themselves.[3] Again, you do not have to be an old man to be a good example, but it helps. Youthful passion is no substitute for a long track record of sexual purity, of leading a family, of handling illness and of resisting the different trials and temptations that beset people at each new life stage.

People ask different questions at different ages. In our twenties we ask "Who am I?" In our thirties we ask "How can I hold all this together?" In our forties we ask "Is there more to life than this?" In our fifties we ask "Can I keep going?" In our

---

[2] Peter echoes 3:1–6 by insisting that God's household should be led by men rather than women. Paul states this in much more detail in his letters.

[3] These verses go alongside 1 Timothy 3:1–13 and Titus 1:5–9. The Greek word *katakurieuō* that is used in 5:3 is the same word Jesus uses in Matthew 20:25 to rebuke the disciples for *lording it over* one another. Church elders are to equip and mobilize an army of leaders. Elders serve churches, not the other way around.

sixties we ask "Am I still needed?" In our seventies we ask "Was it all worth it?" We do not have to have lived through each of these life stages to shepherd people through them, but we do have to be able to answer each of these questions and be taken seriously when we do.

Regardless of our age, Peter encourages us to aspire to some form of church leadership.[4] He still calls himself an *elder*, refusing to view church leadership as a stepping stone towards apostleship. He sees it as an enormous privilege to serve as a deputy to Jesus, the true Chief Shepherd or true Senior Pastor.[5] He has no regrets that he responded to Jesus' command in John 21:15–17: *"Do you love me?... Take care of my sheep."* He encourages us to obey it ourselves. It carries with it the promise of a great reward.

In 5:5–6, Peter addresses the younger men within the church. He tells them not to be frustrated that their time has not yet come to lead.[6] He quotes from Proverbs 3:34 to warn them that God has many things to teach them during the waiting period.[7] Their biggest question ought not to be how to acquire church leadership, but how to acquire the character that church leaders need. At the top of this list is humility, since pride turns God into our enemy. Only those who have a sober view of their own weakness can be trusted to handle his resurrection

---

[4] We are not all called to be church elders but we are all called to lead in some way. Since churches ought always to be going and growing, there is plenty of room for each one of us to lead something.

[5] Peter also refers to Jesus as the true *poimēn* and *episkopos* – the true pastor and elder – in 2:25. This should come as a huge relief to church leaders. The true burden of church leadership is his, never ours.

[6] Peter echoes Psalm 75:2 and 6–7, which says that the Lord alone promotes people *"at the proper time"*. Peter also echoes James 4:10. Premature promotion simply gives us a higher place from which to fall.

[7] James 4:6 also quotes Proverbs 3:34. Humility is perhaps the biggest lesson a potential leader has to learn.

power.[8] It's therefore surely no coincidence that these verses come just before a warning against the Devil's pride.

People don't just ask different questions at different ages. God also calls them to achieve different things. The first two decades of our lives are like winter: lots of spiritual growth is happening but it is largely beneath the surface. Our twenties and thirties are more like springtime: branches begin to grow and it starts to become obvious how much spiritual fruit our lives are going to be able to bear. Our forties and fifties are like summer: growth slows down but we start bearing our greatest fruit. It is harvest time. From our sixties onwards, life is like autumn: some fruit remains but our best strength is gone. Our bodies start to fall apart but our lives still present magnificent colours to those who watch us, provided we have learned to live them well. That's why Peter deals so strongly with the young men here. This is not the season for complaining that they have not yet been given the badge of leadership. This is the season for concentrating on developing the character that will enable their lives to be very fruitful in the long term.

In 5:7, Peter addresses us all. He belongs to a dying generation. He is one of the last eyewitnesses of Jesus' death and resurrection. He therefore assures us from first-hand experience that the Lord cares for us and that we can throw all of our anxiety onto him. This Greek word *epirrhiptō* is also used in Luke 19:35 to describe people *throwing* their cloaks onto the donkey that Jesus rode into Jerusalem. Whatever our life stage, Peter tells us to throw our worries onto Jesus and allow him to ride away with them.

So be encouraged. Whether you are old or young, you have a living hope that overcomes the worries of each life stage. Play the role that God has given you at its proper time, enjoying the different seasons of a life overflowing with resurrection power.

[8] The Greek word Peter uses in 5:5 means literally *to gird oneself* or *put on a belt*. It links back to his command in 1:13 to "*Gird up the loins of your mind.*" We need to be active in our pursuit of humility.

The Devil in Disguise (5:8–14)

Your enemy the devil prowls around like a roaring lion looking for someone to devour.

(1 Peter 5:8)

Any fan of the *X-Men* movies knows that Mystique is a deadly foe. She is a shape-shifter, able to transform her appearance in order to disguise herself as other people. The X-Men have to be on constant alert against her never-ending deceptions.

Peter ends this letter by telling us that the Devil is a far cleverer opponent than Mystique. He warns us that he is a shape-shifter with four main strategies for tricking churches into submission and defeat. As we come to the end of 1 Peter, let's read these verses very carefully. We need to see through these disguises for the Gospel to triumph in the end.

In 5:8–9, Peter tells us that the Devil's first disguise is *persecution*. This entire letter has been about our need to suffer with Jesus, but still this is surprising. Peter says that persecution is deceptive. The Devil comes at us with sharp teeth and claws, but he is merely *like* a roaring lion. Jesus is the true Lion of the Tribe of Judah and he commands us to see the Devil's threats for the bluster that they are.[1]

The Devil wants to fool us that he is stronger than he is. Peter says we can easily resist him if we let the Gospel go to

---

[1] Revelation 5:5 tells us that Jesus is the true Lion. The Devil is just a great pretender.

our heads.[2] The Devil wants to fool us that our sufferings are somehow unique, but Peter points out that believers all around the world are going through precisely the same sufferings as we are. The Devil wants to fool us that we are isolated and alone, but Peter points out that we are part of *"the family of believers"*. We have God as our Father, Jesus as our big Brother and millions of believers as our brothers and sisters. We are far from alone. We are part of the mighty winning team. All we have to do is open our eyes and see through the Devil's first deception.[3]

In 5:10–11, Peter tells us that the Devil's second disguise is *panic*. He wants to make us feel as though the Church is on the ropes and on the run. He wants to rattle our courage and stop us from clothing ourselves in the armour of God. He wants to make us shrill and complaining and aggressive, so that we play right into his hands. The third-century church leader Origen was forced to counter this by telling believers that *"Sometimes we think we are confuting someone, and we speak ill-advisedly. We become aggressive and argumentative as we try to win our case, no matter what language we have to use. When we do this, the devil takes our mouth and uses it like a bow from which he can shoot his arrows."*[4]

Peter warns us not to panic. The Devil's strength is an illusion. Our God is the God of all grace. Our Saviour Jesus has shared with us his eternal glory. He has filled us with his Spirit to make us strong and firm and steadfast. He is the Rock, so his Spirit makes us rock-hard. He is the Living Stone, so his Spirit makes us living stones too. The Devil is the one who ought to

---

[2] Peter uses the Greek word *grēgoreuō* in 5:8 to command us *to be vigilant.* This is the word used in Matthew 26:41 when Peter fails to be vigilant in the Garden of Gethsemane.

[3] Although Peter had authority to bind and loose spirits (Matthew 16:19), he tells us that Satan has already been bound. He does not tell us to bind the Devil, simply to resist him.

[4] Origen says this in his commentary on Psalm 36:3.

panic, not us. Satan's onslaught will only last a little while, but God's power will keep on going forever.

In 5:12–13, Peter tells us that the Devil's third disguise is *division*. This letter has been all about unity in the face of persecution, without any mention of the disunity which dominates his second letter. Nevertheless, Peter is well aware of the Devil's attempts to disguise sinful self-seeking as godly ambition in order to divide us. He therefore bends over backwards to emphasize that he and the other apostles are all on the same team. He confesses that he is just an ignorant fisherman who has needed the help of Silas to write this letter in Greek. Silas was an apostle in his own right and a close teammate of Paul, but there is not a trace of rivalry in Peter's attitude towards him.[5] He tells the believers that he regards Silas as *"a faithful brother"*, who has helped him to encourage them throughout this letter to stand firm and united in *"the true grace of God"*.[6]

Peter also mentions a second colleague. It is no less embarrassing for him, because everybody knew that he had needed Mark's help to write down his account of following Jesus. Irenaeus tells us that *"Mark, the disciple and interpreter of Peter, handed down to us in writing what Peter preached."* Eusebius says that *"Peter's hearers... pleaded with Mark whose Gospel we have, seeing that he was Peter's follower, to leave them a written statement of the teaching which had been given them verbally. They did not give up until they had persuaded him, and so they became the cause of the written Gospel which bears the name of Mark."*[7] Peter is not embarrassed to confess that he

---

[5] Silas was a gifted prophet and apostle, who helped on Paul's second missionary journey (Acts 15:22–40; 1 Thessalonians 1:1; 2:6). He was a Roman citizen (Acts 16:37) and so had better Greek than Peter.

[6] When Peter says in 5:12 that he *testifies* to the true Gospel (*epimartureō*), he uses a Greek word that echoes his claim in 5:1 to be an *eyewitness* to the sufferings of Jesus (*martus*).

[7] Irenaeus of Lyons in *Against Heresies* (3.1.1). Eusebius of Caesarea in *Church History* (2.15.1).

still needs Mark to be on the team to help him with his stumbling Greek words. Despite the fact that Mark was closely linked to the apostles Paul and Barnabas, there is not a hint of rivalry in Peter's words. He is happy to own Mark, not just as a colleague, but also as a beloved son.[8]

In 5:13–14, Peter tells us that the Devil's fourth disguise is *seduction*. We know from the writings of the early Christians that Peter was in Rome when he wrote this letter, so note the odd way he refers to the church there: *"she who is in Babylon"*.[9] This is inspired by the Old Testament book of Isaiah, where the Church is depicted as "Zion" and the seductive culture of this sinful age is depicted as "Babylon". Peter talks very little in his first letter about false teaching, so he ends with a warning to be alert to it as the Devil's fourth disguise. If we resist Satan's attempts to hoodwink us with persecution, panic and disunity, he will try to seduce us into sinful thoughts and deeds in order to undermine our message. We have a copy of a second-century sermon which warns the church against this: *"When the pagans hear the words of God from our mouths, they are amazed by their beauty and majesty. But when they discover that our actions do not match up with the words we speak, they turn from wonder to blasphemy, saying that it must all be an idle story and delusion."*[10]

Peter therefore ends his letter with a loving greeting and with a peaceful blessing. He insists that, though we live *"in Babylon"*, our true home is *"in Christ"*. He signs off his letter full of confidence that we will see through these four disguises of the Devil. He is certain that, whatever Satan may throw against us, the Gospel will triumph in the end.

---

[8] Acts 12:25; 14:14; 15:36–39; Colossians 4:10.

[9] The actual city of Babylon lay in ruins. The small Egyptian garrison town named Babylon was obscure. Peter and John were good friends, and John refers to Rome quite freely as "Babylon" in Revelation 17:5–9.

[10] 2 Clement 13:3.

Part Two:

Precious Faith

(2 Peter)

A New Enemy (1:1–2)

To those who through the righteousness of our God and Saviour Jesus Christ have received a faith as precious as ours...

(2 Peter 1:1)

Not long after Peter dispatched his first letter to the Gentile believers in Asia Minor, the situation took a sudden turn for the worse. Simmering hostility and sporadic persecution suddenly boiled over into full-blown bloodletting and murder. On the night of 18th July 64 AD, a fire broke out near Rome's chariot-racing stadium and quickly spread across the city. Rome burned for a week and suspicious eyes turned towards the Emperor Nero, whose plans to redevelop his capital city had instantly received the go-ahead they needed. The Roman historian Tacitus tells us how Nero responded:

> *To quash this rumour, Nero fastened the guilt and inflicted the most exquisite tortures on a class hated for their abominations, called Christians by the populace. Christ, from whom the name had its origin, had suffered the death penalty during the reign of Tiberius at the hands of one of our procurators, Pontius Pilate, and a most mischievous superstition, thus checked for the moment, again broke out not only in Judea, where the evil began, but even in Rome.... A large number were convicted, not so much for the crime of setting fire to the city as for the fact that people hated them. Mockery of every sort was added to their deaths. Covered with the*

skins of beasts, they were torn by dogs and perished, or were nailed to crosses, or were doomed to the flames and burnt, to serve as nightly illumination when daylight had expired.[1]

Peter was caught up in the mayhem. The New Testament does not tell us how he died; it simply tells us that he died a martyr's death, so we have to rely on the early Christian writings to fill in the blanks for us. They say that he was arrested and imprisoned during Nero's brutal slaughter. Tertullian says that after a short while on death row, *"Peter endured the same suffering as his Lord... bound to the cross."* Eusebius confirms this: *"Peter was crucified at Rome with head downwards, as he himself had desired to suffer."*[2] It helps to know this, because we can tell from 1:12–15 that Peter is on death row and in no doubt about the fact he is about to die. He writes as a dying man, sending a final letter to warn the believers that they have a new enemy.

The first big change we notice between the two letters is that Peter introduces himself here as *"Simon Peter, a slave and apostle of Jesus Christ"* rather than simply as *"Peter an apostle of Jesus Christ"* in his first letter. The three years between 62 and 65 AD had not been easy for him, and he had been forced to put his own teaching into practice daily. He felt like the lowest of the low, a common slave.[3] Another big change is to his opening blessing: *"Grace and peace be multiplied to you"* expands into *"Grace and peace be multiplied to you through the knowledge of God and of Jesus our Lord."* Peter is a man with nothing left. Even his life is about to be taken away from him, yet nobody can

---

[1] Tacitus in his *Annals* (15.44).

[2] Tertullian in his *Prescription Against Heretics* (chapter 36) and *Antidote to the Scorpion's Sting* (chapter 15). Eusebius in *Church History* (3.1.2).

[3] The Greek word *doulos* in 1:1 means *slave* rather than servant. Like Paul, James and Jude in their letters, Peter considers it a privilege to assume the lowest place in society out of love for Jesus.

take away his living hope in Jesus or his utter conviction that the Gospel always triumphs in the end.[4]

Another big change lies in the quality of the Greek text. The grammar in this second letter is often a shambles. We can see why Peter needed Silas to help him write his first letter and why he needed Mark to turn his spoken memories into a written gospel. On death row he lacks the luxury of a better educated scribe. Besides, he cares far more about discharging his final burden than he does about watching his Greek grammar.[5]

But none of these things qualifies as the biggest difference between Peter's two letters. The first one was all about our suffering in the face of persecution, but the second one is all about our new enemy. We might expect this to be Nero, but Peter practises what he preached in his first letter about honouring rulers by refusing to fulminate against the emperor. He tells us that the new enemy is not outside the Church, but within. It is a group of false teachers who are pretending to be believers, while in fact being part of the Devil's shape-shifting strategy to destroy the Church, corrupting the Gospel where intimidation and persecution have failed. Peter's first letter was all about our *living hope*; his second letter is therefore all about our *precious faith*. He writes *"to those who through the righteousness of our God and Saviour Jesus Christ have received a faith as precious as ours"*.

Peter does not address this second letter to the five northern provinces of Asia Minor alone. His message this time is far more universal.[6] The false teachers Peter fights throughout this letter are like jewel thieves plotting an elaborate heist

---

[4] Note the way that Peter says in 1:2 that the more we get to know the Lord the more we will experience his grace and peace. Bible study is of paramount importance because Christian growth is never passive.

[5] 2 Peter is to Peter what 2 Timothy is to Paul. Both are death-row letters that convey an apostle's legacy.

[6] Peter clearly expects in 3:1 that his first letter has also been read all across the Roman Empire too.

against the Church everywhere. They want to replace the true Gospel with an imitation version, which looks quite similar but which lacks any value or any share in its death-and-resurrection power. Peter reminds us firmly in these verses that Jesus is the God of the Old Testament, because who Jesus is lies right at the heart of the true Gospel.

Peter uses the Greek word *isotimos* to tell us that our faith is *equally precious* to his own. The word comes from the noun *timē*, which he used in 1 Peter 1:7 and 2:7 to describe the exceeding value of the Gospel of Christ, and from the adjective *timios*, which he used in 1 Peter 1:7 and 19 to describe how valuable our share in it ought to be to us. This theme hides in the background in 1 Peter but now it bursts into the foreground in the pages of 2 Peter.[7] Peter tells us literally in 1:1 that our share in this precious faith was *received by lot*. God chose us; we didn't choose him. He has entrusted us with the most valuable commodity in human history. We dare not allow the Devil to snatch it away from us.[8]

So get ready for the message of Peter's second letter. We have a new enemy. The Emperor Nero may rage against the Christians in Rome but he is a pale threat compared to preachers in many Christian pulpits. As Peter prepares to lay his life down to guard the Gospel, he calls us to join him in the struggle to preserve the precious faith we have.

---

[7] Some modern scholars try to argue that Peter did not write 2 Peter because the Greek is so inferior. However, the word *timios* is just one of many themed words that bind 1 and 2 Peter very strongly together.

[8] God was the guardian in 1 Peter 1:4 and 5. Now he invites us to become part of his team of guardians.

God Has a Body (1:3–4)

He has given us his very great and precious promises, so that through them you may participate in the divine nature.

(2 Peter 1:4)

Every culture has certain things that it dislikes about the Gospel. Our culture hates the way it clashes with certain scientific theories. People in the first century hated the way it clashed with certain tenets of Greek philosophy. The Christians felt under pressure to adjust their faith in order to find a friendlier hearing. They were looking for a way to make it easier for pagans to accept the Gospel. The false teachers were happy to oblige.

Greek philosophy made a clear distinction between the spiritual and physical realms. The spiritual realm was seen as good, the physical realm as evil. The philosopher Epictetus summed up the pagan view as *"You are a little soul, burdened with a corpse."*[1] This made it very hard for pagans to accept the Gospel. They wanted to be told how to get rid of their physical bodies and ascend to the spiritual realm, not how someone had descended from the spiritual realm to take on a physical body! The idea was as illogical as it was unappealing. God belonged to one kind of nature and people belonged to another, so mixing them together was like trying to mix oil and water – impossible.[2]

I wish we had more precise detail about the way in which

---

[1] Epictetus lived c.55–135 ad. These words are recorded in his "Fragment 26".

[2] John contradicted this very strongly. He insists in John 1:14 that *"The Word became flesh."*

the false teachers attempted to accommodate the Gospel to this pagan worldview. The problem is that most of our non-biblical sources date from several decades after Peter wrote this second letter, so we are left to work out the detail from what Peter says. One thing at least appears quite clear. These false teachers were the early pioneers of what historians now call Docetism.

The Greek word *dokeō* means *to seem* or *to appear*. The Docetists came up with the idea that God had not in fact taken on human flesh at all, but had merely pretended to do so in order to gain a hearing from humans. For most Docetists that was the end of the story, although a more elaborate version claimed that "Jesus" was a human being and "Christ" a separate spiritual being that entered his body in the form of a dove at his baptism and abandoned his body just before his crucifixion.[3] Peter wrote his second letter because many Christians were embracing Docetism as the answer to their evangelistic problem. It seemed a far friendlier way of presenting Jesus to their pagan culture. Peter warns them that it isn't friendly: it spells disaster. Not only is it untrue but it also robs the Gospel of its power, since our living hope relies on the physical death and resurrection of Jesus. To spell out the value of the precious faith that the Docetists are diluting, Peter pens one of the most outrageous verses in the Bible. He says God *"has given us his very great and precious promises, so that through them you may participate in the divine nature"*.

Many readers find what Peter says so baffling that they simply rub their eyes and carry on reading. But slow down a little. This verse alone warrants Peter's description of the Gospel as our most "precious faith". It is nothing short of a spiritual revolution.

First, Peter is saying that Jesus has a human body. He is the flesh-and-blood descendant of Adam and Eve, whose coming

---

[3] This may sound very strange to our ears, but Muslims still believe a modified form of Docetism. The Qur'an teaches that *"They did not kill or crucify him; he was made to appear to them like one crucified"* (4:158).

was predicted in Genesis 3:15. He is the descendant of King David, whose coming was prophesied in such stunning terms that David exclaims literally in 1 Chronicles 17:16–17, *"Who am I, O Lord God, and what is my family that... you have seen me as a forerunner of the Man who is on high."* Peter is saying that the Son of God became a full-on human being when he was conceived in Mary's womb. First Timothy 2:5 says he is still a full-on human being in heaven now. The Greeks were wrong about human flesh. It is redeemable. Jesus proved it by taking on a human body of his own.

Second, Peter is saying that Jesus is still looking for a body. Having ascended to heaven, he now pours out his Spirit on his followers so that they can become God's body on the earth too.[4] John wrote to refute the same false teaching as Peter, so he tells us literally in John 17:21–23 that Jesus prayed, *"Father, in the same way that you are in me and I am in you, may they also be in us... I in them and you in me."* Peter is a fisherman, not a philosopher, so his words are slightly hard to understand. He takes one of the Greek buzzwords used by the Docetists – *phusis*, meaning *nature* – and he tells us that Jesus fills us with the Holy Spirit so that our flesh-and-blood bodies can participate in the divine *phusis.*[5]

Third, Peter is saying that this daily reality of partnering with God's Spirit inside us lies right at the very heart of the Christian Gospel.[6] It is what makes the Gospel such a precious faith. We cannot downplay it without forfeiting everything. God has made us his earthly dwelling place by placing inside us the same Spirit who raised Jesus from the dead. Without this, it would be impossible for us to follow Jesus on the death-and-resurrection pathway at all. *"His divine power has given us*

---

[4] 1 Corinthians 6:15–20; 12:12–27.

[5] The Greek word *phusis* is the root of our English word *physical*. It refers to the essence of God.

[6] Galatians 3:14 says that *"He redeemed us in order... that by faith we might receive the promise of the Spirit."*

*everything we need for a godly life... having escaped the corruption
in the world caused by evil desires."*[7]

There is plenty for us to learn here about how to communicate the Gospel. Peter warns us that the Church's biggest enemy is never its enemies on the outside who seek to martyr its messengers, but the false friends on the inside who seek to modify its message. We cannot doctor the Gospel without diluting it. We cannot make it palatable without making it powerless. We dare not accommodate it to the views of ancient philosophers or modern scientists, because the coming of Jesus demands that people discard their old ways of viewing the world and submit their minds to God.

Peter wants to equip us to resist false teachers, but he also wants to do much more. He wants to excite us afresh with the precious faith we are called to defend. He wants us to reflect and marvel and worship God for placing his divine power inside our human bodies, empowering us to say no to evil desires and yes to his new way of living.[8] Peter is inviting us to participate in the divine nature by partnering together with the Trinity.[9]

What a promise. What a Gospel. What a precious faith. And what a travesty it is whenever Christians dilute it to sound a bit more like the empty messages of the world.

---

[7] Adam and Eve corrupted humanity by sinfully desiring to become like God. By becoming a human, Jesus frees us from our sinful desires and helps us to escape the corruption of the fallen world. Amazing.

[8] The Greek word *aretē*, or *virtue*, is only used five times in the New Testament – in 1:3, twice in 1:5, and once each in 1 Peter 2:9 and Philippians 4:8. We now get to possess the divine virtues we declared in 1 Peter 2:9!

[9] The Greek word *koinōnos* in 1:4 means a *partner* and is the same word used in Luke 5:10 to describe Peter and John as fishing partners. Peter is therefore saying that we get to work as part of the Trinity's team, which is why Jesus refers to *Father, Son and Church* in Revelation 3:12. The Spirit is one with us!

Return on Investment (1:5-11)

> *If you possess these qualities in increasing measure, they will keep you from being ineffective and unproductive in your knowledge of our Lord Jesus Christ.*
>
> (2 Peter 1:8)

Sometimes I wish I had a time machine. If I could only turn back time, I would be mortgage free and never have to think about money again. I live in the investment capital of the world, where stocks and commodities are constantly traded back and forth and where fortunes are quickly lost and made. If only I knew ahead of time which investments would give a good return, I would be like Henry Flagler, the man who spotted the potential of the young John D. Rockefeller's oil business and bought into it on the bottom floor. He multiplied his initial investment 1,250 times over.

However, Peter tells us in his second letter that we have something better than a time machine. We have God's clear instruction about where we ought to invest all our best energies and resources in order to see a phenomenal return. It's one of the reasons why Peter keeps repeating the Greek word *timios* and its sister words.[1] The Gospel is a *precious* faith because its return on investment is quite literally out of this world. So let's read these seven verses slowly. Henry Flagler never found

---

[1] 1 Peter 1:7 (twice), 19 (twice); 2:4, 6, 7, 17 (twice); 3:7; 2 Peter 1:1, 4, 17.

anything half as valuable in John D. Rockefeller's oilfields as we are able to find right here.

Peter tells us in 1:5 that it all starts with an initial investment of faith. That's where the Christian journey always begins. We surrender to the rock of offence and confess that Jesus is the Son of God. We believe that his death and resurrection brings us forgiveness and reconciliation with God. But that's just the first investment. Faith in Jesus' death and resurrection is not how we start out as believers. It isn't just the hallway of Christianity, but the entire house, the garage and the garden too. The death-and-resurrection road has to become our pathway every single day, because that's what it means to invest our lives in Jesus. It costs us everything but the return on our faith investment is enormous. That's the paradox of Christianity.

Peter commands us in 1:5 to *"make every effort to add to your faith goodness."* Christian character is a gift of grace, but that does not mean it is something that we passively receive. Working hard to change ourselves from the outside in will always end in failure, but working hard in partnership with the Holy Spirit to be changed from the inside out always succeeds. The Greek word Peter uses here for goodness is *aretē*, which means *virtue* and is the word he used in 1 Peter 2:9 for the virtuous character of God. When we walk the death-and-resurrection road each day by cooperating gladly with the Holy Spirit as he highlights sin that has to die, the return on our investment is godly character.

Peter carries on his description of what happens when we invest our faith in the Gospel, not just to save us from hell but to fit us for heaven. When faith produces goodness in our hearts it increases our knowledge of God, since this is the natural by-product of our starting to think and act more like him. This greater knowledge of God then increases our self-control, since the more we see how loveable God is the more we grasp how vile sin is. Our growth in goodness, knowledge and self-control then enables us to persevere when times get tough, because it trains us to see past the Devil's disguises to discern the reward of pressing onwards. This perseverance leads in turn to deeper Christian character, since 1 Peter 1:7 tells us it refines our faith like fire. Our initial investment of faith is multiplied back to us many times over and we experience God's resurrection power like never before: in godliness, in affection for one another and in love.[2]

Peter tells us in 1:8–9 that this is the point at which the return on our faith investment really starts to multiply. As any big-shot investor can tell you, the first few investments are really all about building up enough funds to invest in one game-changing moment. Peter says that this moment comes when our personal experience of the death-and-resurrection road turns outwards and we start to apply what we have learned to Gospel ministry. When we decide to invest all the character that we have gained through our faith in a lifetime of active Kingdom partnership with the Holy Spirit, that's the moment when *"these qualities... keep you from being ineffective and unproductive in your knowledge of our Lord Jesus Christ."* It's when crowds get saved, when churches get planted, when cities get transformed and when nations get revived. It's when the Gospel advances rapidly in the way that we admire in Church history books and in Christian biographies. It's when we receive a glorious return on our investment by finally seeing the Gospel triumph in the end.

Many Christians never see this. Peter says they are *"short-sighted and blind"*.[3] They have forgotten that their Christian journey began with their taking the death-and-resurrection

---

[2] The Greek word translated *mutual affection* in 1:7 is *philadelphia*. These last three items on the list therefore refer to love for God, love for believers and love for everyone else.

[3] Peter knows it is impossible to be both *short-sighted* and *blind* at the same time! But since the New Testament often refers to unbelievers as blind, he says short-sighted Christians live like blind unbelievers.

pathway in order to receive forgiveness for their sins. They fail to attribute the fact that the rest of their Christian lives are unfruitful to the fact that they quickly returned to shuffling down the potholed pathways of the world. Perhaps you are among them. Perhaps you have never known great spiritual fruitfulness. Remember what Peter said about the seasons of your life in 1 Peter 5. It is not too late for you to change. Tell the Holy Spirit that you want to make every effort to cooperate with his work inside your heart, to die to your ungodly desires and to be raised to a new way of living in step with him. Tell him that you want to invest your faith in Christian character. Tell him that you want to invest all you have in the death-and-resurrection pathway. This is the inward victory that always precedes public victory.

Peter cheers us on in 1:10–11. He knows he is about to die, so his hopes no longer rest on his own investment portfolio. They rest on ours. He therefore urges us again to *"make every effort to confirm your calling and election."* He has no doubt that true believers are truly saved, but he tells us that part of the return on our investment ought to be an increased assurance of our salvation. When we see the Holy Spirit doing things through us that we could never do on our own, it testifies that we have truly been called and chosen. It assures us that we are about to cross the finish line of faith in glory when we die. We will not skulk across the finish line long after the crowds have gone home, like a lazy marathon runner. The investment of our lives will indeed reap a glorious return when we finally cross the finish line to the rapturous applause of God.[4]

So let's run. Let's make every effort. Let's invest our faith and expect an amazing return.

---

[4] Peter is not saying we will receive no welcome at all if we are lazy, simply that we ought to desire a rich welcome. He is not teaching us salvation by works. In 1:1, he started his letter with *"the righteousness of our God"*.

Ancient Treasure (1:12–21)

We did not follow cleverly devised stories when we told you about the coming of our Lord Jesus Christ in power, but we were eyewitnesses of his majesty.

(2 Peter 1:16)

I recently took my children to see the Crown Jewels at the Tower of London. You didn't have to be a jewellery expert to appreciate the magnificent Koh-I-Noor diamond on one of the crowns. It is as large as an egg, but the guards tell visitors that its true beauty lies, not in its size, but in its ancient history.

The Koh-I-Noor diamond was owned by the Sultan of Delhi and captured by Babur after the Battle of Panipat. It became the centrepiece of the jewel-encrusted throne of the Mughal emperors. Later it was captured and worn by the emirs of Afghanistan and the maharajas of India. Finally, it was seized by the British and worn by Queen Victoria. The diamond is big and beautiful, but its ancient history is what makes it so priceless.

Peter insists that the Gospel is exactly the same, only more so. In case we think that he is labouring the point in his second letter, he insists firmly, *"I will always remind you of these things, even though you know them and are firmly established in the truth you now have. I think it is right to refresh your memory as long as I live."*[1] Remember, these are the urgent instructions of a dying man. This is Peter's last will and testament. He is bequeathing his most treasured possession to us. It is the ancient treasure of the Gospel.

---

[1] Peter echoes Paul in Philippians 3:1. Our task is as much to remind people of what they already know as it is to inform them of what they do not know.

In 1:19–21, Peter reminds us that this ancient treasure has captivated human hearts since the earliest of times. He tells us that the Holy Spirit inspired the writers of the Old Testament to prophesy about the coming of Jesus. Abraham was inspired by the Holy Spirit when he looked at the ram he had just sacrificed and predicted that *"On the mountain of the Lord it will be provided."*[2] The Old Testament prophets were all inspired by the Holy Spirit when they spoke about the Messiah who was to come.[3] David was inspired by the Holy Spirit when he predicted the Messiah's death and resurrection. Forget the Koh-I-Noor diamond. The Gospel is the greatest ancient treasure in the world. We mustn't let false teachers steal it from us.

When I was a child, I loved to read adventure novels about heroes searching for ancient treasure. One of my favourites was *King Solomon's Mines* by Rider Haggard. When Allan Quatermain finds a map that reveals the location of the diamond quarries of the ancient king of Israel, he follows it to one of the remotest and most dangerous parts of Africa. When he finally discovers what he is looking for, he begins to laugh out loud:

> *There we stood and shrieked with laughter over the gems that were **ours**, which had been found for **us** thousands of years ago by the patient delvers in the great hole yonder, and stored for **us** by Solomon's long-dead overseer, whose name, perchance, was written in the characters stamped on the faded wax that yet adhered to the lids of the chests. Solomon never got them, nor David, nor da Silvestra, nor anybody else. **We** had got them.*

Peter feels the same. He refuses to apologize for labouring his point. What the Old Testament prophets delved for now belongs to us in all its glory. The world may still prefer darkness to light.

---

[2] Genesis 22:14; John 8:56. Abraham was on Mount Moriah, part of which is known as Calvary.

[3] Acts 2:16–21, 25–31, 34–35; 3:21–23; 4:11, 25–26; 1 Peter 2:6–8, 22–25.

False teachers may embrace the darkness in their misguided attempts to promote the light. But we are not like them. We prize the light of the Gospel far more than Allan Quatermain ever did the diamond hoard of Solomon.[4]

In 1:16–18, Peter reminds us that the ancient treasure of the Gospel captivated the hearts of the apostles too. Peter knows he is about to die and that the first generation of believers will soon be extinct. He therefore reminds the next generation that *"We did not follow cleverly devised stories when we told you about the coming of our Lord Jesus Christ in power, but we were eyewitnesses of his majesty."* Peter saw Jesus in his heavenly glory on the Mount of the Transfiguration and heard God the Father proclaim over him, *"This is my Son, whom I love; with him I am well pleased."*[5] Like John in his letters, Peter therefore uses his own eyewitness testimony as a trump card against the false teachers.[6] They may preach fine-sounding ideas about Jesus, but Peter was on the mountain to see him as he really is.[7] He and his friends preached and wrote about Jesus through the same Holy Spirit who inspired the writers of the Old Testament.[8]

In 1:12–15, Peter reminds us that the ancient treasure of

---

[4] The Greek word *phōsphoros* in 1:19 means *light-bringer* and was therefore the name of the *Morning Star* that heralds the dawn. The Latin Bible translates the word as *lucifer*, which also means *light-bringer*. Satan wants to claim this name for himself but he is a phoney (1 Peter 5:8; Revelation 22:16; 2 Corinthians 11:14).

[5] This sounds more like Jesus' baptism than his Transfiguration (Mark 1:11; 9:7). However, Peter talks about the latter event because he was not personally there at Jesus' baptism. When the Temple was destroyed in 70 AD, it also helped the Jews to know that earthly Zion was no longer God's *sacred mountain*.

[6] We need to learn from this. People need proof as well as truth to believe the Gospel.

[7] Peter reminds us in 1:16 that the Gospel is not "Jesus wants to help you with your life." It is "Jesus is Lord and he is coming back in power; repent before it is too late for you."

[8] Peter reinforces this by referring to Paul's letters as *"Scriptures"* in 3:16.

the Gospel needs to captivate our own hearts too.[9] He begins verse 12 with the little Greek word *dio*, meaning *therefore*, because the more we understand the Gospel's present beauty and its ancient value, the more we will sacrifice to defend it. Peter says that this is why he is writing this letter, for the Lord has revealed to him that he is about to die. He has known for thirty-five years that he will die a martyr's death, but he slept peacefully in prison because he knew that his time had not yet come.[10] Now this time things are different. Jesus has revealed to him that it is time for him to discard his mortal body like a tent at the end of a camping holiday and to depart for his heavenly home.[11] He needs to pass on the baton to the next generation of believers, so he warns them that if they lose the real Jesus, they have lost everything.[12]

The Koh-I-Noor diamond is protected by sixty soldiers and by a four-foot-thick metal blast door. The ancient treasure of the Gospel is protected by the Holy Spirit at work in us. Peter is dead. His watch is over, but he tells us that our watch has now begun.

---

[9] The Greek word for *to know* in 1:12 is *eidō*, which means literally *to see*. Peter says in 1:13 that he wants to *diegeirō*, or *arouse*, our head knowledge into passionate vision and action.

[10] John 21:18–19; Acts 12:3–7.

[11] Peter refers to his body as a *skēnōma*, which is the same word used in Acts 7:46 to describe the Tabernacle. The Docetists were right to say that flesh and blood will not last forever, but they were wrong to assume that this means God cannot dwell in human flesh. He has made us his Tabernacle and Temple (1 Peter 2:5).

[12] Peter calls his departure from this world his *exodos*, meaning *exodus* or *exit* (1:15), and his entrance into heaven his *eisodos*, meaning *entrance* (1:11). He is about to cross the Jordan and enter the Promised Land.

The First Wrong Step
(1:19–21)

No prophecy of Scripture came about by the prophet's own interpretation of things... Prophets, though human, spoke from God as they were carried along by the Holy Spirit.

(2 Peter 1:20–21)

Many Bibles have the words of Jesus in red letters to differentiate them from the rest of Scripture. The first red-letter Bible was published in 1899 by Louis Klopsch, who believed that *"It could do no harm and it most certainly could do much good."* Actually, that's debatable. According to Peter, if we really want to highlight the words spoken by Jesus in the Bible, we had better print the entire book in red.[1]

The dying apostle has already told us in 1 Peter 1:11 that *"the Spirit of Christ"* inspired the Old Testament prophets. Now he explains what he means. He says that *"No prophecy of Scripture came about by the prophet's own interpretation of things. For prophecy never had its origin in the human will, but prophets, though human, spoke from God as they were carried along by the Holy Spirit."* Since the Greek word *pherō*, which Peter uses for the prophets being *carried along* by the Holy Spirit, is the word that was used for sailing ships being driven by the wind, this is Peter's equivalent of Paul's statement in 2 Timothy 3:16 that all Scripture is *"God-breathed"* – the bits in black ink as well as the

---

[1] Peter's description of the Old Testament Scriptures in 1:19 as *"a light shining in a dark place"* echoes the statement in Psalm 119:105: *"Your Word is a lamp for my feet."* The black letters are as inspired as the red ones.

bits in red. It is a massive statement about the divine inspiration of the Bible.[2] Peter says the writers of the Old Testament did not record their own ideas or conjectures about God. What they wrote down were the words of Jesus as he inspired them through his Spirit.

Peter then goes further. He says that their writings are *"completely reliable"* and that the Gospel simply fleshes out their message in much more detail.[3] He says we must remember this *"above all"*, because the first wrong step towards embracing false teaching is always rejecting the entire Bible as the inspired Word of God.

I became a Christian through a British Baptist preacher named Steve Chalke. Through a series of unlikely incidents, I ended up at a meeting where he spoke from the life of Samson about sin and hell and judgment. It is ironic, given that he would now disown much of what he preached that evening, but as Steve spoke I was profoundly converted. Since I am deeply grateful to Steve for my own salvation, I have watched with horror as he has gradually distanced himself from large sections of the Bible. This single wrong step has led him on a journey towards preaching almost the exact opposite of the message that saved me. I really care for Steve, so I want to use him as an example of how easy it is to succumb to the enemy Peter confronts in this letter. If I am sticking my neck out here, I am doing it to save yours.[4]

Steve Chalke expressed his doubts in a paper published in

---

[2] "Scripture" meant the 39 books of the Old Testament in 65 AD, but 2 Peter 3:15–16 also calls Paul's letters Scripture. Peter is therefore implicitly including what we call the New Testament in this too.

[3] He says literally that they are *"made more reliable"* in Christ. The coming of Jesus does not undermine the Old Testament. It affirms that we need all of it. See also Nehemiah 9:30 and Zechariah 7:12.

[4] For the sake of clarity, I am not saying that Steve is a false teacher in everything, simply that he is the victim of false teaching here. Peter does not name false teachers in either of his letters, so neither shall I.

March 2014. Talking about some of the tricky passages in the Old Testament prophets, he asserted that

> *The biblical texts are... most faithfully engaged with as a collection of books written by fallible human beings whose work bears the hallmarks of the limitations and preconceptions of the times and the cultures they lived in... If the Bible is an ancient dialogue around the gradually growing picture of the character of God, fully revealed only in Jesus, it is also a dynamic conversation which, rather than ending with the finalisation of the canon of the Bible, continues beyond it and involves all of those who give themselves to Christ's ongoing redemptive movement... We may sometimes come to a developed, or even different, view from some of those contained in the canon of scripture. In doing so, however, it always remains our responsibility to explore why the Bible includes the range of voices we find there and what the Spirit of God is teaching us through their inclusion. It is through an acceptance of the humanness of our sacred text, rather than a denial of it, that we discover God's inspiration.*[5]

On one level, I can see why Steve has embraced this view. Those who assert it are very persuasive, but here's the problem: false teachers always are. Peter confronted clever people who claimed to have found a way of presenting the Christian Gospel in a far less offensive fashion to pagan ears, and in doing so he also confronts those who claim to have found a way of doing the same thing today. He says that, yes, it is awkward when God commands the Israelites in the Old Testament to execute his judgment on sinful nations. Yes, it is awkward when he

---

[5] Steve Chalke in an article entitled "Have We Misread the Bible?" (*Christianity Magazine*, March 2014).

condemns sexual promiscuity, adultery and homosexuality.[6] But it is always far more awkward in the long run to explain these Scriptures away. Whenever we do so, we end up with a very different Jesus from the one that Peter witnessed on the Mount of the Transfiguration.

Shortly after he published his controversial paper, Steve Chalke agreed to take part in four video discussions with the British theologian Andrew Wilson. When Steve confessed that he viewed much of the Old Testament as *"an appalling misrepresentation of who God is"*, Andrew asked him what he thought of the New Testament Scriptures that speak about God's judgment, such as the death of Ananias and Sapphira in Acts 5.

Chalke: Even in the New Testament, not just the Old Testament, sometimes I think there are – in the light of who Jesus is and how Jesus lived and what he taught – there are misrepresentations...

Wilson: Peter is talking to them and saying, "You haven't lied to men, you have lied to God," and she spontaneously drops dead of something that's got nothing to do with divine intervention or providence at all? And everybody goes, "Oh goodness, that looks suspicious"? That's terrible exegesis, Steve, surely? That's reading all kinds of our assumptions into the text.

Chalke: It's reading Jesus into the text.

Wilson: Peter knew Jesus pretty well.

Chalke: I'm sure he did... but I do not believe God wipes people out.[7]

---

[6] This is where the denial of certain Scriptures inevitably leads. When Ireland voted in favour of same-sex marriage, Steve tweeted on 23rd May 2015: *"The angels rejoice! God's love triumphs!"* That's not just hard to square with the Old Testament. It's hard to square with Romans 1:22–32 and Luke 15:10.

[7] This transcript comes from the second video debate in March 2014, hosted by *Premier Christianity*.

That's what Peter is warning us against here. He says that the first step towards false teaching in the Church is when teachers start to cherry-pick which Scriptures to believe in based on "reading Jesus into the text" – never noticing how similar their Jesus looks to themselves. As Andrew Wilson points out, Peter knew Jesus pretty well. He warns us that he is an eyewitness of Jesus' ministry. He heard him endorse the Old Testament again and again: *"It is written... It is also written... It is written"* and *"Scripture cannot be set aside."*[8] He warns us that downgrading the authority of certain passages of Scripture is always the first wrong step on a journey that quickly leads us to a false Jesus.

---

[8] Matthew 4:4, 7, 10; John 10:35. In contrast, the snake asks Eve in Genesis 3:1, *"Did God really say?"*

Ignorance (2:1–12)

These people blaspheme in matters they do not understand.

(2 Peter 2:12)

Peter wasn't a Greek philosopher. He was a Jewish fisherman. We might therefore have expected him to feel a little bit intimidated by the intelligence of the false teachers and by their clever grasp of pagan culture. If he was, then he hid it very well. He insists that people do not fall for false teaching due to their sophisticated study and their enlightened education, but due to their fatal ignorance of the facts of the Gospel.

In 2:1, Peter warns us that false teachers are ignorant about Jesus. Their subtle questioning of Scripture always leads to their *"denying the sovereign Lord who bought them"*. Muhammad believed that God had called him to restore the Arab people to the ancient faith of the Jews and Christians.[1] In Surah 3:42–55 of the Qur'an, he affirms that Jesus is the Word of God, the Messiah, the Holy One, the one born to a virgin, the miracle worker, the one who died and rose again, the one God calls us to obey and the one God has appointed to show us the way to heaven. His message won a hearing with seventh-century Arabs because it sounded like a return to Christianity, minus a few of the things that most offended Arab culture, yet in denying that Jesus is the Son of God and that he died on a cross Muhammad made a fatal error. He supplanted the real Jesus with a false messiah who has

---

[1] This statement should not be seen as controversial. Muhammad tells anyone who struggles to understand his words that they should ask their Jewish and Christian friends to clarify them (Qur'an 10:94).

no power to save. Peter likens such false teachers to the false prophets of ancient Israel because, although they mean well, their ignorance of God always spells disaster.[2] Ignorance isn't bliss. It's spiritually fatal.

In 2:2–3, Peter warns us that false teachers hate the truth. Although they love to present themselves as intellectuals, they seek to supplant the facts with their *"fabricated stories"*.[3] They sidestep the biblical discernment of their listeners by using funny anecdotes and half-truthful testimonies that manipulate people's emotions. Peter urges us to spot the *"depraved conduct"* and *"greed"* that lurk behind the glossy packaging of their message.[4] They may look progressive and compassionate, but they are self-centred and sinful.

In 2:4–9, Peter uses three Old Testament examples of ignorant talkers who were silenced by God's judgment.[5] The angels who sided unthinkingly with Satan in his primordial rebellion were expelled from heaven and became demons.[6] The people of Noah's generation who sided unthinkingly with Satan through their complacency were destroyed in the Flood. The people of Sodom and Gomorrah who sided unthinkingly with

---

[2] Peter repeats verses that false teachers fool themselves as well as their hearers. In the next chapter we will tackle the question of whether this means that a Christian can lose their salvation. For now, just remember that Peter denied Jesus (Matthew 26:69–75) and had to be corrected for his false teaching (Galatians 2:11–14).

[3] Since the name "Christian" was still a term of abuse, Peter refers to Christianity as *"the way of truth"* (2:2) and *"the way of righteousness"* (2:21). See also Acts 9:2; 19:9, 23; 24:14, 22.

[4] The Greek word *emporeuomai* in 2:3 means *to make merchandise* out of something. Peter is warning us that they are clever marketeers, whose *"fabricated stories"* stand in stark contrast to his own message in 1:16.

[5] We will see later that Jude's letter is very similar to 2 Peter 2. Peter writes mainly to Gentiles, so he keeps the Old Testament references concise. Jude writes mainly to Jews so he explores these stories in more detail.

[6] Some demons are already being punished in hell (Luke 8:31). Only a proportion are still roaming the earth. Jesus affirms 2:4 in Matthew 25:41, telling us that he created hell as the place of punishment for Satan and his demons. It is tragic that any human should ever choose to join them there.

Satan through their sexual depravity and their lack of concern for the poor were destroyed by fire and sulphur. Peter uses a few of the Old Testament Scriptures most downplayed by false teachers in order to warn us that they are *"an example of what is going to happen to the ungodly"*.[7] Peter's Greek is clumsy as he issues this urgent warning, but he does not care.[8] Despite his clumsy speech, he is wise like Noah and Lot. However well-spoken the false teachers are, it is they who are ignorant fools.[9]

In 2:10–12, Peter warns us that false teachers tend to be ignorant rather than deliberately evil. They do not know they are false teachers, because they repackage the Gospel so convincingly that they even fool themselves.[10] It is ironic, given that the false teachers claimed to have a better grasp of Greek philosophy and a cleverer way of presenting the Gospel palatably to pagans, that Peter says they are *"like unreasoning animals, creatures of instinct, born only to be caught and destroyed, and like animals they too will perish".* When they mollify the pagans by denying that God inhabits human flesh, Peter says that they are fleshly! When they claim to argue on the same spiritual plane as the Greek philosophers, Peter says their arrogance offends angels and demons in the heavenlies![11] When they claim to be deep thinkers who have grasped the truth about Jesus, Peter

---

[7] These stories are affirmed by Jesus in Luke 10:18 and 17:26–33. False teachers have not rediscovered the lost message of Jesus. They are ignorant of the real Jesus.

[8] Peter writes in Greek but it is clear that he thinks like a Jew. For example, he uses a Hebraism at the end of 2:12, saying literally that false teachers *"will be destroyed with destruction"*.

[9] Since he is writing mainly to Gentiles, Peter uses the word *Tartarus* for hell in 2:4, the only time the word is ever used in the New Testament. In Greek thought, Tartarus was the place of eternal, conscious punishment.

[10] The Greek word translated as *arrogant* in 2:10 is *authadēs*, which means literally *self-pleasing*. They believe they are packaging the Gospel better for God, but in reality they are chasing results and avoiding persecution.

[11] The Greek word translated as *celestial beings* in 2:10 is *doxai*, which means *glorious ones*. For all they claim to have higher knowledge than a simple fisherman like Peter, they know nothing about spiritual things.

says *"these people blaspheme in matters they do not understand."* Sounding clever-thinking is not the same thing as being clever. Peter says that they know nothing about real Christianity.

We should find this warning very sobering. Peter is saying that false teachers are difficult to spot. They don't hang a skull and crossbones from the lectern while they are preaching. You don't hear "The Imperial March" from *Star Wars* playing as they turn around the corner. Their teaching is found on the bestseller lists in Christian bookshops, presenting itself as a fresh take on the Gospel which will make it more appealing to a new generation. Their teaching is found in Christian churches whenever people despise the authority of Scripture and the lessons that 2,000 years of Christian thinking have taught us. False teachers *"secretly introduce destructive heresies"*, because the Devil loves to come at us in disguise. They are often totally unaware that their little nips and tucks have created a modified Jesus who is powerless to save anyone.

We should also find what Peter says encouraging. He says that there is a simple antidote to false teaching: preaching the truth of the Gospel. He tells us to imitate Noah, *"a preacher of righteousness"*, whose short-term failure to convince his own generation resulted in salvation for the human race. The same Spirit of Jesus who inspired him still wants to inspire us today.[12] Peter also tells us to overcome the immorality of the false teachers by grieving like Lot over Sodom and by demonstrating the truth of the Gospel through our better way of living.

Noah and Lot were seen as foolish by their neighbours. Nevertheless, they were truly wise and their neighbours were ignorant fools. Peter therefore urges us not to be intimidated by false teachers. If we keep on proclaiming the true Gospel and living as true children of God, the Gospel will never fail to triumph in the end.

[12] 1 Peter 3:18–20 tells us that the Spirit of Jesus preached through Noah. He only saw seven converts, but he was hugely successful in the long run. All we have to do to defeat false teaching is continue to preach the truth.

Toxic Returns (2:13–22)

They will be paid back with harm for the harm they have done.

(2 Peter 2:13)

Peter began his second letter by convincing us that the Gospel delivers a return on investment that is, quite literally, out of this world. He said that when we invest our faith in the real Jesus, it yields godly character. When we reinvest this character, it yields self-control, which itself yields perseverance, which yields even godlier character and begins the whole investment process all over again. Henry Flagler's investment of his money in John D. Rockefeller's oilfields made it into the history books, but the investment of our faith in the Gospel will echo throughout eternity.

Now Peter warns us that there is a flipside. Whenever a person invests their faith in a false gospel, the return on their investment is proportionally toxic to their soul.

In 2:13, Peter uses the language of Greek commerce when he tells us that *"they will be paid back with harm for the harm they have done."* Nobody knows who began the tulip mania that gripped the Netherlands from 1635 to 1637. All we know is that an entire nation went so mad that at the height of the bubble a single tulip bulb changed hands for sixteen times the average yearly salary. Dutchmen mortgaged their houses and invested everything in bulbs which were inedible and only flowered for two weeks of the year. On the day the bubble burst, they were bankrupted and ruined. Peter warns us that a similar Day of

Judgment is coming for those who invest their lives in a false gospel.[1]

In 2:14–16, Peter says that faith in a false gospel affects people's *eyes*. It poisons the way they view the world.[2] When we bring Jesus down to our own level, we start to act like little gods and train ourselves to see other people in terms of what they can do for us.[3] We look at people's bodies and burn with lust.[4] We look at their possessions and burn with greed. We become like the false prophet Balaam in the book of Numbers, who took a bribe to curse the Israelites and taught their enemies how to seduce them into sexual sin to separate them from the Lord.[5] Balaam was rebuked by a donkey, and we are rebuked by a fisherman.[6] We must not throw away our faith for such toxic returns.

In 2:17, Peter says that sinful eyes quickly affect people's *hearts*. Don't miss the progression here or the way that these verses mirror the more positive promises of 1:5–9. The New Testament repeatedly warns us that what we choose to look at today will become what we value tomorrow and what we do the day after.[7] Proverbs 4:23 says the same: *"Above all else, guard*

---

[1] Peter is talking about false teachers but what he says is equally true for anyone who believes their message. After all, every false teacher starts out as a victim of false teaching.

[2] The Greek word translated *to seduce* in 2:14 and *to entice* in 2:18 is *deleazō*, which means *to bait a hook*. When fish catch sight of bait and decide to bite, it is one of the last things that they ever see.

[3] Peter says that they *gymnazō*, or *train themselves like athletes*, in greed. 1 Timothy 4:7 and Hebrews 5:14 also use the word *gymnazō* to encourage us to *train ourselves like athletes* in godliness.

[4] Peter says literally that their eyes are full of *an adulteress*, not just full of *adultery*. Whenever people discard the real Jesus, they quickly target individuals and possessions as the object of their self-centred desires.

[5] Numbers 22:1–25:18; 31:8, 14–16. Balaam is also used as a picture of the modern-day false teacher in Jude 11 and Revelation 2:14.

[6] Peter calls Balaam's donkey a *"speechless animal"* to echo *"unreasoning animals"* in 2:12.

[7] For example, in Matthew 6:22–23; 12:34; 15:18; Philippians 4:8; James 1:14–15.

your heart, for it is the wellspring of life." Peter uses the language of wellsprings and of rainclouds when he warns us that false teaching always promises much but delivers little. It creates a spiritual drought in the hearts of all who succumb to its lies. It is to the soul what drinking poison is to the body.

In 2:18–19, Peter says that sinful eyes and hearts soon start to affect people's *mouths*. False teachers make a lot of noise about the power of their doctored message but they cannot free themselves, let alone those who believe them.[8] Since they are preaching a false Jesus, the Holy Spirit refuses to work with them, so they cannot appeal to people's consciences before God. All they can do is appeal to the sinful desires of unregenerate flesh and offer people worldly self-help dressed up in Christian clothes. It is tragic to read about the lives that were destroyed by the Dutch tulip mania, but it is far more tragic to see people reaping the toxic returns of putting their faith in a false gospel today.

In 2:20–23, Peter says that sinful eyes, hearts and mouths affect people's actions, which in turn dictates their *eternal destiny*. He has already warned us that false teachers are heading towards *"swift destruction"* (2:1), *"condemnation"* (2:3), *"destruction"* (2:3) and *"punishment on the day of judgment"* (2:9). He has already told us that they *"will perish"* (2:12) as *"an accursed brood"* (2:14) and that *"blackest darkness is reserved for them"* (2:17). Now he states explicitly that the final return on their foolish investment will be to spend eternity in hell.[9] The fact that they heard about Jesus and chose to turn *"the sacred command that was passed on to them"* into a false gospel makes them even guiltier than they would have been had they

---

[8] Peter stresses the irony of false teachers preaching freedom while remaining slaves themselves. In a parallel verse, Jude 19 stresses the irony of their claiming to be spiritual while not even having the Spirit.

[9] Some Greek manuscripts add *"forever"* to the end of 2:17. Whether or not this belongs in the text, Peter clearly has hell in mind here. Compare 2:17 with 2:4, Jude 6 and 13, and Matthew 25:30.

never heard the Gospel at all.[10] Peter is so aghast at their fate that he quotes from Proverbs 26:11, likening them to dogs that eat poisonous food that they have already vomited because it made them ill, learning nothing from their past experience.[11] He also likens them to pigs that are washed clean but resent the experience, rushing straight back to wallow in the mud.[12] Learning nothing from their experience of Jesus, the false teachers strip the Gospel of its power in their futile attempts to make it sound more palatable to the world.[13] They turn the message which ought to have carried them to heaven into a one-way ticket to hell.

Peter has already assured us elsewhere that a genuine Christian cannot lose their salvation.[14] What he is doing here is mirroring 1:10, where he urged you to invest your faith in the true Gospel in order to *"confirm your calling and election"*. He does not want you to be like Balaam, who looked like a genuine believer but whose actions proved his profession of faith to be a lie. Peter wants you to grasp that the same Jesus who invested his lifeblood in you (2:1) is holding back his judgment so that you can invest your everything in him (2:3).[15] Peter denied

---

[10] Jesus also says that increased revelation makes us guiltier (Luke 12:47–48; Matthew 10:15; 11:21–24).

[11] In 1:1, *precious faith* presents the Gospel as a divine gift to be received. In 2:21, *sacred command* presents the Gospel as a divine order to be obeyed. Jesus is King as well as Saviour.

[12] Proverbs 26:11 only speaks about the foolish dog. Peter adds his own equivalent proverb about a pig because it was particularly filthy to his Jewish eyes. Both proverbs echo the talk of dumb animals in 2:12.

[13] Peter's words echo Matthew 12:43–45. Experiencing the Gospel needs to result in our repentance and in our being filled with the Holy Spirit. Satan is all too eager to fill spiritual vacuums.

[14] We are told this is impossible in John 10:28, 1 Peter 1:5 and 1 John 5:18. However, this does not stop Peter and John from issuing a similarly sober warning to one of their converts in Acts 8:18–24.

[15] 2:1 does not say that the false teachers *were* saved, but that Jesus died so that they *could be* saved. He invested everything in them, but they decided to invest everything in their own man-made Jesuses instead.

Jesus three times, so he is not embarrassed to ask you bluntly if you are trusting in the real Jesus yourself. He pleads with you to invest your whole life in the real Gospel, having no share in the toxic returns of a false gospel.

Remember the Story
(3:1–9)

I want you to recall the words spoken in the past...
They deliberately forget.

(2 Peter 3:2, 5)

In the Steven Spielberg movie *Amistad*, John Quincy Adams can see that the judges of the Supreme Court will only free a group of African slaves if they are given a chance to tell their stories. The former US president, played by Anthony Hopkins, has to convince their advocate, played by Morgan Freeman, that this is how people always make big decisions. He has shown the court *what* they are – a group of Africans – but he hasn't described *who* they are. He hasn't talked about their families, their abduction and their struggle for survival. He will only win their freedom if he remembers to tell their story.[1]

In 3:1, Peter says something similar as he starts to bring his second letter to a close. He tells the believers that their victory over the false teachers depends on their remembering the Christian story – not just *what* they are, but *who* they are in Jesus. Peter tells them that his aim in both his letters has been to help them view themselves correctly.[2] He echoes what he said in 1:12–15: *"I will always remind you... It is right to refresh your*

---

[1] *Amistad* (DreamWorks Pictures, 1997).

[2] Peter says literally in 3:1 that he wrote both letters *"to fully awaken your genuine mind in remembering"*. This verse does not necessarily mean that 2 Peter was written to the same group of believers in Asia Minor. It simply means that 1 Peter was in wide circulation by the time he wrote 2 Peter. See Colossians 4:16.

memory." The way to overcome false teachers is to remember our story.[3]

In 3:2, Peter tells us where to look to find the Christian story. *"I want you to recall the words spoken in the past by the holy prophets,"* he says, referring to what we now call the Old Testament.[4] We need to remember that we are the children of Noah, the preacher of righteousness who was saved out of a sinful generation. We need to remember we are the children of Abraham, the man God commanded to turn his back on civilization to become a tent-dwelling nomad in a foreign land. We need to remember that we are heirs to the promises that the Lord gave to the Israelites after rescuing them from slavery in Egypt. We need to remember that we serve the true Son of David, the one greater than Solomon, who is building a Temple out of the living stones that he is quarrying from the nations of the world. Peter told us in his first letter that such recall brings us victory over persecution. Now he tells us that it brings us victory over false teachers too.

Peter has not finished: *"I want you to recall... the command given by our Lord and Saviour through your apostles"* – in other words, the early gospels and letters that make up much of our New Testament.[5] It isn't enough for us to know the story of Israel before the coming of the Messiah. We also need to know how Jesus has reconstituted it by appointing twelve apostles to become twelve new patriarchs for God's reconstituted people. We need to grasp that we are citizens of the New Jerusalem at the heart of Babylon, that we are the people of heaven scattered

---

[3] Peter calls the next generation of Christians to remember in 1:9, 12, 13, 15, 20; 3:1, 2, 8.

[4] Although we tend to see "the prophets" as just the final books of the Old Testament, the apostles saw Moses, Samuel and David as prophets too (Acts 2:29–30; 3:21–24). This is shorthand for the entire Old Testament.

[5] *"Your apostles"* is probably meant to emphasize that Gentile believers have as much a share in the Bible's story as any native-born Jew. Peter treats Paul's letters as divinely inspired Scripture in 3:15–16, just as he did the Old Testament in 1:19–21. Paul does the same with Luke's gospel in 1 Timothy 5:18.

throughout the earth to proclaim the rule of King Jesus and that this proclamation is the world's greatest story. False teachers may make initial gains, but the Gospel will triumph in the end.

In 3:3-7, Peter tells us that false teachers deliberately forget this story. They sound very intelligent when they modify the Gospel to help it travel with the prevailing winds of culture, but underneath their rhetoric lurks an eagerness to justify their immoral desires. They sound pretty convincing when they point out that Jesus has not come back from heaven as promised and that the Second Coming might therefore be just a metaphor, but Peter tells us *"they deliberately forget"* the Bible's story.[6] They choose not to recall the fact that history began when God's Word created dry land out of water.[7] They choose not to remember the complacent certainty of Noah's generation that God would never judge the world, even as the rainclouds gathered.[8] They deliberately forget the story because they do not want to face up to the fact that the Day of Judgment is approaching for those who refuse to surrender their lives to God.[9]

In 3:8-9, Peter therefore charges us solemnly: *"Do not forget."* He reminds us of the words of Moses in Psalm 90:4, because God has delayed the return of his Son from heaven in order to save more people. His slowness does not mean inactivity. Having talked very bluntly about hell in 2:4, 2:17 and 3:7, Peter tells us that God has delayed the Second Coming

---

[6] The Greek word *parousia* in 3:4 is a technical term for the Second Coming of Jesus. If people had already grown impatient waiting for it in 65 AD (see a similar reference to *"scoffers"* in Jude 17-18), we should not be surprised that many people have done so in our own day too.

[7] Note the way that the false teachers undermine themselves in 3:4 by referring to the universe as *"creation"*, even as they deny that God created it. Their choice of words reveals what they truly know.

[8] Peter says in 3:5 that people reject the Gospel, not for intellectual reasons, but for moral ones. They do not want to believe so they choose to forget. Keep proclaiming the facts about Jesus until they listen.

[9] Peter declared in Acts 2:16-17 that *"the Last Days"* had begun. However, he uses a future tense in 3:3, just as Paul does in 2 Timothy 3:1-2, to recognize that *"the Last Days"* will go on for quite some time.

because he does not want anyone to end up there. This is not the time for forgetting and for siding with scoffers. It is the time for recalling our story and for calling many sinners to surrender to God.

I find these verses very encouraging. So should you. Peter is telling us that false teaching thrives on ignorance and on fabricated stories that entertain the mind and move the heart while hiding the truth. It can never succeed as long as Christians remember the Bible's story and carry on proclaiming it to the world. The truth will always triumph in the end, if we awaken our own memory of God's story and proclaim it to others.

John Quincy Adams concludes his lesson by teaching us that *"In the courtroom, whoever tells the best story wins."* Peter tells us that we are part of the best story in the world and that simply telling it will ensure its final triumph over the false teachers. As he prepares for his execution, he charges us to continue his mission after he has gone. He commands us to remember the story.

Does God Get What God Wants? (3:9)

He is patient with you, not wanting anyone to perish,
but everyone to come to repentance.

(2 Peter 3:9)

Peter made a statement at the end of those few verses about remembering our story that requires a little more unpacking. Peter told us that God does not want anyone to perish in hell. He wants everyone to come to repentance and to experience heaven. But what does that mean, given that the majority of people on the earth today are not followers of Jesus? It is so confusing that it makes Rob Bell ask:

> God wants all people to be saved and to come to a knowledge of the truth. So does God get what God wants? How great is God? Great enough to achieve what God sets out to do, or kind of great, medium great, great most of the time, but in this, the fate of billions of people, not totally great. Sort of great. A little great.... Hell is not forever, and love, in the end, wins.[1]

Rob Bell is asking a very good question, even if his answer takes him somewhere very different from Peter. If you have never asked yourself this question, then slow down and reflect on

---

[1] Rob Bell in *Love Wins* (2011). Sadly, Rob turns his confusion into doubt that the Bible can be true. He told Oprah Winfrey in a TV interview on 15th February 2015 that *"The church will continue to be even more irrelevant when it quotes letters from 2,000 years ago."*

what Peter means. Then go one better. Ask God to answer the question for you. I remember grappling with this many years ago and concluding that too much of our theology is spent discussing God rather than interacting with God. I decided to lay this question before God on my knees. As I prayed, he directed me to the story of Balaam.

Peter mentioned Balaam in chapter 2 as the perfect picture of a false teacher. When we read his story in Numbers 22–24, however, it is confusing. Is he obeying God or isn't he? When he asks the Lord if he should go and help the enemies of Israel, he is told, *"Do not go."* When he asks a second time, he is told, *"Go with them."* Confused yet? It gets worse. The Lord uses a donkey to rebuke him for going, as he was told, yet responds to Balaam asking the question for a third time by saying, *"Go with the men."* All of this only makes sense when we grasp that God has two wills, not just one. He has both a "perfect will" and a "permissive will".

God's perfect will is that every single person he has created should love and worship him. He does not want anyone to perish in hell. Paul tells us in 1 Timothy 2:4 that God *"wants all people to be saved and to come to a knowledge of the truth"*. The Lord confirms this in Ezekiel 18:23 and 33:11: *"I take no pleasure in the death of the wicked, but rather that they turn from their ways and live."* Peter is therefore highlighting for us that God always has a bias towards saving people rather than punishing them for their sin.

Nevertheless, God's permissive will allows people to reject his desire to save them. Luke 7:30 states this explicitly: *"The Pharisees and the experts in the law rejected God's purpose for themselves."* Peter cannot be saying that God limits his perfect will by allowing our wills to override his own, since he is clear throughout his letters that people can only be saved if they *"have*

been chosen according to the foreknowledge of God the Father".[2]
What overrides God's perfect will is not our choices, but his own permissive will. God sometimes chooses not to get what he wants in order to get something that he wants even more.

We can see this most clearly in Judas Iscariot's betrayal of Jesus. Peter tells the crowds in Jerusalem that Jesus *"was handed over to you by God's deliberate plan and foreknowledge".* Jesus even commanded Judas to *"Do what you came for, friend... that the writings of the prophets might be fulfilled."*[3] Nevertheless, the Bible also says it was a sinful act inspired by Satan that resulted in the death of God's Son and the eternal destruction of Judas.[4] God allowed his permissive will to override his perfect will because he saw the big picture. He gave up what he wanted (Judas to repent and be saved) because he wanted something more (to make a way for many millions of others to repent and be saved).

Most of us find this pretty hard to understand. This shouldn't surprise us. If we could understand the mind of God, he would not be God at all. Later on today I need to clean out my tropical fish tank. The fish will not understand why I am disrupting their environment, because I am a more intelligent being than they are. I can see the big picture in a way that they cannot. The same thing is true of God with us.[5]

What should we therefore do with Peter's statement? The first thing it should make us do is *worship God*. If a thousand of our years are like a day to him and one of our days is like

---

[2] Peter talks about God's election of who to save in 1 Peter 1:1, 1:2, 2:8 and 2:9, and 2 Peter 1:10 and 2:3. We are also told literally in 2 Peter 1:1 that God has *allotted* us a share in his salvation.

[3] Acts 2:23; Matthew 26:50, 56. Jesus identifies one of these prophecies as Psalm 41:9 in John 13:18. Peter identifies two others as Psalm 69:25 and 109:8 in Acts 1:15–20.

[4] Matthew 26:24; Luke 22:3; John 13:2, 27; 17:12; Acts 1:18, 25.

[5] God drops hints throughout the Bible why he might allow his permissive will to override his perfect will. For example, Romans 9:22–23 suggests it reveals the full depth of his character so that we can worship him.

a thousand years, we need to praise him for having thoughts that are on an altogether higher plane than ours. We may not be able to understand fully how his perfect and permissive wills dovetail together, but we can understand his heart to do us good. We can worship him for being able to see the big picture in a way that we cannot.

The second thing that Peter's statement should make us do is *call unbelievers to repentance.* Jesus has delayed his return from heaven to give them time to embrace *"the will of my Father who is in heaven"*. Although the Psalmist tells us that *"Our God is in heaven; he does whatever pleases him,"* Jesus says that God has decided to work out his will on earth through our prayers: *"Your kingdom come, your will be done, on earth as it is in heaven."*[6] God has commanded us to call unbelievers to repentance before Jesus returns to call a sudden halt to history. God will get what he wants through our obedience today.

The third thing that Peter's statement should make us do is *expect a massive Gospel harvest.* God has revealed to us that his perfect will is the salvation of a great multitude. The name Jesus does not mean "The Lord Judges", but "The Lord Saves"! His very name is a promise of fruitfulness. We must never forget that this is the Bible's story, a story that ends with John's vision in Revelation 7:9 of *"a great multitude that no one could count"*.

We may not fully understand how God's perfect and permissive wills interact with each other, but we can rest assured that on the Last Day, when we do, it will make us worship him throughout eternity for the way in which his wisdom achieved for him precisely what he wanted in the world.

---

[6] Psalm 115:3; Matthew 6:10; 7:21; 12:50; 1 John 2:17.

After Earth (3:10–13)

But in keeping with his promise we are looking forward to a new heaven and a new earth, where righteousness dwells.

(2 Peter 3:13)

During eight frantic summer days in 1940, a third of a million soldiers were evacuated from the French beaches of Dunkirk to the safety of Britain. Their exit surrendered mainland Europe to the Nazis, but failure to evacuate would have meant the capture of the British army and of Britain itself. Prime Minister Winston Churchill was jubilant: *"In the midst of our defeat glory came to the Island people, united and unconquerable; and the tale of the Dunkirk beaches will shine in whatever records are preserved of our affairs."*[1]

Peter knows that the false teachers have a similar view of the world. The reason they struggle to believe that God took on human flesh is that they have fallen hook, line and sinker for the Greek idea that physical matter is evil. They view salvation as evacuating our wretched bodies and being promoted to live on a purer, spiritual plane. They teach people to behave like beleaguered British soldiers queuing for the ships at Dunkirk.

But that isn't the Christian Gospel at all. After the Dunkirk evacuation, Winston Churchill told a crowded House of Commons that *"We must be very careful not to assign to this deliverance the attributes of a victory. Wars are not won by evacuations... We shall go on to the end. We shall fight in France."*

---

[1] Both of the quotations in this chapter come from Winston Churchill's memoirs, *Their Finest Hour* (1949).

Peter reminds us that history will not end with our evacuating the earth and surrendering it to the Devil. It will end with Jesus invading this fallen earth at his Second Coming and remaking it as it was always meant to be.

So don't misunderstand Peter when he tells us that Jesus will destroy the earth and skies with fire.[2] This is not the act of a painter throwing his unwanted portraits onto the fire, but the act of a goldsmith carefully melting metal so he can recast it into something better. Peter tells us that Jesus is coming back to melt the elements of this fallen world so that he can fulfil the promise of Isaiah 65:17 and 66:22: *"I will create new heavens and a new earth... The new heavens and the new earth that I make will endure before me."* Jesus describes this as the *"rebirth"* of the universe in Matthew 19:28, and Peter describes it as God *"restoring"* the universe in Acts 3:21.[3] Peter therefore reminds us that the Christian hope is not evacuation, but restoration. It is a promise that the Gospel will triumph in the end.

As Christians, we need to remember this. Ludwig Feuerbach was not being entirely unfair when he observed that *"Nature, the world, has no value, no interest for Christians. The Christian thinks only of himself and the salvation of his soul."*[4] Even at the time of year when we celebrate the Son of God taking on human flesh, we sing Christmas carols which ask him to *"Fit us for heaven to live with Thee there."*[5] We talk at funerals as if our loved ones have triumphed by vacating their bodies to spend eternity as disembodied spirits in heaven. We talk about the

[2] When the Bible talks about the "new heavens", it is not saying heaven needs to be remade. The Hebrew and Greek words for "heaven" and "sky" are the same. It is therefore talking about our earthly skies and space.

[3] The Greek word *palingenesia* in Matthew 19:28 means literally *"being born again"*. It is the same word that Paul uses for a person being born again in Titus 3:5.

[4] The nineteenth-century German philosopher says this in *The Essence of Christianity* (1841).

[5] This is what Christians teach their children to sing in the final line of "Away in a Manger".

"rapture", as if our true home is in heaven. Peter will have none of this.[6] I find Tom Wright very helpful when he observes that

> *At no point in the gospels or Acts does anyone say anything remotely like, "Jesus has gone into heaven, so let's be sure we can follow him." They say, rather, "Jesus is in heaven, ruling the whole world, and he will one day return to make that rule complete"... To see the death of the body and the escape of the soul as "salvation" is not simply slightly off course, in need of a few subtle alterations and modification. It is totally and utterly wrong. It is colluding with death. It is conniving at death's destruction of God's good, image-bearing human creatures, while consoling ourselves with the (essentially non-Christian and non-Jewish) thought that the "really important" bit of ourselves is "saved" from this wicked, nasty body and this sad, dark world of space, time and matter! As we have seen, the whole of the Bible, from Genesis to Revelation, speaks out against such nonsense.[7]*

That's why we mustn't glaze over at this point in Peter's letter. He believes that a proper understanding of the end of the story will enable us to live very differently today. Knowing that every element in the periodic table is about to be destroyed and re-forged will change the way we live. It will sever our addiction to the fading pleasures and fleeting popularity of this present world order. It will help us to withstand persecution from outside the Church and false teaching within the Church. It will deafen our ears to the bullying cry of unbelievers that Christians are on the wrong side of history. We know how history is going to end – with Jesus bringing down heaven and fusing it together

---

[6] I explain why "rapture theology" is such a serious misunderstanding of Matthew 24:40–41, 1 Thessalonians 4:16–17 and Revelation 20:1–10 in my book *Straight to the Heart of Revelation*.

[7] Tom Wright in *Surprised by Hope* (2007). Another good book on this is Randy Alcorn's *Heaven* (2004).

with the new earth as the eternal dwelling place of God and humankind.

Make no mistake about it. God took on human flesh in order that some of the elements of this fallen universe might be nailed to the cross with him and buried in his tomb. He did it so that, when he rose again, he might make some of the elements of God's new universe burst onto the stage of this fallen world through his resurrection body. That's why Paul talks excitedly about Jesus being *"the firstfruits of those who have fallen asleep"* and says his resurrection means *"the redemption of our bodies"* and of *"the whole creation"*.[8] Even now, as Jesus sits enthroned in heaven, his ascended body proclaims that the elements of the new earth are not incompatible with the elements of heaven. We can be certain that what Peter prophesies will take place because the miracle has already begun.

Tom Wright again: *"The message of Easter is that God's new world has been unveiled in Jesus Christ and that you're now invited to belong to it... Christian holiness consists not of trying as hard as we can to be good, but of learning to live in the new world created by Easter, the new world which we publicly entered in our baptism."* A proper knowledge of how history is going to end will make us holy and godly and eager to proclaim the Gospel to unbelievers to quicken the great Day when Jesus returns.[9]

So don't fall for the mistakes of Greek paganism. Jesus did not take on a human body so that we can be rid of ours. The Christian Gospel is not a promise of evacuation. It is the promise that heaven is going to land on the beaches of this world and capture it from the evil one, so that we can live with God on earth forever. Peter says it is the promise of *"new birth into a living hope through the resurrection of Jesus Christ from the dead"*.[10]

---

[8] 1 Corinthians 15:20; Romans 8:18–25.

[9] 2 Peter 3:12 is ambiguous. It could either mean *"as you wait eagerly for the coming of the day of the Lord"*, or *"as you wait for **and speed up** the coming of the day of the Lord"*. The thrust of 3:9 suggests the latter reading.

[10] 1 Peter 1:3. For more detail on what this means, read Revelation 21–22.

Final Warning (3:14–18)

Therefore, dear friends, since you have been forewarned, be on your guard.

(2 Peter 3:17)

In February 2003, a gang of jewel thieves robbed the Antwerp Diamond Centre. The centre's owners had considered its vault impregnable: two floors below ground, sealed by a lock with 100 million possible combinations and protected by magnetic fields, heat detectors and seismic sensors. Nevertheless, by posing as diamond dealers to win the trust of the security guards, a gang of Italian thieves was able to escape with $100 million worth of diamonds and gold. Peter therefore uses his dying words to issue us with a final warning never to forget that Satan is plotting a similar jewel heist against us.

In 3:14, Peter reminds us that protecting the jewel of the Gospel demands our greatest efforts. He began this letter by telling us that we cannot save ourselves through our own actions, but only through receiving God's free gift of grace and peace. Now he ends it by clarifying that this is not an excuse for spiritual complacency. He uses the Greek word *spoudazō*, which means *to labour diligently*, when he tells us that our hope in God's grace ought to motivate us to *"make every effort to be found spotless, blameless and at peace with him"*.[1] This is the tension of Christianity. No amount of effort can turn us into

---

[1] This same Greek word is also used in 2 Peter 1:10 and 15, Ephesians 4:3, 2 Timothy 2:15 and Hebrews 4:11.

something we are not, yet no amount of effort must be spared in becoming the people we now are.[2]

Peter warns us that believers who abdicate their spiritual responsibility make easy pickings for the Devil. While we console ourselves with passive platitudes about letting go and letting God, Satan rifles through the bank vaults of our souls and steals the power of the Gospel from us. As Peter prepares to pour out his life for Jesus, he uses his dying breaths to urge us to live on and pour out our own lives in active service for Jesus too. God has declared us to be holy and has promised to make us part of his holy new creation. We must make every effort to be found living out this holiness when he returns.

In 3:15–16, Peter reminds us that protecting the jewel of the Gospel demands our solidarity as a team. He displays none of the blinkeredness that afflicts many modern scholars when they try to drive a wedge between the writings of Peter and of Paul. Conscious that he is about to die, he commends Paul as *"our dear brother"* and encourages his readers to turn to Paul's letters after his own departure. He tells them to view Paul's letters as *"Scriptures"* alongside the Old Testament.[3] This is quite some statement from the one who told us in 1:20–21 that the Holy Spirit inspired the ancient prophets to write the Word of God. Peter says that the best way to resist false teachers is for us to accept that the same Holy Spirit also inspired the words of Paul.[4] His letters may include concepts that are hard to understand, but they are not as hard as the false teachers would

---

[2] Jude expresses the same paradox in the parallel verses in Jude 20–21. Although we are saved by grace, Jude tells us that we need to "build ourselves up in our most holy faith" and "keep ourselves in God's love".

[3] This Greek word *graphē* is the same word that was used in 1 Peter 2:6 and 2 Peter 1:20 to refer to Old Testament *Scripture*. It is also used over 30 times elsewhere in the New Testament to refer to the Old Testament Scriptures. Peter is telling us to consider Paul's letters to be part of the inspired Word of God.

[4] Paul in turn affirms the divine inspiration of the gospels, calling Luke 10:7 *"Scripture"* in 1 Timothy 5:18.

have us believe.[5] The same Spirit who inspired Paul to write will also inspire us to read when we study Paul's letters in an attitude of prayerful humility.

Note that Peter says the antidote to false teaching is studying the Bible. This cannot have been an easy thing for the fisherman to say. The stumbling Greek text of this letter reinforces the unkind way in which the Jewish leaders dismissed him as *"unschooled and ordinary"*, but his own lack of education does not make him despise it in others.[6] He tells us that people normally fall for false teaching because they are *"ignorant and unstable"*.[7] It stems from their refusal to study the wisdom that the Lord gave to Paul.[8] The Greek word that Peter uses for their rough-handed treatment of Scripture is *strebloō*, which means *to torture someone on the rack*, and Peter had first-hand knowledge of the cruel Roman arsenal of torture devices. As he rubs his own sore shoulders, he warns us to guard against allowing the false teachers to dislocate our doctrine.

In 3:17, Peter reminds us that protecting the jewel of the Gospel therefore requires vigilance. Many readers get confused when Peter warns us not to share in the fate of those who try to destroy God's Word and end up destroying themselves. It sounds like a contradiction, since Peter has told us elsewhere that we cannot lose our salvation.[9] We need to remember

---

[5] Peter commands us literally in 3:15 to *"count the patience of our Lord as salvation"*. He is making a deliberate link back to his warning against the false teachers in 3:9.

[6] The Greek word *agrammatos* in Acts 4:13 means *unlearned* or even *illiterate*. Peter wrote quite poorly. Even if you find reading difficult, Peter still urges you to devote yourself to diligent Bible study.

[7] The Greek word for the twelve disciples is *mathētēs*, which means *student* or *learner*. Peter calls the false teachers *hoi amatheis*, which means they are *unstudied, unlearned* and *undisciplined ones*.

[8] Although Paul condemns the wisdom of this world in 1 Corinthians 1:17, Peter says he wrote with heaven's wisdom. The power of the Gospel is not that it is ill thought through or poorly reasoned, but that it cuts across our earthly worldview and replaces it with the true worldview of heaven.

[9] For example, he promised us in 1 Peter 1:4–5 that God himself has placed a guard on our salvation.

that Roman guards were executed if they lost a prisoner or possession that had been entrusted into their hands.[10] Peter is urging us to guard the Gospel as diligently as the Roman soldiers in the gloomy dungeon are guarding him as he scribbles his final words. It helps us here that Jude 24 parallels this verse, completing Peter's train of thought for us. Whereas Peter warns us not to *"fall from your secure position"*, Jude assures us that God *"is able to keep you from falling"*. The Lord will guard our salvation if we prove that it is genuine by guarding it diligently in the face of error.

In 3:18, Peter signs off his letter with a final call for us to grow in grace by growing in our knowledge of Jesus as the only true Messiah, Lord and Saviour of the world. In his first letter he spoke eighteen times about "suffering", and this is now the thirteenth time in his second letter that he has spoken about "knowing". Peter uses his dying words to underline the main theme of this letter, pointing us to the Scriptures and urging us to study them diligently so that we can foil the jewel heist that the Devil is plotting against us. If the owners of the Antwerp Diamond Centre had known that thieves were coming, they would have been prepared. But we do know that false teachers are coming. They have already come. *"Therefore, dear friends, since you have been forewarned, be on your guard."*

There is a battle raging for the Gospel. We must not be duped like the security guards at the Antwerp Diamond Centre into trusting greedy thieves disguised as diamond dealers. Peter died but the Gospel didn't. It triumphed in the end. We do not know the names of the false teachers today, but we give the names "Nero" and "Caesar" to our dogs. We give the name "Peter" to our children and "St Petersburg" to one of our great cities.

Because of Peter and his friends, the Gospel has been

---

[10] This had happened to Peter's guards in Acts 12:19 when he escaped from death row many years earlier.

passed down through the centuries to you and me. Now it is our turn to protect it from jewel thieves. Let's guard it as our precious faith and see the Gospel finally triumph in the end.

Part Three:

Holy Faith

(Jude)

Me Too (1–2)

Jude, a servant of Jesus Christ and a brother of James.

(Jude 1)

Jude was the me-too man of the New Testament. Whenever he appears in Scripture, he seems to be in someone else's shadow. He was an also-ran, a hanger-on, an afterthought.

The first time we meet Jude, he is firmly in the shadow of his older half-brother Jesus. The people of Nazareth reject his brother's ministry by asking in Matthew 13:55 and Mark 6:3, *"Isn't this the carpenter's son? Isn't his mother's name Mary, and aren't his brothers James, Joseph, Simon and Judas?"* Judas was the Greek form of the name Judah, but when the me-too man of the New Testament found himself in the shadow of Judas Iscariot, he forfeited his very name. Although he introduces himself in the Greek text as Judas, we know him as Jude because the English translators of the Bible decided to anglicize his name to remove any confusion between him and his big brother's betrayer. Even today Jude's life remains in someone else's shadow. It can't have been easy for him.[1]

Even after the ascension of Jesus to heaven, Jude remained in the shadow of another older brother. When James became the leader of the church in Jerusalem, Jude continued to be mentioned as an afterthought alongside him. We are told that all of Jesus' half-brothers were highly sceptical of his ministry,

---

[1] The other disciple named Judas dealt with this problem by changing his name to *Thaddeus* (Matthew 10:3; Mark 3:18; Luke 6:16; John 14:22; Acts 1:13). The writer of this letter introduces himself as the brother of James, and the way he talks in Jude 17 shows that he is not one of the Twelve.

but we are only told about his post-resurrection appearance to James. This is deemed explanation enough for the conversion of Jude and for the fact that he was there with the believers on the Day of Pentecost.[2] Even when Paul lists Jude among the emerging group of apostles who stood alongside the Twelve, he mentions James by name but not Jude.[3] He had been the me-too man of the New Testament for many years before he wrote his letter in around 65 AD.[4]

When Jude wrote his letter, things actually got worse. Despite the fact that several early Christians quote from his letter and it appears in the earliest list of the books of the New Testament, it has not been universally appreciated over the centuries.[5] Many readers object to the way Jude entertains Jewish legends and apocryphal stories. Other readers object to the way that Jude so closely echoes 2 Peter – at least twenty of its twenty-five verses have direct parallels in Peter's second letter. Martin Luther declared that

> *No one can deny that it is an extract or copy from St. Peter's second epistle, so very like it are all the words. He also... quotes sayings and stories that are found nowhere in the Scriptures... Therefore, although I praise the book, it is an epistle that need not be counted among the chief books, which are to lay the foundation of faith.*[6]

---

[2] Mark 3:21–35; John 7:3–10; Acts 1:14; 1 Corinthians 15:7.

[3] Galatians 1:19; 1 Corinthians 9:5.

[4] We can date Jude's letter from its similarity to 2 Peter, from the fact that he fails to mention the destruction of the Temple in Jerusalem and from the fact that his readers had evidently known the Twelve personally (verse 17).

[5] Jude is quoted and affirmed by Clement of Alexandria, Tertullian, Origen and Athanasius. The list of New Testament books in the "Muratorian Fragment" dates back to c.170 AD.

[6] Luther says this in the "Preface to the Book of Jude" in his German translation of the Bible.

In fairness to Jude, Martin Luther also cast doubt on Hebrews, James and Revelation because they contradicted his own views. Luther was simply one in a long line of people to under-appreciate Jude and to leave him in the shadows. But I want to show you why Jude's letter really matters. He points the way to three important things for us to follow.

First, Jude points the way towards *great humility*. At no point does he attempt to assert his own importance. Long before Thomas Hardy ever wrote his novel, the me-too man of the New Testament was very happy to own the title of Jude the Obscure. Nobody in the ancient world introduced himself as someone's brother – you would introduce yourself as somebody's son – but Jude is happy to begin his letter by describing himself as *"a brother of James"*. Nor does he boast that he is the son of Mary or the half-brother of Jesus.[7] He simply introduces himself as *"a servant of Jesus Christ"*, or more literally as *"a slave of Jesus Christ"*.[8] He is very happy to remain in the shadows of Church history because he wants us to understand that the task of defending the Gospel has not been entrusted to mighty preachers like Peter alone. It has also been entrusted to an army of nobodies, like you and me. While false teachers love to boast about their own importance, guardians of the Gospel are always happy to confess their nothingness and to keep the spotlight pointing firmly onto Jesus.

Second, Jude points the way towards *great clarity*. Peter wasn't wrong to end his second letter by confessing that Paul's writings can be difficult to understand, but he was a fine one to talk. His second letter is one of the most clumsily written and hardest-to-follow letters in the whole of the New Testament.

JUDE: HOLY FAITH

138

---

[7] Mary is not mentioned at all in the New Testament after Acts 1:14. Like Jude, she also bows out of the spotlight to focus all the attention on Jesus as her own Saviour and ours (Luke 1:47).

[8] James also describes himself as Jesus' slave at the start of his own letter. Unlike the relatives of Muhammad in the early days of Islam, James and Jude both downplay the importance of their family links with Jesus.

The fact that Jude strongly echoes 2 Peter is therefore of crucial importance to us. Wherever Peter is unclear, Jude clarifies what he meant to say. Take for example the way that many people wonder whether 2 Peter 3:17 tells us we can lose our salvation. Jude clarifies in the very first verse of his letter by assuring us that Christians are *"those who have been loved and called in God the Father and who have been kept in Jesus Christ"*.[9]

Third, Jude therefore points the way to *great stability*. Unlike Peter, he is not writing from a death-row dungeon. He is not preparing for crucifixion and he is in no doubt that the Gospel will triumph over the false teachers in the end. His opening prayer is very similar to the opening prayer in both of Peter's letters – *"Mercy, peace and love be yours in abundance"*[10] – but his closing prayer is far more lavish than Peter's: *"To him who is able to keep you from stumbling and to present you before his glorious presence without fault and with great joy – to the only God our Saviour be glory, majesty, power and authority, through Jesus Christ our Lord, before all ages, now and for evermore! Amen."*

Jude is happy to remain the me-too man of the New Testament, but don't let that fool you that his letter is unimportant. It may be short but it is also very sweet. It gives us clear and humble assurance that, however hard the Devil tries to rob us of our holy faith through the subtle scheming of false teachers, he can never win. Jude writes in complete assurance that God's promise is true: The Gospel will triumph in the end.

---

[9] This is a literal translation of the most accurate Greek manuscripts. A variant reading in some Greek manuscripts is that Christians are *set apart as holy* in God (*hagiazō*) rather than *loved* in God (*agapaō*).

[10] Note the similarity between Jude 2 and 1 Peter 1:2 and 2 Peter 1:2. The two men clearly knew each other well and had worked closely together.

Spot the Difference (3–4)

I felt compelled to write and urge you to contend for the faith that was once for all entrusted to God's holy people.

(Jude 3)

The great Swedish scientist Alfred Nobel argued that *"One can state, without exaggeration, that the observation of and the search for similarities and differences are the basis of all human knowledge."* If we want to understand the message of Jude, it therefore helps to note the similarities and the differences between his letter and 2 Peter.

The similarities between the two letters are obvious. Jude 1–2 echoes 2 Peter 1:1–2, Jude 4–13 echoes 2 Peter 2:1–17, Jude 16 echoes 2 Peter 2:18, and Jude 17–25 echoes 2 Peter 3:1–4 and 14–18. Both letters are written to *"dear friends"* as a warning to stand firm against the lies of the false teachers. They also share so many common words and phrases that one letter has to be a reworded copy of the other.[1] Peter is less likely to have done the copying, since he was cut off from the outside world in prison and the Greek text of his letters is worse than Jude's. If he had copied the words of a better writer, we would expect his second letter to be as refined as the first one, which he wrote with the help of Silas. Jude therefore appears to have done the copying, but he is not slavish about it, because he evidently has a different readership in mind.

---

[1] It is possible that Peter and Jude simply travelled together as part of the same preaching team and then wrote down their common message separately. However, even the structure of their letters is very similar.

Peter refers to the Gospel as the "precious faith", because he is writing primarily to Gentile believers who had no right to hold such a valuable jewel in their hands at all. He reminds his readers of their past ignorance, of their pagan ancestry and of their foreign education, because he wants them to understand that the Gospel has granted them admission into God's people.[2] Jude refers to the Gospel as the *"holy faith"*, because he is writing particularly to Jewish believers who need to understand that the Gospel has always been the key marker of God's people.[3] He reminds them that the Gospel is *"the faith that was once for all entrusted to God's holy people"* and that the false teachers who are trying to deceive them are *"individuals whose condemnation was written about long ago"*.[4] He wants them to see that the battle raging in their churches is the same one that raged throughout ancient Israel in the pages of the Old Testament. Don't miss this difference, because it is vital if we want to understand why Jude's letter is in our Bibles. It does not merely repeat Peter's second letter. It rephrases it differently for the Jewish reader.

Jude tells the Jewish believers in verse 3 that he originally intended to write a letter like 1 Peter. His elder brother James had been murdered by the Jewish Sanhedrin in 62 AD, so he had intended to write a letter about withstanding persecution. He wanted to tell them that, although the priests and rabbis were out to get them, they were the true heirs of the faith of Israel: *"I was very eager to write to you about the salvation we share."* Before he could put pen to paper, however, he heard that the false teachers who had infiltrated churches across the Gentile world

---

[2] Peter shows us that his readers are primarily Gentile believers in 1 Peter 1:14, 1:18, 2:9–12, 3:6 and 4:3.

[3] The Greek word *hagioi* simply means *saints*, but in verse 3 it refers to God's people in the Old Testament.

[4] The Greek word *prographō* in verse 4 means *to write beforehand*, so it could technically mean that the false teachers were *marked out* for condemnation long ago. However, since Jude then launches into 12 verses of Old Testament overview, he clearly means that they were *"written about"* in the Jewish Scriptures.

were also gaining a hearing in churches across the Jewish world. He hastily took a copy of Peter's second letter and reworded its warning in better language for the Jews. He warned them not to turn their backs on God's Law and embrace the immorality of Greek culture.[5] They must not let the Docetism of the pagans seduce them away from Jesus as the Jewish Messiah and the holy God of Israel.[6]

Jude tells his Jewish readers that they of all people ought to be able to spot *a different Gospel*. Since the Lord entrusted the Gospel once and for all to men like Abraham and Moses and David, those who know the Jewish Scriptures ought to be able to spot Greek false teaching a mile away. We noted in 2 Peter 2:4 that the dying apostle paid lip-service to Greek mythology by using the pagan word "Tartarus" to describe the horrors of hell, reminding his Gentile readers that their own culture's campfire stories testify that the Gospel is true. Note the way that Jude does something similar when he uses language from the Old Testament prophets to refer to hell in verse 7 as *"the punishment of eternal fire"*. Note also the way that he pays lip-service to Jewish campfire stories by quoting from the "Testament of Moses" and the "Book of Enoch" in verses 9 and 14–15. He wants to convince his readers that their Jewish culture testifies that the Gospel is true.

First-century Jewish culture was conservative. Twenty-first-century Western culture is not. Perhaps that makes it all the more important that we understand what Jude means when he calls the Gospel *"the faith that was once for all entrusted to God's holy people"*. He is telling us that the Gospel is more than a jewel to be guarded. It is the family heirloom of the Jewish nation.

---

[5] Jude's older brother James had taught the Jewish believers that Christianity was the fulfilment of their Law, not an excuse for them to abandon it. See Acts 21:17–24; James 1:25; 2:8–12; 4:11–12.

[6] I explain in *Straight to the Heart of Hebrews and James* that James took highlights from his preaching to the church in Jerusalem and put them in a letter to the wider Jewish community. Jude now does the same.

Abraham did not invent it. He was given it by God. We therefore have no right to modify it by surrounding it with pagan ideas at the high places of modern philosophy. Unless new teaching is a rediscovery of the ancient faith of the Jews, Jude insists it is false teaching. The Gospel isn't just precious. It is also holy.

Jude tells his Jewish readers that they of all people ought to be able to spot *a different Jesus*. He points out in verse 17 that many of them have spent time with some of the original twelve disciples. They have been taught by James, the half-brother of Jesus, and they are reading a letter written by another half-brother who lived in his shadow. Gentiles who had not witnessed the ministry of Jesus might fall for the lies of the false teachers, but surely not the Jews. They knew that Jesus claimed to be the *Christ* – the Greek translation of the Hebrew word *Messiah*.[7] They knew that he claimed to be the *Sovereign Lord* of the Old Testament.

Jude tells his Jewish readers that they of all people ought to be able to spot *a different lifestyle* among those who listened to the false teachers. Peter called them *"lawless"*, so Jude expects the Jewish believers to spot that these are *"ungodly people"* preaching *"unbridled lust"* and *"shameless immorality"*.[8] Toxic teaching always produces toxic fruit in the lives of those who listen. Those who had been taught by the original apostles ought to see this more clearly than anyone.

Jude gives us a second copy of Peter's letter because we need to hear its message twice. He may have Peter's three denials in mind when he echoes 2 Peter 2:1 by warning his

---

[7] This was, after all, why Jude and his brothers thought that Jesus was a madman (Mark 3:21–35; John 7:1–10). We are crazy ourselves if we think such claims could be made by a merely human teacher.

[8] The Greek word *asebēs*, or *ungodly*, is used in Jude 4 and 15, 1 Peter 4:18, 2 Peter 2:5 and 3:7, and in only three other places in the New Testament. The word *aselgeia*, meaning *unbridled lust* or *shameless immorality*, is used in Jude 4, 1 Peter 4:3, 2 Peter 2:7 and 2:18, and in only five other places in the New Testament.

Jewish readers not to *"deny Jesus Christ our only Sovereign and Lord"*. False teaching is poison to the soul. We need to kill it before it kills us.

The Language of the Jews (5–16)

The archangel Michael, when he was disputing with the devil about the body of Moses... Enoch, the seventh from Adam, prophesied...

(Jude 9, 14)

The language we use to communicate truth with other people often spells the difference between our being listened to and our being ignored. We discover this in Acts 21:37–22:2. A Roman commander dismisses Paul as a dangerous terrorist until he hears him speaking in the educated language of the ancient world. *"Do you speak Greek?"* he exclaims and quickly allows Paul to explain the Gospel to him. The Jewish crowd try to stop Paul, but we are told that *"When they heard him speak to them in Aramaic, they became very quiet."* People who seem very hostile to the Gospel can often be persuaded to listen if we speak the Gospel in the right kind of language.

That's the irony when people discard Jude's letter because he quotes from Jewish campfire stories. That's not a reason for us to ignore his letter. It's the reason we should treat it as a masterclass in how to communicate the Christian message in a manner that will be heard. Instead of criticizing, let's read these twelve verses very slowly. As we watch the way that Jude presents the Gospel in the language of the Jews, we can learn to share with those around us in a manner that will make them want to sit up and listen.

It really helps us here that Jude 7–16 is a deliberate reworking of 2 Peter 2:4–18, and that Jude has just denounced people for tampering with the Christian message in verse 3. It means that his reworking of Peter's message displays the difference between tampering with the Gospel and tailoring it to our hearers. Knowing that the Gospel is our *"holy faith"* does not mean that we can be lazy in how we share it. We dare not modify God's message, but nor must we fail to contextualize it. Let's learn from Jude as he gets the Jewish believers nodding by demonstrating that the Christian message is the very thing their culture is longing for.

In verse 5, Jude wins the Jewish believers onto his side by adding an extra Old Testament story to the list in Peter's letter.[1] The Exodus from Egypt was one of the defining moments in Jewish history, so Jude uses it to convince his readers that they are in grave danger. If God did not spare the Exodus generation for refusing to put their faith in him, they dare not insult God by siding with false teachers instead of with the apostles, now that a far greater Exodus has come.

In verses 6–7, Jude echoes Peter by reminding his readers that the Lord judged the angels who joined in Satan's rebellion. He also echoes Peter when he reminds us that Sodom and Gomorrah and the other cities of the plain were destroyed for their *"sexual immorality and perversion"*. But don't miss the subtle differences in Jude's language. Peter refers to hell as "Tartarus", the deep abyss in the Underworld where the Greeks believed that wicked men and women were punished when they died, whereas Jude echoes the words of the Old Testament prophets by referring to hell as *"the punishment of eternal fire"*.[2] Peter uses Lot's anguish in Sodom to connect with Gentile

---

[1] In order to do this he omits Peter's mention of Noah's Flood. He knows that he will connect better with his Jewish readers by quoting instead from Noah's great-grandfather Enoch in verses 14–15.

[2] See for example Isaiah 33:14; 34:10; 66:15–16, 24. Note that Jude agrees entirely with Peter that hell was created for demons rather than for humans, that all demons will eventually go there (Matthew 8:29; 25:41; Luke 8:31) and that any person who chooses to go there with them will remain there forever.

believers living in pagan cities, whereas Jude uses the sinfulness of Sodom to convince Jewish believers that the false teachers are promoting a lifestyle that is anathema to their Jewish culture. Jude is very skilful in the way that he presents Jesus in the language of the Jews in order to persuade Jewish believers to hold on to the Gospel.

In verses 8–10, Jude expands on Peter's statement that the false teachers are guilty of blaspheming angels. Knowing that this is far more offensive to Jews than it is to Gentiles, he reminds his readers of the old Jewish legend about the burial of Moses. Deuteronomy 34 says that Moses died alone on Mount Nebo and yet was buried on the mountain, so a question had arisen over who had buried him. A Jewish campfire story taught that the archangel Michael had rescued his body from Satan and had buried him.[3] Jude is not endorsing this legend any more than Paul is endorsing the writings of the pagan Greek poets Epimenides and Aratus when he uses their words to present the Gospel to a group of Athenians in Acts 17:28. Jude is simply building a bridge towards his readers so that they will accept what he is saying: If even an archangel dared say no more than *"The Lord rebuke you!"* to Satan, the false teachers are patently deluded in the offhand way in which they share their dreams about angels and demons.[4] Rather than being offended by the way Jude handles this story, let's be instructed. Tim Keller explains:

> *As soon as you express the gospel, you are unavoidably doing it in a way that is more understandable and accessible for people in some cultures and less so for others... If you forget the first truth – that there is no*

---

[3] This ancient campfire story was written down in the "Testament of Moses" in the first century AD. The name *Michael* is Hebrew for *Who is Like God?* He appears in Daniel 10:13, 10:21 and 12:1, and in Revelation 12:7.

[4] Even the Lord himself rebukes Satan in Zechariah 3:2 by saying *"The Lord rebuke you!"*

*culture-less presentation of the gospel – you will think
there is only one true way to communicate it, and you are
on your way to a rigid, culturally bound conservatism. If
you forget the second truth – that there is only one true
gospel – you may fall into relativism, which will lead to a
rudderless liberalism. Either way, you will be less faithful
and less fruitful in ministry... Do contextualization*
consciously.[5]

Jude refuses to tamper with the Gospel, but he is adamant that
it has to be tailored to a specific group of hearers. In verse 11,
he echoes the way that Peter compares the false teachers to
the Old Testament villain Balaam, but he also adds two more
comparisons of his own. If the Jewish Christians believe the false
teachers, they are on the side of Cain in Genesis 4 and of Korah in
Numbers 16. Jude takes another Jewish campfire story in verses
14–15 and points out that even Enoch, the great-grandfather of
Noah, prophesied against false teachers such as these.[6] There
is nothing new about their evil doctrine. Such lies pre-date the
Flood and will remain until the return of Jesus from heaven. The
Jewish believers, of all people, ought to be ready to defend the
holy faith of Israel from its enemies.

Jude won his battle to gain a hearing for the Christian
message by presenting it in the language of the Jews. Now he
expects us to study our own culture and to do the same. God has
revealed his message of salvation once and for all, but he also
wants to teach us how to present his timeless truth in a timely
manner. He wants to teach us how to gain a hearing from our
friends and neighbours for the message that Jesus is the Saviour
for whom their culture has been searching for so long.

---

[5] Timothy Keller in *Center Church* (2012). If you are interested in learning more
about how to contextualize the Gospel – how to build bridges towards people
when you share it – this book is a great place to start.

[6] These ancient campfire stories were finally written down in the first century
BC in the "First Book of Enoch".

Giving and Grabbing (5–19)

These people are... shepherds who feed only themselves.

All of us can list examples of church leaders who went bad. They ran off with the church's money or they seduced the church's women or they tampered with the church's teaching. Each time it happens, people wring their hands and ask themselves how they can have been so blind to the leader's flaws. That's why Jude's letter is still so relevant. He gives us a simple test to assess the true agenda of any church leader. He tells us to take a step back and consider: Are they into giving or are they into grabbing?

In verse 6, Jude points out that a grabbing agenda always comes from the Devil. No church leader has ever looked more impressive than the angels who rebelled with Lucifer, the light-bearing angel who served alongside Michael in heaven. God had given them everything, yet it was still not enough for them. They did not want to bear light for the Lord, but to grab the limelight from the Lord. Jude tells us that whenever we see a leader who is more into grabbing than giving, that same spirit is at work within them.

In verse 7, Jude points out that this spirit caused the destruction of Sodom and its neighbouring cities. Ezekiel 16:49–50 lists the sins of Sodom as pride, complacency, social injustice and sexual immorality, all of which are expressions of a desire to suck things out of people instead of serving them. Jude particularly singles out the fourth item on Ezekiel's list when he tells us that the people of Sodom *"gave themselves up to sexual* sin". The Greek word he uses is *ekporneuō*, which is one of the roots of our English word pornography and speaks of exploiting others for our own sexual gratification. Jude adds literally in Greek that *"they went after a different type of flesh"* – not so much a reference to their desire to have sex with angels (since Genesis 19 says they thought the angels who visited Sodom were men), but a reference to their desire to have sex with men instead of women.[1] When church leaders lust in secret over members of their congregation, whether male or female, Jude warns us that the church is in grave danger. It always is whenever its leaders are more into grabbing than giving.[2]

In verse 11, Jude points out that Cain's problem was that he was a grabber through and through. Although his father Adam told him to give glory to the Lord by offering a blood sacrifice, he refused. He sacrificed the work of his own hands in order to grab all the glory for himself. Jude points out that Balaam was also a grabber, who viewed religion as a means of making money and who was even willing to promote sexual sin among God's people in return for pay. Jude says that Korah was the same. He tried to grab a position of spiritual leadership within Israel in order to gain prestige in the community. Jude expects us to know that Cain was banished and that Balaam and Korah were killed. God takes all this business of giving and grabbing very seriously.[3]

In verses 12–13, Jude tells the Jewish believers that if they apply this simple test to their church leaders, they will spot false

---

[1] Many modern scholars deny that Jude is talking about gay sex, but this is how Jude's words have been understood for the past 2,000 years of Church history. They are echoed by Romans 1:18–32, 1 Corinthians 6:9–11 and 1 Timothy 1:10. The fact we struggle with this simply reinforces how much we need Jude's letter.

[2] Jude echoes 2 Peter 2:16 by calling such leaders *brute beasts* in verse 10. Phoney leaders think themselves clever, but if they are governed by their self-centred desires, they are no better than animals.

[3] See Genesis 4; Numbers 16; 22–25; 2 Peter 2:15; Revelation 2:14.

teachers a mile away.[4] Do they act like *"shepherds who feed only themselves"*, guzzling the free food and drink at the church's shared meals without thinking about serving the needs of the poor and the hungry?[5] Then they are untrustworthy. They are *"clouds without rain"* and *"autumn trees, without fruit and uprooted"*, making loud promises about how much their teaching will benefit their hearers but yielding nothing in their lives but spiritual barrenness and famine.[6] Do they commit to serving a community of believers for the long haul, or do they move on as soon as the offer of a better congregation comes along? If it is the latter, they are as unstable as the *"wild waves of the sea"* and as the *"wandering stars"*. They are rootless and fruitless imposters and charlatans. Unless confronted, they will drag those they lead down with them into their own impending destruction.[7]

In verses 14–16, Jude uses the prophecies of Enoch to point out that having the wrong leaders does not merely rob churches of God's power. It actually makes them part of the problem. The Final Day when Jesus returns from heaven at the head of an army of angels will be a day of many surprises.[8] Jude does not want us to wait until that moment to spot that many so-called Christian leaders, Christian speakers and Christian writers are in fact *"ungodly sinners"*. He says that we can spot

---

[4] The Greek word for *shepherding* in verse 12 is *poimainō*, the root of the Greek noun *poimēn*, meaning *pastor*.

[5] It is not clear precisely what Jude means here by *"love feasts"*. It might refer to the church celebrating the Lord's Supper together, or it might refer to the whole church eating together as a big family.

[6] If you live in a rainy country, put yourself in the sandals of a first-century Jew. Clouds that fail to produce rain might be good news for us, but they spelled disaster for a Middle Eastern farmer. See Proverbs 25:14.

[7] Jude is alerting us to false teachers, so don't miss the way his letter specifically highlights those who deny the Bible's teaching about homosexuality, other sexual sin and the eternal nature of hell.

[8] The *hagioi*, or *holy ones*, in verse 3 were the ancient people of Israel. The *hagioi* in verse 14 are the holy angels. Enoch was taken into heaven thousands of years before Jude wrote his letter (Genesis 5:21–24), but his prophecies were preserved in the Jewish oral tradition and written down in the first century BC.

them right now from the fact that, unlike Jude, they cannot bear to live in anyone else's shadow. They are grumblers and malcontents and constant critics, who even refuse to be led by Jesus himself, daring to pass judgment on the words of the Bible instead of letting it pass judgment on them.[9] On the Last Day, any boaster who has flattered weak-minded people into giving them a church leadership position will be revealed as the self-centred sinner that they truly are.

In verses 17–19, Jude therefore urges his readers to make a sober assessment of their leaders. Since Jude is writing to Jewish believers in around 65 AD, he expects many of them to remember the original twelve apostles. Those men were givers who warned their hearers that many grabbers would come, dividing congregations and despising the Bible's teaching in pursuit of *"their own ungodly desires"*.[10] The apostles warned that such people would minister out of their own *"natural instincts"*, since they would not be true believers and would therefore not have the Holy Spirit to rely on.[11]

If you are a church leader, you ought to find these verses sobering. Take a pause from reading to consider whether any of the things that Jude lists could apply to you. Ask the Lord to make you like the godly church leaders described in 1 Timothy 3:1–13, Titus 1:6–9 and 1 Peter 5:1–4. Repent of your grabbing and commit yourself to giving.

If you are not a church leader, you ought to find these verses pretty sobering too. Jude is telling you that the type of leader you follow dictates the kind of Christian you will become. He is telling you to apply a simple test to your leaders today: Are you being influenced by grabbers or by givers?

---

[9] The Greek word *mempsimoiros* in verse 16 means *fate-blamer* rather than *fault-finder*. It refers to discontented people who complain about their lot in life because their agenda is all about grabbing, never giving.

[10] A scoffer is somebody who asks, *"How can you believe the Bible when it says that? It's just a primitive myth!"*

[11] The Greek word *psuchikos* in verse 19 means *empowered by the human soul*. False teachers may be very gifted but they are not filled and empowered by God's Spirit.

Inwards, Outwards, Upwards (20–25)

But you, dear friends, by building yourselves up in your most holy faith and praying in the Holy Spirit, keep yourselves in God's love.

(Jude 20–21)

Jude's letter is not the shortest in the New Testament. Two of John's letters and one of Paul's are even shorter. Nevertheless, Jude's letter feels very brief and hurried. We have barely begun it when we find ourselves in its six verses of conclusion. Jude uses these six verses to outline three ways for us to respond to his short letter. He tells us to look inwards and outwards and upwards if we want to see the Gospel triumph in the end.

In verses 20–21, Jude tells us to look inwards. Although he calls the Gospel *"the grace of our God"* in verse 4, he does not believe that receiving God's grace ought to lead to passivity. He echoes 2 Peter 3:14 when he tells us to make every effort to build ourselves up in our most holy faith and to keep ourselves in God's love. That's the paradox of the Christian life. It is a heavy burden and a daily battle, but one that Jesus carries for us and strengthens us to win. Jude therefore tells us to put ourselves in a position to receive all that God wants to give us. We cannot make ourselves grow and flourish as Christians, but we can certainly stop ourselves from growing and flourishing.

Jude says that one of the primary ways for you to grow in *"your most holy faith"* is through *"praying in the Holy Spirit"*. I wish that Jude were clearer here, because we can interpret this instruction in two different ways. Jude might be telling us to look inwards and to cooperate with the Holy Spirit as he reveals to us the topics about which God wants us to pray. This would tie in with Zechariah 12:10, Romans 8:26–27 and Ephesians 6:18. On the other hand, he might be telling us to look inwards and to cooperate with the Holy Spirit as he enables us to pray in tongues, a special prayer language given us by God. This would tie in with 1 Corinthians 14:4 and 14:14–15. The British missionary Jackie Pullinger interpreted Jude's instruction in the second of these two ways and later shared it as the secret to her extraordinary fruitfulness in seeing hundreds of drug addicts in the Walled City of Hong Kong saved and set free:

> *I gave in. "All right, Lord – this doesn't make sense to me, but since You invented it, it must be a good gift, so I'll go ahead in obedience and You teach me how to pray."... Every day I prayed in the language of the Spirit. Fifteen minutes by the clock. I still felt it to be an exercise. Before praying in the Spirit I said, "Lord – I don't know how to pray, or whom to pray for. Will You pray through me – and will You lead me to the people who want You." And I would begin my fifteen-minute stint. After about six weeks I noticed something remarkable. Those I talked to about Christ believed. I could not understand it at first and wondered how my Chinese had so suddenly improved, or if I had stumbled on a splendid new evangelistic technique. But I was saying the same things as before. It was some time before I realized what had changed. This time I was talking about Jesus to people who wanted to hear. I had let God have a hand in my prayers and it produced a direct result. Instead of my deciding what I wanted to do for God and asking His blessing I was asking Him to do His will through me as I prayed in the language He gave me. Now I found that person after person wanted to receive Jesus. I could not*

be proud – I could only wonder that God let me be a small part of His work.[1]

Personally, I think that both of these two possible interpretations are valid. If Jude is vague, then it is probably deliberate. He wants us to "pray in the Holy Spirit" by allowing him to guide what we pray for in our own languages, and he wants us to "pray in the Holy Spirit" by asking God to give us the gift of tongues so that we can pray in a language we do not understand. It isn't either or. He wants us to take Paul seriously when he says, *"I will pray with my spirit, but I will also pray with my understanding… I thank God that I speak in tongues more than all of you."*[2]

In verses 22–23, Jude tells us to look outwards. He encourages us to build up other people in their holy faith too. Unlike the false teachers, who view other people in terms of what they can get out of them, we are to serve our fellow Christians in the same manner that Jesus has served us. We need to pastor different people in different ways. Those who vacillate between faith and doubt require our merciful patience as they grow to maturity.[3] Those who fall for the lies of false teachers require our urgent intervention to rescue them. Those who spread false teaching require our firm discipline, as we temper our mercy towards them with a solemn warning that their actions suggest they are not true Christians at all. Jude assures us that self-centred wolves can be defeated through such wise shepherding. He addresses these instructions to all of us, not just to leaders, because every believer has a role to play.[4]

---

[1] Jackie Pullinger in her autobiography *Chasing the Dragon* (1980).

[2] 1 Corinthians 14:15, 18. Like Paul in 1 Corinthians 1:7, Jude says that we should expect such spiritual gifts to last until Jesus returns from heaven. We still need them just as much today.

[3] The Greek word *diakrinō* in verse 22 means *to be of two judgments*. It was used in verse 9 to describe Michael's dispute with Satan. When Christians dither in two minds they need our mercy, not our anger.

[4] Take note: Jude does not blame the Devil for false teaching within the Church. He blames Christians for allowing it to take root in the Church

In verses 24-25, Jude ends his letter by telling us to look upwards. These are probably the most famous verses in Jude's letter, because they are used by many church traditions as a doxology in their worship services. They assure us in the face of conflict that, if our salvation began with God, we can rely on him to keep us saved until the very end. They remind us that God is our eternal Saviour and that Jesus is our eternal Lord. The ultimate triumph of the Gospel in our lives does not rely on our own faithfulness but on his. The security of our salvation does not depend on our ability to keep hold of God but on God's ability to keep hold of us. The English Puritans put it this way:

> *They whom God hath accepted in His Beloved, effectually called, and sanctified by His Spirit can neither totally nor finally fall away from the state of grace, but shall certainly persevere therein to the end, and be eternally saved... True believers may have the assurance of their salvation divers ways shaken... yet they are never utterly destitute of that seed of God and life of faith that... by the operation of the Spirit this assurance may, in due time, be revived.*[5]

That's how Jude ends his letter, assuring us that persecution outside the Church and false teaching within the Church are no match for the glory, majesty, power and authority of God. However much the Devil hates our holy faith, he cannot destroy it. Those God saves he also protects. He will ensure the Gospel triumphs in the end.[6]

---

unchallenged.

[5] *The Westminster Confession of Faith* (1646). Other verses that talk about the "perseverance of the saints" are John 10:28, Romans 8:35–39, Philippians 1:6, 1 Thessalonians 5:23–24, 2 Timothy 1:12 and Hebrews 7:25.

[6] Jude is a personal example of this. He once dismissed his older half-brother's claims as those of a madman. Now he proclaims that Jesus truly mediates God's glory, majesty, power and authority forever.

Part Four

True Knowledge

(1 John)

The Man Who Was There (1:1-4)

We have seen it and testify to it.

All eyes were on William Pitt the Elder as he hobbled into the Houses of Parliament on 7th April 1778. The aged former prime minister was only able to walk with the aid of crutches, but he refused to let his decrepit body rob him of a chance to speak his mind. In middle age, he had masterminded the British victory over France in the Seven Years War. In old age, he had repeatedly warned the British government that if it tried to tax the American colonies, it would lose them. Now he was determined to spend whatever strength was left to him on warning Parliament not to heed the threats of enemies abroad and of weak men at home by surrendering prematurely to France.

"My Lords, I rejoice that the grave has not closed upon me; that I am still alive to lift up my voice... My Lords, any state is better than despair. Let us at least make one effort; and if we must fall, let us fall like men!" The very act of speaking these words proved too much for William Pitt the Elder. As he finished his speech, he clutched his chest in agony and collapsed in a fit on the floor. He was carried out of the Houses of Parliament to die, but the words that he had spoken long outlived him. The final appeal of an old man strengthened the resolve of a nation and drew it back from the precipice of ruin.

That's the kind of picture that we need to have in mind when we read John's three letters. By now it is around 90 AD and the apostle is aged somewhere between eighty-five and

158

ninety-five. He has been following Jesus for over sixty years. Over the past twenty-five years since Peter and Jude wrote their letters, he has watched an entire generation of Christians die. Peter and Paul have been executed by Emperor Nero. Mark has been murdered by a lynch mob in Egypt. Other leaders have been martyred as missionaries to the fringes of the Roman Empire. John is the sole survivor of the twelve original disciples, and even he has had to flee the destruction of Jerusalem and set up home in Ephesus, on the west coast of modern-day Turkey.[1]

Irenaeus tells us that *"John the Lord's disciple, the one who leaned back on his chest, published a gospel whilst living at Ephesus in Asia... John made his permanent home in Ephesus until the time of Trajan."*[2] John wrote his five books of the New Testament during his twilight years in Ephesus in order to save the Church from disaster.[3] Things had worsened since Peter and Jude had written about our *living hope*, our *precious faith* and our *holy faith*. False teachers had attracted large followings and had gained a loud voice in many churches. An early form of what is now known as "Gnosticism" had infiltrated many congregations. John therefore hauls his ageing body into the fray, like William Pitt the Elder, in order to call believers back to faith in the real Gospel. He says in 2:26 that *"I am writing these things to you about those who are trying to lead you astray."*

John's first letter is all about *true knowledge*. The word "Gnostic" comes from the Greek word *gnōsis*, which means *knowledge*, because the false teachers claimed to offer people special knowledge about God. John therefore talks about *knowing* and *knowledge* a whopping forty-five times in the five chapters

---

[1] John was the sole surviving member of the Twelve, but there were other eyewitnesses still alive in the churches. Note his *"we"* in these four verses and in John 21:24.

[2] Irenaeus wrote this in c.180 AD in *Against Heresies* (3.1.1 and 3.3.4). Trajan became emperor in 98 AD.

[3] John 21:23 suggests that people were amazed at John's extreme old age by the time he wrote his gospel. Revelation 1:9 suggests that John wrote during Emperor Domitian's wave of persecution in c.95 AD.

of his first letter.[4] That's more than twice as often as Peter and Jude use those words in all their letters put together. John insists firmly that the Gospel alone imparts true knowledge of God. The abstract ideas of false teachers may sound impressive, but talk is cheap. John is an eyewitness of what the Lord Jesus came down to earth to do. Note the way that he echoes the start of his gospel in the opening four verses of this letter, asserting eight times his authority as an eyewitness to the ministry of Jesus: *"We have heard... We have seen with our eyes... We have looked at... Our hands have touched... We have seen it and testify to it... It appeared to us... We have seen... We have heard."*[5]

John's second and third letters are all about *true love*. It wasn't easy for the believers to know how to respond to the false teachers. Surely the most Christian response was to tolerate them and to try to woo them back to the truth through acceptance and love? In any case, it wasn't hard to see that Emperor Domitian might at any moment launch a far worse wave of persecution against the Church than anything cooked up by his predecessor Nero. Surely this was a moment for unity, not division, in the face of a powerful enemy? John therefore does more than merely teach us how to spot false teaching. He also tells us how to deal with it when we find it. These three letters could not be more relevant to us today.

When the eighteenth-century politician Horace Walpole reflected on the actions of William Pitt the Elder, he concluded that he *"found the nation at the lowest ebb in point of power and*

---

[4] He also talks about *knowing* over 100 times in his gospel. Note the way that these opening four verses echo the big themes of his gospel: Jesus is *the Word* (John 1:1) and *the Life* (John 11:25 and 14:6), who alone can grant *eternal life* (John 3:16) and *complete joy* (John 15:11 and 16:24). Unlike Peter and Jude, John does not name himself at the start of his letter, but this echo confirms the early Church's united testimony that John wrote it.

[5] In the face of Docetism, John 20:19–29 particularly emphasizes the fact that he and his friends saw, felt and touched the physical resurrection body of Jesus. The Greek word used in 1 John 1:1 for *touching* is *psēlaphaō*, the same word that is used in Luke 24:39.

reputation... [and] roused us from this ignoble lethargy". They clashed frequently, but Walpole was forced to acknowledge that *"It were ingratitude to him to say that he did not give such a reverberation to our stagnating councils, as exceedingly altered the appearance of our fortune. He warded off the evil hour that seemed approaching, he infused vigour into our arms, he taught the nation to speak again as England used to speak to foreign powers."*[6]

That is my prayer for you as you read John's three letters. In an age of spiritual lethargy, my prayer is that John's words will rouse you to action. In an age of unthinking compromise, born not of wickedness but of ignorance, my prayer is that John's words will instruct you and give you a strong backbone for battle. In an age where the Church speaks with such uncertainty, with such timidity and with such longing for this world's approval, my prayer is that John's words will teach you to speak as Christians spoke before, in an age when the Church advanced in astonishing ways through God's power.

The apostle John speaks as a voice from a dying generation to the one that lives on. He reminds us: *"That which was from the beginning, which we have heard, which we have seen with our eyes, which we have looked at and our hands have touched – this we proclaim."*

---

[6] Horace Walpole in his *Memoirs: Volume III*.

The Fixer (1:2–4)

We write this to make our joy complete.

When reading John's letters, it isn't hard to tell that he was an uneducated fisherman. He uses shorter sentences and a much smaller vocabulary than either Paul or Luke. Instead of structuring his arguments according to the strict rules of Greek logic, he goes round in circles as he states the same argument three times.[1] It isn't hard to believe that this is the man that the Jewish leaders dismissed as an ignorant fisherman alongside Peter in Acts 4:13. But don't let that fool you that John had the same role to play as Peter in God's plans for the Church. He had been kept alive longer than his friends because he had his own particular role to play.

162

When Jesus had called the fishing partners to follow him on the shores of Lake Galilee, he had hinted at different plans for Peter and John. He found Peter fishing and promised to enable him to catch great nets full of people through his evangelistic preaching, but he found John fixing nets that had been damaged through the hard demands of long hours of fishing. The Greek word that is used for John *fixing* nets in Matthew 4:21 and Mark 1:19 comes from the word used to describe church leaders *equipping* Christians to follow Jesus fruitfully in Ephesians 4:12.[2] The account of John's calling, therefore, hints that he was destined to become God's fixer. He would pick up his pen to

---

[1] As we will see later, John repeats the same argument in 1:5–2:28, 2:29–4:6 and 4:7–5:12.

[2] The verb *katartizō* and its noun *katartismos* refer to the work of *fixing, completing, preparing* or *perfecting*.

write at a time when the Church's nets were damaged and there was lots of urgent fixing to be done.

John wrote his gospel after those of Matthew, Mark and Luke. He repeats little of what they say because he wrote to fill in what they missed out. John deepens our understanding of Jesus by describing his inner thoughts and by saying that we can think like him by being filled with the Holy Spirit. The second-century church leader Clement of Alexandria observes that *"John, perceiving that the outward facts had been set forth in those gospels, urged on by his friends and inspired by the Spirit, composed a spiritual gospel."*[3]

John also wrote Revelation to complete what was lacking in our view of Jesus from the four gospels. He introduces us to Jesus, not as he used to be when he walked the shores of Galilee in weakness before his death and resurrection, but as he is now, sitting in glorious triumph on the Throne of heaven. It is easy to forget who Jesus is, so John reminds us that without this knowledge we are fishing with broken nets and are likely to catch next to nothing. He tells us, *"Dear friends, I am not writing you a new command but an old one, which you have had since the beginning."*[4] The Church's nets need to be fixed in each generation and God appointed John to be one of their earliest fixers.

First, John fixes our view of *the Christian message*. He uses a phrase in 1:2 that is his own equivalent of Matthew's *"kingdom of heaven"* and of Mark and Luke's *"kingdom of God"*. Sixteen times in his gospel and six times in his first letter, he describes the Gospel as the promise of *"eternal life"*. He wants this thought to stop us from cowering before a hostile emperor or a hostile media, since we have a hope that nobody can take away from us. The worst that they can do is propel us into its undying arms. More than that, since the Greek phrase *zōē aiōnion* can also be

---

[3] Quoted by Eusebius of Caesarea just after 300 AD in his *Church History* (6.14.7).

[4] 1 John 2:7; 3:11; 2 John 5.

translated *"the life of the eternal age"*, John reminds us that the Gospel is far more than a promise for tomorrow. It is meant to be our very real experience today. We are meant to feast so fully on the delights of the coming age that we are able to bring down its power to people living in this age that is passing away.[5] If the Church remembers this, its powerful preaching will never fail to catch a crowd of eager converts, but it never will if its nets are broken through forgetfulness.

False teachers always have impressive arguments. They cannot be fought by logic alone, but this does not present a problem if we remember that *"the kingdom of God is not a matter of talk but of power."*[6] John wants to mend our broken understanding of the Gospel so that we can speak to the need we see around us and say with him and his fishing partner in Acts 3:6, *"Silver or gold I do not have, but what I do have I give you."*

Second, John fixes our view of *the Christian calling.* He uses the same Greek word in 1:3 to describe our fellowship with God that Luke 5:10 uses to describe Peter and John's fishing partnership.[7] Left to our own devices, we always downgrade the idea of fellowship to the nodding of our heads at God in the hope that he will maybe nod back in return and to the shallowest of interactions between Christians after a Sunday service. But John is a practical fisherman. He knows what partnership truly means. It isn't about waving to one another or lamenting the fact that there are too many fish in the lake and not enough in the boat. It is about rolling up our sleeves and committing to work hard together as a team.

God has committed to work hard with you. Because the

---

[5] See Hebrews 6:5. John tells us in John 17:3 and in 1 John 5:13 and 20 that *eternal life* is not just about our getting into heaven when we die, but about our getting heaven down to earth while we still live.

[6] 1 Corinthians 4:19–20; 1 Thessalonians 1:5; 2 Timothy 3:5.

[7] The word for *partner* in Luke 5:10 is *koinōnos.* The word for *partnership* in 1 John 1:3 is *koinōnia.*

Father loves the Son, he sent him into the world. Because the Son loves the Spirit, he poured him out on his earthly followers after he had completed his own assignment and ascended back to heaven. Today he invites you to be an active partner in God's family business: *"When the Advocate comes, whom I will send to you from the Father – the Spirit of truth who goes out from the Father – he will testify about me. And you also must testify."*[8]

Third, John fixes our view of *the Christian experience*. He says in 1:4 that he wrote this letter *"to make our joy complete"*.[9] Let's face it: Christians aren't always marked by their glad faces. John says that this is because our nets are broken. We think too much about trying to win God's approval and not enough about how much we already have it in Jesus. We think too much about the problems that lie before us and not enough about the power of the eternal age to overcome them as we partner with the Holy Spirit.

So let's listen to God's fixer. Let's believe him when he tells us that our nets are broken. Let's submit gladly to the way he mends them through his letters. John wants to teach us that the only way forward is to go back to the promises of Jesus, *"that my joy may be in you and that your joy may be complete"*, and that we *"may have life, and have it to the full"*.[10]

---

[8] John 15:26–27. Jesus deliberately refers to the *Father, Son and Church* in Revelation 3:12.

[9] Some Greek manuscripts say *'your joy complete'*, but in most John includes himself in the work of fixing.

[10] 1 John 1:4 strongly echoes John 10:10, 15:11, 16:24 and 17:13. It is echoed in turn in 2 John 12.

Signs of Life (1:5–2:28)

His anointing teaches you about all things... That anointing is real, not counterfeit.

(1 John 2:27)

One of my friends is almost eighty. He has some fascinating stories to tell – or at least he has the very first time that you meet him. The problem is that he instantly forgets what he has told you. He repeats the same old stories over and over again, sometimes even in the same conversation. It is one of the signs that his mind is getting old.

A lot of people think that John must have suffered from the same problem, because the ageing apostle repeats the same argument three times in this letter. He adds some fresh perspective with each retelling, but this repetition still strikes many readers as very strange. We therefore need to know a little bit about what was happening in Ephesus and the surrounding cities in the final fifteen years of the first century. It helps us to see that John wasn't losing his mind. Far from it. He writes with the skill of an old master.

It is clear from John's opening statement about seeing and touching Jesus that the Docetists were still very active when he wrote this letter, claiming that Jesus had not truly taken on human flesh but had merely pretended to do so in order to make people listen to him. The second-century writer Irenaeus tells us that one of the most active false teachers at Ephesus was Cerinthus, a man who had studied comparative religions in Egypt and who made a firm distinction between "Jesus" and "Christ". He claimed that Jesus was a normal man who had been born to both Mary and Joseph, and that a spiritual being named "Christ" had entered his body at his baptism, abandoning him just before his crucifixion. Cerinthus attracted a large following, since this removed many of the Greek objections to Christianity: the virgin birth, the idea of God taking on human flesh and the idea of God's Son dying like a common criminal.[1]

We also discover in Revelation that John was fighting a false teacher named Nicolas and a woman who pretended to be a prophet. Revelation warns people to keep away from their *"so-called deep secrets"*, suggesting strongly that they were early Gnostics who claimed to initiate their followers into a deeper knowledge of God.[2] Many Christians were confused over whose teaching was right and whose was wrong, so John repeats a simple test for them to follow. After describing the test for a third and final time, he explains in 5:13 that *"I write these things to you who believe in the name of the Son of God **so that you may know that you have eternal life**."*

John agrees that we need deeper knowledge of God, but he warns us not to look for it in this world's philosophy dressed up in Christian clothes. He tells us to look for it in our experience of the Holy Spirit. As we examine our lives, can we see any evidence of the life of the age to come breaking out in our hearts? Can we see any signs that we are engaged in active partnership with the Trinity? John repeats in 1:5–2:28, in 2:29–4:6 and in 4:7–5:12 that this is the only secret knowledge that truly matters. If we see any signs of spiritual life in our sinful hearts, it is proof we have God's Spirit in us and are therefore saved, since we could not bear such spiritual fruit on our own.[3] If we see no clear signs of spiritual life in our hearts then – no matter how much

167

---

[1] Irenaeus tells us about Cerinthus in *Against Heresies* (1.26.1, 3:2.1, 3.3.4 and 3.11.1).

[2] Revelation 2:6, 15, 20, 24. Irenaeus says that the Nicolaitans were led by the Nicolas who is mentioned in Acts 6:5, but the evidence for this is not convincing. Nicolas was a common first-century name.

[3] John 3:3–8. See also John 1:13; 6:63; Ephesians 2:1–10; Titus 3:4–7.

we may protest to the contrary – John says that we are not saved at all. John says that the key to all true Christian confidence lies in our active experience of the Holy Spirit.[4]

John's first sign of life is that *we find ourselves living like Jesus* (1:5–2:6, 2:29–3:10 and 5:1–5). This can only be a miracle. Although ancient false teachers and modern self-help paperbacks assure us that we have the power to change ourselves, we know from bitter experience that it simply isn't true. We know the way we ought to live but we choose not to do so. Even when we try to make the right choice, we discover what Paul describes in Romans 7–8 as *"the law of sin and death"* at work within us, stopping us from following through on our good desires and dragging us back towards our wicked ones. John therefore tells us to examine our lives to see the ways that God has changed us. If we are no different from the way we were before we prayed to become Christians, there was evidently something wrong with our prayer. If we can see clear changes, John encourages us to rejoice over each little miracle as a proof of our salvation.

John's second sign of life is that *we find ourselves loving like Jesus* (2:7–11, 3:10–24 and 4:7–21). He singles out love because the New Testament repeatedly says it is the mother of every other Christian virtue.[5] Unbelievers may love passionately, but they tend to reserve their love for those who love them back. To love those who hate us requires the inner miracle that Paul describes in Romans 5:5: *"God's love has been poured out into our hearts through the Holy Spirit, who has been given to us."*[6] John therefore argues that if we see no signs of sacrificial love in our hearts, we are fooling ourselves that we are saved. Conversely, if

---

[4] Romans 8:9, 16; 1 Corinthians 12:13; 2 Corinthians 1:21–22; 5:5–6; Ephesians 1:13–14.

[5] Matthew 22:37–40; Romans 13:8–10; Galatians 5:14; James 2:8.

[6] Matthew 5:43–48; Luke 6:32–36. Jesus is not saying that unbelievers never display sacrificial love for others, simply that to do so consistently requires God to work a miracle in our hearts by his Holy Spirit.

we see any traces of the love of Jesus flowing out of our hearts, it is a certain sign we have eternal life through faith in him.

John's third sign of life is that *we find ourselves believing in the real Jesus* (2:18–28, 4:1–6 and 5:6–12). He is not at all surprised that many people preach a very different Jesus. After all, who would choose a Christ who insists that our lives must revolve around him and not around ourselves? Who would choose a Christ who judges us instead of indulging us whenever we refuse? Who would choose a Christ who demands that we walk the death-and-resurrection road with him each day? The answer is nobody – nobody, that is, except for those whose sinful spirits have been made alive by the Holy Spirit. Nobody except for those who have been born again and who therefore think very differently from the unregenerate world. It is such a miraculous turnaround for anyone to acknowledge the real Jesus that John says it is a sign of their salvation.

So don't imagine that John repeats himself throughout this letter because his old age has befuddled his senses. He does so because his old age has given him great clarity of mind. In six decades of following Jesus he has discovered three foolproof signs of a real Christian, which cut through the confusion of our mixed-up world. *"I write these things to you who believe in the name of the Son of God **so that you may know** that you have eternal life."*

What John Saw (1:5–2:6)

If we confess our sins, he is faithful and just and will forgive us our sins and purify us from all unrighteousness.

(1 John 1:9)

Confidence isn't always a virtue. If it isn't based on truth, it can spell disaster. I will never forget the week my voice broke and I answered the phone sounding for the first time like a man. My father often received phone calls for marriage counselling and this was one of them. Hearing my baritone voice, the woman unleashed on me a cascade of self-revelation before I was able to reply. She gave me detail about her husband's latest indiscretion that no thirteen-year-old should ever have to hear. It was only when she finally paused for breath to unleash a fresh burst of unwanted information that I was able to interrupt her awkwardly: *"Erm – I think you want to speak to my father!"*

John is confident throughout this letter. He states his eyewitness credentials and assures us that he is able to help us know for sure that we have eternal life. But how can we tell whether his confidence is well placed? Does he have true knowledge or does he merely have the same false confidence that proved so embarrassing to the woman who phoned my father's home? John predicts our question because, as he states his argument for the first time, he tells us what he saw as one of the original twelve disciples.[1]

---

[1] *"If we claim... If we claim... If we claim"* challenges us that our confidence may be misplaced (1:6, 8, 10). John says in 1:5 that he bases all of his confidence in *"the message we have heard from him and declare to you"*.

When John started following Jesus, he was an arrogant man. That may sound strange to you, given that he was a common fisherman, but he liked to think of himself as something of a hero. For a start, his family was well connected in Jerusalem. He was on such good terms with the high priest that he was able to gain entrance to the palace even when security was high. He was so impressed with his own abilities that he once asked Jesus to appoint him as his right-hand man in heaven.[2] John assures us in 1:5-7 that his confidence is no longer based on arrogance. Three years with Jesus had demolished his youthful arrogance once and for all. When he saw that the high priest was unable to point out a single sin that Jesus had committed, he was forced to recognize that he was nothing by God's standards: *"God is light: in him there is no darkness at all."*[3]

John had seen the very best religious teachers standing alongside Jesus. He was there to hear him challenge the rabbi Nicodemus: *"No one can see the kingdom of God unless they are born again."* He was there to hear him warn the religious that *"Many will say to me on that day, 'Lord, Lord'... I will tell them plainly, 'I never knew you. Away from me, you evildoers!'"*[4] That's why in 1:8-10 he bases all his confidence, not on religious devotion, but on a free and frank confession of our sin. *"If we claim to be without sin, we deceive ourselves and the truth is not in us. If we confess our sins, he is faithful and just and will forgive us our sins and purify us from all unrighteousness."*[5] John writes with confidence because he saw enough of Jesus to grasp that all our confidence must be in God, and not in ourselves.

John had not merely seen how far the best of us fall beneath

[2] John 18:15–16; Mark 10:35–41.

[3] This is why self-deception is so damaging to our relationship with God and with other believers. Light and darkness cannot mix. We need to take off our masks and be honest with each other.

[4] John 3:1–12; Matthew 7:21–23.

[5] John tells us in 1:9 that the blood of Jesus grants us two things, not just one. It grants us *forgiveness* from the penalty of sin and *purification* from the filth of sin. God wants us to believe in him for both.

God's standards. He had also seen God's willingness to forgive the very worst of us. He writes with confidence because he saw Jesus intervene to save the life of a woman who was about to be stoned to death for adultery, saying to her, *"I do not condemn you; go now and leave your life of sin."* He had seen the way that Jesus responded to the rabbis when they complained that he extended friendship to prostitutes and traitors and other notorious sinners. He had heard Jesus express God's love for the repentant in his reply: *"It is not the healthy who need a doctor, but those who are ill. I have not come to call the righteous, but sinners."*[6]

That's why John assures us in 2:1-2 that we can have every confidence that God will forgive us if we throw ourselves on his mercy. It isn't wishful thinking. It is the fruit of his having seen Jesus on the cross forgiving one of the thieves who hung next to him and crying out for his Father to forgive his executioners. John tells us to be confident because our forgiveness does not depend on whether or not our own prayers and sacrifice are good enough, but on whether or not Jesus's prayers and sacrifice are good enough. These two verses can be translated, *"If anybody sins, we have a defence attorney before the Father – Jesus Christ, the Righteous One who averts God's anger against our sins."* There is nothing uncertain about John's confidence here. With a defence attorney like Jesus we simply cannot lose.[7]

172

John was there to see God's great sign to us that the sacrifice of Jesus is good enough to atone for all our sins. John had gone into the tomb and handled the empty grave clothes. He had seen the risen Jesus several times. He knew more than anyone that Jesus is alive. The false teachers may talk about him in the past tense as a great teacher and a great example, but John talks about him in the present tense as our closest friend.

---

[6] John 8:1–11; Mark 2:15–17.

[7] The Greek word for *defence attorney* in 2:1 is *paraklētos*, the same word Jesus uses to describe the Holy Spirit helping us in John 14:16, 14:26, 15:26 and 16:7. See Romans 8:27 and 34, and Hebrews 7:25.

John's confidence flows from the fact that he has walked for over half a century with the risen Jesus and that he has helped two generations of believers to walk with him too.

We can therefore trust John's confidence in 2:3–6. We can believe him when he assures us that the Gospel unleashes God's resurrection power in the lives of those who truly know him. The Holy Spirit refuses to back up the self-improvement plans of the false teachers, but he rushes to apply the death and resurrection of Jesus to the heart of anyone who embraces true knowledge of him. If you can see no evidence of a miraculous change to your own lifestyle, this is serious. You need to find a Christian friend and ask them to lead you into genuine salvation. But if you can see evidence of God's miraculous work within your heart, this should give you confidence to say with John: *"We know that we have come to know him if we keep his commands."*

So do you pass John's test? Do you see clear signs of God at work in your life? Do you see the humble confession of 1:5–10, the robust faith of 2:1–2 and the active experience of 2:3–6? If you do, then praise God for it. Our godly actions have no power to save us but they bear powerful witness that we are saved. If you see no clear signs, do something about it. Tell God that you want to know Jesus today through your confidence in the things John saw.

The Whole World (2:1–2)

He is the atoning sacrifice for our sins, and not only
for ours but also for the sins of the whole world.

(1 John 2:2)

John was an unlikely world traveller. He was a Galilean through and through. Although Luke describes the body of water on which he fished as a lake, to John it was the Sea of Galilee. He was so travel-shy that he confesses in his gospel his fear of travelling to Jerusalem, revealing that at one point he even locked the door of his lodgings for fear of the Judeans. When Jesus commanded John and his friends to take the Gospel from Judea to the ends of the earth, they were therefore terrified. They would have much preferred to stay at home.[1] Nevertheless, John moved to Ephesus and wrote a gospel which emphasizes that Jesus came to earth to save people from every nation of the world.[2] He does it again here in 2:2, telling us to be confident that Jesus *"is the atoning sacrifice for our sins, and not only for ours but also for the sins of the whole world"*.

Some people misunderstand this verse. They think that John is saying that Jesus died for everybody and that eventually everybody will therefore be saved. When we looked at a similar verse in 2 Peter 3:9, we reflected on why we find this idea so attractive. Most of us have loved ones who have died without putting their faith in Jesus, so we find it comforting to think that God's love towards them might have overruled their

---

[1] John 6:1; 11:7–8; 20:19; 21:1; Acts 1:8. John's view of Lake Galilee is so out of proportion that many English Bibles even translate the Greek word *sea* as if it ought to mean *lake*.

[2] See John 1:29; 3:16; 4:42; 12:32.

indifference towards him. Most of us have unbelieving friends who seem to lead good lives, so it would be nice to think that the blood of Jesus is powerful enough to overrule their rejection of it. But that is not what John is saying here. Quite the contrary. He is telling us that sin is so serious that the whole world needs the atoning sacrifice of Jesus.[3] He is echoing the message of his gospel that *"Whoever believes in the Son has eternal life, but whoever rejects the Son will not see life, for God's wrath remains on them."*[4]

Other people take John's words to mean that, while outright atheists are excluded, God will accept the sincere faith of the devotees of any of the great world religions. If somebody happened to be born in Tibet or Saudi Arabia, God will treat their faith in the local gods as if it were faith in Jesus. I hope you can see that this is also the very opposite of what John is saying here. He is writing from a city which was very proud of its Temple of Artemis, one of the seven wonders of the ancient world, but instead of applauding their devotion to the goddess John ends this letter with a solemn warning to *"Keep yourselves from idols."* Remember, this is the man who stood up with Peter and risked death to declare in Acts 4:12 that Jesus died for the whole world because none of the world's religions carries any power to save: *"Salvation is found in no one else, for there is no other name under heaven given to mankind by which we must be saved."*

John cannot be telling us here that Jesus was punished for the sins of everybody in the world. God is not unjust, so he never punishes two people for the same sin. If Jesus bore the penalty

---

[3] The Greek word *hilasmos* in 2:2 means *propitiation* or *an act which appeases wrath*. It was a word from the Temple that warns us we need a sacrifice to avert God's righteous anger towards our sin. The death of Jesus was not a sign that God is now more lenient towards sin, but that he is unwavering in his judgment of it.

[4] John 3:36; 1 John 5:12. A global summit of church leaders at Constantinople in 553 AD ruled firmly that "universalism" (the belief that God will ultimately save everybody) is an entirely unbiblical view.

for every sin, everybody must be saved, but of course the rest of the Bible says that this is not the case. The great Puritan thinker John Owen observes that

> God imposed his wrath due unto, and Christ underwent the pains of hell for, either [1] all the sins of all men, or [2] all the sins of some men, or [3] some sins of all men. If the last, some sins of all men, then have all men some sins to answer for, and so shall no man be saved... If the first, why then are not all freed from the punishment of all their sins? You will say, "Because of their unbelief; they will not believe." But this unbelief, is it a sin or not? If not, why should they be punished for it? If so, then did Christ undergo the punishment due to it, or not? If He did, why must that hinder them more than their other sins for which He died?... If He did not, then He did not die for all their sins.[5]

John must therefore be saying the same thing as Paul in 1 Timothy 4:10, that Jesus *"is the Saviour of all people, and especially of those who believe"*. He reminds us that the Gospel invitation is for everybody everywhere. Although he is a reluctant traveller, he has made his home in a pagan city because he believes God has chosen to save many people who live there. No one is so sinful or so entrenched in another religion that they are beyond the reach of God's salvation. John saw the way that Jesus embraced lepers and adulterers and repentant rabbis, so he speaks with the tender voice of a father in 2:2, calling his readers *"my little children"* for the first of seven times in this letter.[6] As one of the final survivors from the first generation of Christians, he tells those who come after him that God's mercy stretches to each

---

[5] John Owen wrote this in 1648 in *The Death of Death in the Death of Christ* (1.3).

[6] Whereas Paul tends to call his readers *"brothers"*, John calls them *teknia mou*, which means literally *"my little children"* (2:1, 12, 28; 3:7, 18; 4:4; 5:21).

one of them. Even the interest with which we are reading his letter is proof that God has chosen to begin a saving work in our hearts.[7]

If this is true, it is the best news that anyone can hear. If God is truly willing to save anyone – regardless of their sinfulness, their religion, their race and the hatred that they have presented towards him until now – then we need to travel the whole world with it – starting with our neighbours and work colleagues, but also doing all we can to reach people hundreds and thousands of miles away. We need to warn the world that anybody who denies their sin will be punished for it, while anybody that confesses their sin will find that God's Son has already borne their punishment away. We need to pass on the testimony of 1 John 4:14: *"We have seen and testify that the Father has sent his Son to be the Saviour of the world."* We need to ask them with Charles Spurgeon:

> *Whom did Christ die for? Will you answer me a question or two, and I will tell you whether He died for* ***you***. *Do you want a Saviour? Do you feel that you need a Saviour? Are you this morning conscious of sin? Has the Holy Spirit taught you that you are lost? Then Christ died for you and you will be saved... I can not only say to you that you may be saved, but what is better still, that you will be saved... For if Christ has died for you, you cannot be lost. God will not punish twice for one thing. If God punished Christ for your sin, He will never punish you.*[8]

---

[7] See John 1:13; 6:37, 44, 65; 15:16; 2 John 1, 13. Jesus died for everyone potentially, so the moment anybody shows any sign of faith in his cross, it is a clear sign that God is at work in their heart.

[8] Spurgeon preached this sermon on "Particular Redemption" at his church in London on 28th February 1858, arguing that God never punishes sin twice. He died for all potentially, but we must receive it specifically.

The Miracle Maker (2:3–11)

We know that we have come to know him if we keep his commands.

(1 John 2:3)

John knew Jesus as the Miracle Maker. He was there when Jesus turned water into wine at a wedding banquet. He was there when Jesus healed a lame man who had been an invalid for thirty-eight years. He was there when Jesus fed a crowd of over 5,000 people with only five loaves and two fish. He was there when Jesus walked on water, healed a man who had been born blind and called the dead man Lazarus to step out of his tomb. The miracles in John's gospel ought to leave us breathless.

178

John also knew what it was like to partner with Jesus as Miracle Maker, performing *"many signs and wonders among the people"* after the Day of Pentecost. When he and Peter saw a lame man on their way to a prayer meeting, they healed him. When this attracted crowds of ill and demonized people to John and his friends, *"all of them were healed."*[1] We might have therefore expected John to treat his miracles as proof that his teaching was true, yet he was aware that false teachers can perform counterfeit miracles of their own. What they cannot do, he tells us, is counterfeit the work of the Holy Spirit inside a Christian. John says that if we want proof that we are saved, we need to look for the Miracle Maker at work in our hearts. We need to look for things that only God can do.

In 1:5–7, John stated this as the main argument of his

---

[1] Acts 2:43; 3:1; 5:12–16. Peter gets most of the limelight early on in Acts, but John was very active too.

letter.[2] He pointed out that the hearts of those who have been born again are as radically different from the hearts of those who have merely assented to religious doctrine as light is radically different from darkness. Later on in this letter he will use other vivid contrasts: between life and death, between love and hatred, between truth and lies, between righteousness and lawlessness, between the children of God and the children of the Devil, between the Christ and the Antichrist, between heaven and hell, and between love for Christ and love for the world. For now, he restricts himself to repeating the most common metaphor that he uses in his gospel.[3] Since God is pure light, we can tell whether or not we truly know him by looking into our hearts and asking if we can see evidence of his light at work within us.

In 1:8–2:2, John warned us to pay particular attention to how we respond to the challenge of God's Word. If we resist its definition of good and evil, either by debating it or by ignoring it, we are like insects that scuttle under a rock for fear of the light. We can tell we are not saved if we try to claim that we are right and God is wrong, but we can tell we are saved if we side with God's Word against ourselves. That is something that only those who are born again will ever do. Instead of kicking and screaming, God's Word quickly has them confessing and surrendering.

In 2:3–6, John points out that only the Miracle Maker can ever make us *live like Jesus*. It is easy to claim that we know God, but true knowledge of him is always backed up by the Holy Spirit transforming our innermost desires to become like his. Since sinful people hate the real God and resent his commands, it proves we have been born again if we love him and eagerly surrender even to his costliest commands. Matthew, Luke and

---

[2] 1:5–7 belongs with 2:3–11. John is simply conscious that we may think he is saying that unless we are perfect we are not Christians. He therefore breaks off to clarify through a brief aside on forgiveness for sin.

[3] See John 1:4–5, 7–9; 3:19–21; 8:12; 9:5; 11:9–10; 12:35–36, 46, 13:30.

Paul also tell us that true conversion always results in a new manner of living. John is simply echoing the rest of the New Testament when he insists that *"We know that we have come to know him if we keep his commands."*[4]

In 2:7–11, John points out that only the Miracle Maker can ever make us *love like Jesus*. Sin made Adam try to pin the blame on Eve, it made Cain murder Abel and it has made the human race live at war with one another ever since. Being reconciled to God always starts to undo the toxic results of the Fall by transforming our hearts towards other people. Over fifty years have passed since Jesus told his disciples in John 13:34 that this lies at the heart of Christianity – *"A new command I give you: love one another. As I have loved you, so you must love one another"* – so John points out that the command is now both old and new. It has been around for a long time, but it is new to our thinking. It is nothing like the way we used to live before the Miracle Maker began his work inside us.[5]

We tend not to think of love for other people as a miracle. That's odd because Paul gives his great definition of Christian love right at the heart of three chapters of teaching about miracles. In 1 Corinthians 12, he promises that the Holy Spirit will grant us power to perform great signs and wonders. In 1 Corinthians 14, he promises that the Holy Spirit will enable us to speak in supernatural languages and to prophesy so accurately that unbelievers fall down and confess that we truly know God. It is no less of a miracle, therefore, in 1 Corinthians 13 when he describes the love that only the Holy Spirit can work in our hearts:

---

[4] Matthew 3:8; Luke 3:8; Acts 26:20; Galatians 5:19–24; Ephesians 4:1; Philippians 1:27; Colossians 1:10; 1 Thessalonians 2:12. John also echoes his own teaching in John 15 when he talks about *living in God* in 2:5–6.

[5] In Matthew 5:21–22, Jesus supports John's statement that hatred makes us like the murderer Cain.

Love is patient, love is kind. It does not envy, it does not boast, it is not proud. It does not dishonour others, it is not self-seeking, it is not easily angered, it keeps no record of wrongs. Love does not delight in evil but rejoices with the truth. It always protects, always trusts, always hopes, always perseveres. Love never fails.

We need to read those verses slowly. This kind of supernatural love is never anything short of a miracle.

John therefore tells us to look for signs of this God-given love within our hearts. If we find the same dog-eat-dog attitude which dominates this sinful world, he warns us that we do not truly know God. We may claim to know him but we are blinded by the Devil and still living in darkness.[6] We are fooling ourselves that we know God, because it is no more possible for people to draw closer to God without drawing closer to one another than it is for the spokes of a bicycle wheel to travel inwards to the hub without drawing closer to one another.[7] Praying a prayer and joining a church do not guarantee that we are genuine believers, because those who are not born again can do both of these things. Loving other people with the sacrificial love of Jesus, on the other hand, is never man-made. It is always proof that God is at work on the inside.

So look inside yourself. What do you see? Ask the Holy Spirit to come and impart to you the kind of love that only God can give to those who truly know him.

---

[6] Note the progression of Ephesians 2:1–10 into 2:11–22. Unless we exhibit this progression, 1 John 2:11 warns us we are tragically deluded: *"They do not know where they are going."*

[7] John 21:15–17. To emphasize this, John refers to his readers in 2:7, not as children, but as *beloved ones* (*agapētoi* in the most reliable Greek manuscripts) or as *brothers* (*adelphoi* in less reliable manuscripts).

The World is Not Enough (2:12–17)

Do not love the world or anything in the world. If anyone loves the world, love for the Father is not in them.

(1 John 2:15)

We don't have to read much of John's writings to spot that he has a few favourite words. Near the top of the list is the Greek word *kosmos*, which means the world. John uses this word more than all the other New Testament writers put together. In his first letter alone he uses it more times than Matthew, Mark, Luke and Acts combined. We therefore need to understand what he means by it if we want to grasp the meaning of the letter.

John actually uses the word *kosmos* in three distinct ways. The first way is very positive, describing the human race and universe that God created and still rejoices over. It is in this sense that we are told in John 3:16 that *"God so loved the world that he gave his one and only Son."* The second way is far more negative, describing the way that the universe has fallen under the Devil's influence through human sin. It is in this sense that 1 John 5:19 says that *"The whole world is under the control of the evil one."* The third way is somewhere in between the first two, describing life as a battlefield in which our true spiritual state is revealed by our devotion to the things of this transient age or to the things of eternity. It is in this sense that we are told in John 12:25 that *"Anyone who hates their life in this world will keep it for eternal life."* It helps to understand these three distinct ways in which John uses the word *kosmos*, because he uses it twenty-four times in his first letter. It enables us to see that the six verses in 2:12–17 are not merely an aside. They are a fierce call to war.

In 2:12–14, John addresses three groups of people. The first group are young Christians who feel tempted to go along with the false teachers in the hope of accessing some of their so-called secret knowledge.[1] John tells them to rejoice in the forgiveness that is theirs in Jesus and in the fact that they know God as their Father.[2] This is the only true knowledge that satisfies. The second group are long-standing believers who feel tempted to despair about the inroads the false teachers are making into their churches.[3] John reminds them that their many years of Christian experience have given them a unique role to play in the battle. He talked in terms of *"we"* at the start of his letter because, like him, they have a testimony of many years of walking with the real Jesus that no dynamic young preacher can sweep away.[4]

The third group are the warriors in the churches. John calls them "young people" but, since he is aged around ninety, this could refer to anybody under the age of sixty![5] He tells them that there is a war raging in the world between light and darkness, between heaven and earth, between God and the Devil. He reminds them that they are strong enough to fight and that

---

[1] Given that John refers to his readers throughout this letter as his *"dear children"*, it is highly improbable that he is referring to actual children here. These three groupings are more about our maturity than our age.

[2] John says in 2:12 that our forgiveness comes on account of the name of Jesus. Like a bankrupt who is given a joint bank account with a billionaire, our union with Christ makes all his righteousness our own.

[3] John uses a Greek word that means *"fathers"* but this same word is translated as *"parents"* in Hebrews 11:23. He is therefore addressing the long-standing women of the church as well as the long-standing men.

[4] Although many of these older Christians were converted in the Church's early days, John's main point here is that they know Jesus *"who is from the beginning"* (John 1:1). They can detect a false Jesus a mile away.

[5] Again John addresses these instructions to the *"young men"*, but they are equally true for the young women.

their victory over the Devil is guaranteed by the fact that the Word of God lives inside them.[6] They must not waste their lives pursuing man-made philosophy or possessions that are passing away. God is calling them to be his front-line troops in the battle to proclaim true knowledge of him to the nations of the world.

In 2:15–17, John therefore gives us the first of many exhortations in this letter to live for the eternal age which has now begun through the death and resurrection of Jesus, not for the old world order that is coming to an end. This choice lies at the heart of the three signs of life that he says can make us confident we are genuine believers. We will only live like Jesus, love like Jesus and follow the real Jesus if we gladly die to what this temporary age has to offer us. False teachers try to dress Jesus up as the best way of achieving this world's objectives – a better marriage, a better bank balance, a better version of ourselves – but the real Gospel commands us to die to this world's objectives and to live for the priorities of heaven. That's why Paul prays so passionately in Galatians 6:14, *"May I never boast except in the cross of our Lord Jesus Christ, through which the world has been crucified to me, and I to the world."*

So look inside yourself again. Which life are you living for? For the praise and pleasures and possessions of your fleeting life in this fallen world, or for the eternal life that John constantly refers to in his gospel and his letters? John warns us frankly that our answer to this question reveals whether or not the Miracle Maker has begun a work of salvation in our hearts. Anyone who hates the things of this world and loves the things of heaven shows clear signs of having been reborn through God's Spirit, but *"if anyone loves the world, love for the Father is not in them."*

For the sake of shorthand, the New Testament often calls this choice between two different ways of living a choice between "earth" and "heaven", but don't misunderstand this to mean a

---

[6] John expects us to see this as a reminder of his teaching in John 1:1, 5:38 and 15:1–17.

choice between "now" and "later".[7] John is clear that Jesus is eternal life (5:20) and that eternal life has therefore already broken in upon us (1:2). Eternal life is not just something for us to enjoy when Jesus returns, but something for us to begin enjoying now (5:11). John does not tell us to look within our hearts for these three signs in order to know that one day we will have eternal life, but *"so that you may know that **you have eternal life**"*, right here and right now (5:13).

The battle is therefore not a question of time, a choice between life now or life later, but a choice between two types of life. John deliberately echoes Eve's temptation in the Garden of Eden in Genesis 3:6 when he warns us in 2:16 against chasing after *"the lust of the flesh, the lust of the eyes, and the pride of life"*.[8] Those who truly know God can see that this world is a failed bank. They are no longer willing to invest their life in it. Their eyes are open to God and their ears are closed to the Devil. They want to invest all they have in the bank of heaven.

They surrender their lives gladly to the Holy Spirit within them and they allow him to teach them to live like Jesus, to love like Jesus and to follow the real Jesus.

---

[7] For example, in Matthew 6:19–20; Philippians 3:19–20; Colossians 3:1–2.

[8] The Greek word for this world's *life* in 2:16 is *bios*. It is not even worthy of bearing the same name as the *zōē aiōnion*, or *eternal life*, that has been given us by the man who came from heaven.

Christ and Antichrist
(2:18–28)

Who is the liar? It is whoever denies that Jesus is the Christ. Such a person is the antichrist – denying the Father and the Son.

(1 John 2:22)

Near to where I live there is a brilliant Maze of Mirrors. My children love it whenever I take them there. Its floor-to-ceiling mirrors mean that we see hundreds of versions of ourselves chasing one another through the maze. Often we run straight past one another, thinking that we are running past a reflection. At other times we crash at full speed into one of the walls, thinking we have found a real person. As long as you don't mind coming home with a few bruises, a trip to the Maze of Mirrors is a lot of fun.

But the Maze of Mirrors surrounding John wasn't fun. It was deeply troublesome and confusing. So many different versions of Jesus were being preached in Asia Minor that most people had lost track of which one of them was real. Cerinthus described "Jesus" and "Christ" as two people.[1] Nicolas and the prophetess had their own versions of Jesus too. There were probably many other false Jesuses in addition, now lost to history, which is why John introduces another of his favourite

---

[1] John appears to have Cerinthus particularly in mind when he talks in 2:22 about denying that "Jesus" is "Christ". However, he is also issuing a far more general warning for any generation.

words in these verses. Nobody else in the Bible ever uses the word *"antichrist"*, but John uses it five times in his letters.[2]

First things first. Let's understand what John means by this word, since it is commonly misunderstood. In English the prefix *anti-* means "opposed to" (as in antiseptic, antisocial, anti-ageing and anti-aircraft), but in Greek the prefix *anti-* also means "instead of".[3] John is therefore not so much talking here about the enemies of Christ as he is about false versions of Christ. He is echoing Jesus's warning that *"False Christs and false prophets will appear and perform great signs and miracles to deceive."*[4] He is telling his readers not to be surprised that there are so many differing versions of Jesus on offer in their cities. How they respond to them is the third way to tell if they are genuine believers.

In 2:18, John points out that we are in the final stages of world history. Peter called it *"the last days"* when he preached on the Day of Pentecost, but that was already sixty years ago. Now John calls it *"the last hour"*.[5] We are pitched in fierce hand-to-hand combat as we seek to plunder as many souls as possible from Satan's crumbling kingdom before the real King Jesus returns. It should therefore not surprise us that the Devil has sent the spirit of the Antichrist into the world to try to minimize his losses.[6] Jesus prophesied that he would do this and, sure enough, John tells his readers that the spirit of the Antichrist has a whole factory-full of imitation Jesuses who are entirely unable to save.

---

[2] He uses the word in 1 John 2:18 (twice), 2:22 and 4:3, and in 2 John 7.

[3] For example, in Greek Jesus says in Matthew 20:28 that his death is a death *"anti"* many.

[4] Jesus uses the word *pseudochristos*, meaning *false Christ*, in Matthew 24:24 and Mark 13:22. John prefers the word *antichristos*, meaning *alternative Christ*. Only the real Christ gives real *chrisma*, or *anointing* (2:20, 27).

[5] On that basis we must be in the final minutes! John's choice of words conveys great urgency.

[6] 1 John 4:3 tells us that a powerful demon is at work behind the many alternative messiahs in the world.

In 2:19, John tells us that this is the third way that we can tell whether or not we truly know God. Anyone who goes after a false Jesus cannot really have the Holy Spirit, since God's Spirit always leads us to the Son of God. The real tragedy for many people who leave the Church is not that it shows they are backslidden, but that it shows their faith was only ever a human response to God and never the miraculous work of the Holy Spirit.[7] That's what Paul means when he tells us in 1 Corinthians 12:3 that *"No one can say, 'Jesus is Lord,' except by the Holy Spirit."* Anyone can say those three simple words, but without the Holy Spirit nobody truly means "Jesus" or "Lord". Only the Miracle Maker can motivate us to make the real Jesus the real Lord of our lives.

That's why it isn't very helpful when Christians rush to label as the Antichrist a politician, a religious leader or the latest bogeyman to hit the news. Although the New Testament suggests that one particular individual will wreak more havoc than the others, its main emphasis is that the spirit of the Antichrist is at work everywhere.[8] We see its fingerprints every time people start to preach a Jesus of their own making. The most frightening thing about John's words is that those deluded by the spirit of the Antichrist evidently looked like true believers until they were wooed by the false teachers. That's why we need to be so careful as left-wingers if we preach a left-wing Jesus, or as right-wingers if we preach a right-wing Jesus. If the Christ that we believe in has suspiciously similar views to our own, we are no better than the Soviet leader Mikhail Gorbachev when he tried to claim that *"Jesus was the first socialist."*[9]

[7] We find this hard to stomach because their faith once looked so genuine, but John is adamant in 2:19. The spirit of the Antichrist is very good at its job of deceiving.

[8] Even as he describes the greatest *"man of lawlessness"* in 2 Thessalonians 2:3–10, Paul warns us that *"the secret power of lawlessness is already at work"* in many individuals.

[9] Mikhail Gorbachev said this in the London *Daily Telegraph* on 16th June 1992.

In 2:20–23, John tells us that only the Holy Spirit can make people want to follow the real Jesus. Unbelievers flock to hear about Jesus the prosperity provider because their true god is money. Unbelievers love to hear about Jesus the gay-rights activist because their true god is unfettered sexual freedom. Their faith in a false Jesus is proof that they have not been born again and are therefore incapable of loving the real Jesus. We should find these verses sobering, because there are even more false Jesuses on offer today than there were in Ephesus back in John's day.[10] It sounds ridiculous now that Malcolm X tried to claim that *"Christ wasn't white; Christ was black,"* but the truth is that anyone not born again wants to believe that Jesus is just like they are.[11] John says the spirit of the Antichrist wants to turn us all into antichrists, worshipping a little version of ourselves.

In 2:25–28, John emphasizes the encouraging flipside of this. If we have surrendered our lives to the real Jesus – the one that John describes in great eyewitness detail in his gospel, the one who is not a little version of ourselves but who offends us and calls us to die to ourselves every day – we can have complete confidence that we are truly saved. Only the Holy Spirit could have performed such a miracle of faith in our hearts. If you can see signs of this miracle in your own heart, John tells you to recognize it as a deep work of God's Spirit: *"The anointing you received from him remains in you, and you do not need anyone to teach you. But as his anointing teaches you about all things and as that anointing is real, not counterfeit – just as it has taught you, remain in him."*[12]

189

---

[10] In stating that any teaching which denies that Jesus is the Son of God comes from the spirit of the Antichrist, John says non-Christian religions are not alternative ways to God. They are demonic deceptions.

[11] Malcolm X famously made this claim in an interview with *Playboy* in May 1963.

[12] John is not downplaying our need for Bible teachers. This letter is full of Bible teaching! He is simply saying that those who have God's Spirit do not need the "secret knowledge" on offer from the false teachers. These verses echo John 16:12–15, as well as John 6:56–69, 14:23, 15:1–17 and 17:20–23.

What kind of Jesus are you following? Don't be fooled by the Maze of Mirrors. Ask the Holy Spirit to reveal the real Jesus to you as you study the words of his disciple John.

Repeat Symptoms
(2:29–4:6)

This is how we know that he lives in us: we know it by the Spirit he gave us.

(1 John 3:24)

The great fourth-century theologian Jerome told a story about John's final years as a very old man in Ephesus. When he preached one Sunday on *"Little children, love one another"*, he hit a home run. Everyone was deeply moved by the power of his message. When he preached the following Sunday on *"Little children, love one another"*, a few eyebrows were raised but the sermon was just as powerful the second time. When he preached a third Sunday running on *"Little children, love each other"*, some of the church leaders took John to one side. They complained that he was starting to repeat himself. They had heard it all before. John smiled and gave them a simple reply: *"This is what the Lord commanded, and if this one thing shall be obeyed then it shall be enough."*[1]

We do not know for sure whether Jerome's tale about John really happened, but we do know that he was not afraid of repeating himself when it was needed. He repeats his response to the false teachers three times in this letter. We have just seen that it is a call for us to look inside our hearts for things that only God can do. If we *live like Jesus* (1:5–2:6), *love like Jesus* (2:7–11) and *believe in the real Jesus* (2:18–28), we can be sure that the Holy Spirit has brought our spirits to life and is at work

---

[1] Jerome tells us this story in his *Commentary on Galatians*, commenting on Galatians 6:10.

in our hearts. Now John gives us exactly the same instructions again. We are to look inside our hearts to see if we are *living like Jesus* (2:29–3:10), *loving like Jesus* (3:10–24) and *believing in the real Jesus* (4:1–6). These three symptoms of God's work within us are so impossible to fake that John can tell us in 5:13, *"I write these things to you… **so that you may know** that you have eternal life."*

Understanding this helps us to become spiritually discerning. We really need to be. The original recipients of John's letter merely had to discern whom to permit to preach in their church. Most of us have several different churches we could choose to attend, plus tens of thousands of online preachers only a mouse click away. At the same time, our smartphones, computers and TVs bombard us with enough non-Christian messages to fill 174 newspapers every single day.[2] No generation in Church history has been in such need of spiritual discernment as ours.

The main question to ask is not whether we find a particular church's worship songs uplifting. The fourth-century hymn-writer Arius penned such great music and lyrics that his songs were still in use 200 years after the Council of Nicaea had condemned him as a heretic! The main question is not whether we find ourselves nodding at a particular author or preacher, whether our children are making friends on a Sunday or whether the church has a selection of ministries that need our gifting. None of those things is bad, but all of them are secondary. The primary question has to be whether a church is helping us to see more of God at work within our hearts. If they are not influencing us to love Jesus more, to live for Jesus more and to get to know the real Jesus more, we ought to run a mile. However glossy or shiny a church's ministry, it is a man-made

---

[2] From a study by the University of Southern California published in *Science Express* (10th February 2011).

work unless it yields fruit in our lives that only God can bring about.

Understanding these three symptoms of any true work of God makes us spiritually mature. Too many Christians suffer from spiritual constipation. They puff and strain to grow in godliness, but for all their red faces they never appear to get anywhere. John calls us to a very godly lifestyle because he knows that Christian character is not the result of our own work. It is the work of the Holy Spirit or it doesn't work at all. John uses similar language in this letter to the language in his gospel because he wants to point us back to the words of Jesus. His talk about our "living in Jesus" is meant to make us recall the words of Jesus in John 15:5: *"I am the vine; you are the branches. If you remain in me and I in you, you will bear much fruit; apart from me you can do nothing."* Christian maturity does not stem from our own determination to act differently, but from the Holy Spirit living inside us and making us different. On our own, we puff and pant and achieve nothing, but God's Spirit brings more than rebirth. He brings us to maturity.

Understanding this also grants us true spiritual fruitfulness. If we need any proof that the Church's nets are broken today, it is surely in our evangelism. The Western Church has been declining for so many years that many have forgotten that it is not meant to be this way, but the answer is not to start pushing harder in evangelism. John repairs the Church's nets by telling us that we need far more than one more push for victory. We need to learn an altogether different way of partnering with the Holy Spirit.

Much of our evangelism operates on worldly principles. We see it as a work of the mind, so we look for opportunities to instruct unbelievers in basic Christian theology. As a result, we wonder why they are unwilling to listen and even less willing to follow. Alternatively, we see it as a work of the heart, so we look for opportunities to scare them with talk of hell or to move them emotionally with our testimony. We have forgotten that true conversion is only ever a work of the Holy Spirit. It is never simply man-to-man or woman-to-woman. It is always a confrontation between the Holy Spirit and the spirit of the Antichrist. It is always an expression of the principle that Jesus outlines in John 3:6: *"Flesh gives birth to flesh, but the Spirit gives birth to spirit."*

John does not tell us that people are converted through an intellectual understanding of how the death and resurrection of Jesus saves us. He does not tell us that they are converted by feeling fear or hope, but by responding to the Holy Spirit's work within them. Like the thief on the cross, they may understand very little of the workings of the Gospel, but when they hear about the real Jesus they find themselves believing in him. This is John's third sign that we truly know God, but it is the one from which the other two flow. That's why John gives such a simple criterion for salvation in 5:13: *"I write these things **to you who believe in the name of the Son of God** so that you may know that you have eternal life."* Evangelism isn't difficult. It is impossible. It means working in partnership with the Holy Spirit. It means trusting the Miracle Maker to raise people's dead spirits to life as we tell them about the real Jesus so that they can believe in him.

That's why John does not apologize for repeating himself so much throughout this letter. His call for us to look out for the work of God's Spirit in our hearts bears a lot of repeating. It is the key to all spiritual discernment, all spiritual maturity and all spiritual fruitfulness. It has always been the secret of all true Christianity.

Perfect (2:29–3:10)

No one who lives in him keeps on sinning. No one who continues to sin has either seen him or known him.

(1 John 3:6)

When people misunderstand what John is saying in these verses, they can either fall into pride or plunge into despair. Those may sound like polar opposites, but they both spring from the same misunderstanding. They are based on an assumption that, as John repeats his first sign of true conversion, he is telling us that real Christians never commit sin.

John Wesley never taught this explicitly, but his pamphlet *A Plain Account of Christian Perfection* led many others to do so. He made much of John's warning that anyone who carries on sinning cannot truly know Jesus (3:6) and his promise that anyone who has truly been born again through God's Spirit cannot continue in sin (3:9). He argued that

> *There is such a thing as perfection; for it is again and again mentioned in Scripture. It is not so early as justification; for justified persons are to "go on unto perfection" (Hebrews 6:1). It is not so late as death; for St. Paul speaks of living men that were perfect (Philippians 3:15)... Therefore all our preachers should make a point of preaching perfection to believers constantly, strongly, and explicitly; and all believers should mind this one thing, and continually agonise for it.*[1]

---

[1] John Wesley published *A Plain Account of Christian Perfection* in 1766.

For every person that this kind of teaching encourages, there are at least two or three that it drives to despair. If we are meant to assess whether or not we truly know God by looking for absolute perfection in our hearts, which of us can honestly raise a hand? One of my friends resigned his job as a church pastor and almost lost his faith entirely because he mistakenly believed that this was what these verses required of him. We ought to spot at once that this is a misinterpretation, since John clearly expects these verses to increase our confidence that we are truly saved, not take it away. Let's therefore read these verses slowly in order to follow what John is actually saying.

In 2:28–3:3, John tells us that those who have been born again through the Holy Spirit's work in their hearts are now children of God. This is the biggest difference in the way that John lists his signs of life this second time round. The first time round he said that they were proof we have come to dwell "in Christ". This time he says that they are proof we have been adopted as *"children of God"*.[2] It is important that we grasp this, because John is neither saying that unbelievers never do anything good nor that believers never do anything bad (in fact, he tells us explicitly in 3:2 that we will never know sinless perfection until Jesus returns). Rather he is telling us that, since God is completely righteous and pure, our adoption as his sons and daughters will always result in our starting to display some clear family likeness. Those who belong to this world will find it harder and harder to understand the decisions we make and the way that we live. As we look at our own hearts we will begin to see heaven's values driving our behaviour more and more, not the values of the fallen world.[3]

---

[2] Unbelievers are only God's children in the loose sense that he is their Creator (Acts 17:28–29). John says that we can only truly call God our Father when we are adopted into Christ. See John 1:12 and Galatians 3:26.

[3] See 2 Corinthians 3:18. We do not "purify ourselves" by gritting our teeth and trying to be holy, but by actively cooperating with the Holy Spirit who now lives inside us so that he can make us more like Jesus.

In 3:4-6, John tells us that this never happens to those who listen to false teachers. Since they believe that knowing God is all about receiving secret revelation, they have no desire to grow in practical godliness. Without the Holy Spirit on the inside, they have no idea that the Greek philosophers were wrong to claim that how we use our bodies makes no difference to the state of our souls. They never experience the way that God's Spirit always makes those who are born again delight in obedience to God's Law, so John points out that "lawlessness" and "sinfulness" are essentially the same thing.[4] If we continue to act as *"children of disobedience"*, it is a sign that we have fallen for a false version of Jesus.[5] But if we find ourselves viewing sin very differently from before, it is a sign that we have come to know the real Jesus and become children of God.[6]

In 3:7-10, John presses home this point to prevent false teachers from leading us astray. He says that there are two types of people in the world: the children of the Devil and the children of God. We are either at peace with the world's way of living and happy to abide by its moral code, or we are at war with the world and committed to living by heaven's moral code. It is in this sense that he is able to declare that *"No one who is born of God will continue to sin, because God's seed remains in them; they cannot go on sinning, because they have been born of God."* He is not telling us that all Christians are sinless (he explicitly denied this in 1:8-10), but that all Christians inevitably sin less! Their lifestyle begins to be characterized by righteousness instead of sin, by light instead of darkness and by the divine seed of life that has been planted within them by God their Father instead

---

[4] The Greek word *hamartia* means *sin* and the Greek word *anomia* means *rejection of the Law*. John says that in rejecting the moral standards of God's Law the false teachers have become teachers of sin.

[5] This is the literal way in which both Ephesians 2:2 and Colossians 3:6 describe unbelievers.

[6] If 3:6 were a promise of sinless perfection, it would not be a promise that individual Christians can become perfect but a statement that all Christians already are. 1 John 5:21 tells us that this clearly isn't true.

of by the fallen human seed that was planted within them by their natural fathers.[7]

So don't let these verses fool you that your relationship with God has somehow made you sinlessly perfect in the way you live. Ask any of your friends and family and they will tell you that it hasn't! When John talks in 4:12 and 18 about your being *"made perfect in love"* the Greek word *teleioō* is better translated as being *"made mature in love"*, and the pride that says we are already fully mature is the arch-enemy of love. Enjoy each step towards greater godliness, but remember that God has called you to a lifetime of learning.

At the other end of the scale, don't allow these verses to make you doubt your relationship with God because you are aware of sin in your heart. The fact that you admit your sin is proof the Holy Spirit is at work within you![8] The children of lawlessness always seek to hide their sin behind excuses, but you are walking in the light as 1 John 1:7 says true believers always do.

Instead, see each fresh admission of sin and each new step towards greater godliness as equal reasons to be confident that you have truly been born of God. Rejoice with John that they mean the divine seed of God's Spirit inside you is growing to maturity: *"See what great love the Father has lavished on us, that we should be called children of God! And that is what we are!... All who have this hope in him purify themselves, just as he is pure."*

---

[7] The Greek word for *seed* in 3:9 is *sperma*. If God has fertilized our spirit, holiness is guaranteed to grow.

[8] John 16:8 tells us that frank confession of sin doesn't mean we are not Christians. It means that we are!

How to Fight the Plague (3:8)

The devil has been sinning from the beginning. The reason the Son of God appeared was to destroy the devil's work.

(1 John 3:8)

Not long after God created it and declared it very good, a terrible plague broke out on planet Earth. When the Devil persuaded the first humans to side with him against God, sin started to infect everything in their once-perfect home. Their relationships turned sour, first with God and then with one another. Their bodies began to get old and sick, and eventually to die. The world became full of hatred and murder and theft and sexual exploitation and poverty and war. Even the beautiful possessions that God had made for them to enjoy became corrupted and started to possess them. You know the story. You experience it every day. It is the riddle that every religious teacher needs to solve.

John's three signs of true spiritual life draw our attention to the fact that, without the real Jesus, we have only man-made solutions to this problem. Like the Gnostics, we can ignore the material world and go hunting for experiences that will lift us to a higher spiritual plane. Like the ascetics, we can treat our bodies harshly to starve the physical and feed the spiritual within us. But John tells us that neither of these can ever produce the three signs of life that only ever flow out of the Gospel. They can only do for us what the people of Eyam did in Derbyshire, England, in the seventeenth century.

In August 1665, a large delivery of cloth arrived from London at the tailor's shop in Eyam. Within days the tailor was dead. When large numbers of his customers also exhibited the same telltale symptoms of bubonic plague and died, it became clear that the cloth from London was infested with plague-carrying fleas. The village leaders therefore decided that they had only one option. They banned any further deliveries, closed all the roads in and out of town, and cut Eyam off from the rest of the world.

That's what religious teachers always have to do if they do not preach the real Jesus. They can only offer people strategies for damage limitation by cocooning themselves off from the world, because they possess no plague-busting power. John says that so-called Christian leaders can be guilty of this too. They rely on damage-limitation strategies instead of on the Gospel. They turn their churches into closed-off quarantine zones away from the world, using religion in the same way that unbelievers use money, as a hedge of protection behind which their people can shelter in their own group of friends and their own separate schools. But here's the thing: over half of the people of Eyam died because their quarantined community was already infected with the plague. Damage limitation is not the same thing as damage reversal.

Whenever Christians withdraw from the world to escape the plague of sin, it never works. That's because sin is something in here and not just out there. Far too many of the monks who responded to the greed of medieval Europe by taking vows of poverty went on to become some of the greediest landowners of their age. Far too many of the priests who responded to the sexual sin of modern Europe by taking vows of celibacy were later exposed as paedophiles. Most of the Christian groups that have turned inwards to escape ungodliness throughout Church history have ended up becoming very ungodly themselves. That's because the plague of sin is not just out there in the world.

It is in us. The heart of the human problem is the problem of the human heart.

That's where the Gospel is different from every man-made remedy. It is neither Gnostic nor ascetic. It isn't about *flight*, but about *fight*. In 3:8, John tells us that God's solution to the plague of sin is not quarantine, but confrontation: *"The devil has been sinning from the beginning. The reason the Son of God appeared was to destroy the devil's work."* Jesus did the opposite of fleeing from the world. He stepped into it to confront its plague head on. Adam chose to side with the Devil against God in the garden. Jesus chose to side with God against the Devil in the desert. Adam looked at the tree of knowledge and said to God, "Not what you want but what I want." Jesus looked at the tree of Calvary and said to God, "Not what I want but what you want." Having stepped into Adam's shoes and succeeded wherever Adam failed, Jesus then took the plague of sin upon himself when he died on the cross. The Devil and his demons crowed in triumph, thinking that they had won, but on the third day Jesus rose from the dead and proclaimed that he had just destroyed the plague of sin forever.

John therefore pleads with us not to settle for man-made strategies of damage limitation. If we withdraw from the world to be rid of its plague, we will discover that our hearts are just as infected as the tailor's shop in Eyam. Our only path to freedom lies in asking God to fill our hearts with his Spirit and to change us through his resurrection power. When Jesus touched people they discovered that the power of heaven always triumphs over the plague of this world. Lepers were made clean. Corpses were made alive. Samaritans were made part of God's people. That's why 3:8 and 4:4 are the two pivotal verses in this second section of John's letter. Our lives will never be transformed through withdrawal from the world, but only through recognition that Jesus has stepped into it: *"The reason the Son of God appeared was to destroy the devil's work... The one who is in you is greater than the one who is in the world."*

The Devil is desperate to keep you from understanding this. That's why the spirit of the Antichrist is working overtime. John tells us in his gospel that Jesus said it was for the good of his followers that he left the world, so that he could come and live in their hearts through the Holy Spirit and send them out into the world to cure the plague of sin in others through his resurrection power (16:7 and 20:21). John tells us that his great prayer was that the Devil would fail in all his attempts to stop us (17:15–18).[1] Since we make trouble for the Devil simply by being in the world, proclaiming the real Jesus to people, extending the love of Jesus towards people and displaying the lifestyle of Jesus to people, we must never make the mistake of trying to cocoon ourselves away from the world. We mustn't surrender territory to the Devil that is ours.

Many historians see the villagers of Eyam as heroes for their self-imposed quarantine. Dying in isolation was their very best scenario without any cure for the plague. But we are not like them. Our lives proclaim to the world that the Gospel can cure anybody from the inside out. Damage-limitation strategies are completely out of place in our churches, because we proclaim good news: *"The reason the Son of God appeared was to destroy the devil's work... The one who is in you is greater than the one who is in the world."*

---

[1] Note the way 3:8 echoes John 8:44. John constantly points us back to his gospel to understand his letter.

The Orbit of the Son
(3:11–24)

This is how we know what love is: Jesus Christ laid down his life for us. And we ought to lay down our lives for our brothers and sisters.

(1 John 3:16)

When Nicolaus Copernicus began to suspect that the earth revolves around the sun and not the other way around, he knew his new way of viewing the universe would be far from popular. He feared that the world would find it scandalous, even irreligious, so he kept it to himself. He only dared to publish his theory a few weeks before he died.

When Galileo Galilei began to voice his own view that the earth revolves around the sun, he discovered that the great astronomer's fears had been entirely justified. The Roman Inquisition threatened Galileo to silence, issuing him with an injunction in 1616 that required him to *"abandon completely... the opinion that the sun stands still at the centre of the world and the earth moves, and henceforth not to hold, teach or defend it in any way whatever"*.

When John describes the difference between false teaching and true Christianity, he is saying that the Gospel is a revolution of Copernican proportions. He turns up the contrast as he repeats his three signs that we truly know God, warning us this second time round that embracing the Gospel means going to war against the world's fallen way of thinking. When he restated in the previous verses that only the Holy Spirit can empower us to live like Jesus, he described us as children of God living in a world that is populated by the children of the Devil. Now as he restates that only the Holy Spirit can empower us to love like Jesus, he describes us as people whose lives follow a very different orbit from the lives of the unbelievers living all around us.

In 3:11–15, John points out that before the Holy Spirit brought us to new birth our lives used to revolve around ourselves. We were once like Cain, who could not bear the sight of his younger brother Abel's godly lifestyle and murdered him to hide it from his view.[1] We should therefore not be surprised that the world hates us for following Jesus.[2] It is proof that we truly know God. It means that everyone around us can tell our lives no longer follow the orbit of our self-centred world. It is clear to everyone that our lives have changed direction to revolve around God's Son and the eternal life of heaven.[3]

In the first half of 3:16, John describes our new orbit. Perhaps it is mere coincidence that John 3:16 and 1 John 3:16 are so similar: *"God so loved the world that he gave his one and only Son... This is how we know what love is: Jesus Christ laid down his life for us."* On the other hand, perhaps the similarity is no coincidence at all. Perhaps the Lord wants to use it to leave us in no doubt that his love always involves painful sacrifice. It is more than a mushy feeling. It is more than uttering kind words. It means allowing the Holy Spirit to redirect our lives to revolve around something greater than ourselves.[4]

---

[1] This is John's only reference to an Old Testament character in his letters, and he never quotes directly from the Old Testament in any of them. He was evidently writing to a largely Gentile group of believers.

[2] John's gospel also tells us that our love for others (15:17) will cause unbelievers to hate us (15:18–27). We should expect a genuine Christian lifestyle to attract many enemies and not just many converts.

[3] The Greek word *metabainō* in 3:14 means *to pass from one place to another*. We have not simply embraced a new way of thinking. The Holy Spirit has taken us out of Satan's realm and birthed us into God's Kingdom.

[4] When Jesus commands us in John 15:12 to *"love each other as I have loved you"*, he immediately emphasizes in 15:13 that this means self-sacrifice:

In the second half of 3:16 and in 3:17–18, John spells out for us what this means. He uses the Greek word *opheilō* to tell us literally that we *are debtors* to other people.[5] Since Jesus gave up everything to save us, we now owe it to those around us to give up everything for them. If we do not feel stirred to pour out our worldly possessions for the sake of those in need, we do not possess God's love; if we do not possess God's love, we do not possess God's Spirit; and if we do not possess God's Spirit, we do not know God at all.[6] The things we do, say and feel are therefore of paramount importance. When God's love makes our lives revolve around the needs of others, it provides us with powerful proof that we are truly saved. Only the new birth that the Holy Spirit brings could ever produce such a Copernican revolution in our hearts.

In 3:19–22, John keeps emphasizing that the sight of such sacrificial love at work in us ought to give us clear assurance we are saved. He says it is quite normal for us to doubt our salvation from time to time, since our hearts are fallible and fickle, but that *"if our hearts condemn us, we know that God is greater than our hearts, and he knows everything."* Galileo supposedly left the courtroom where he was forced to deny that the earth moves around the sun muttering under his breath in Italian, *"E pur si muove!"* – meaning *"And yet in spite of that it does move!"* When we are shocked by our own lack of love, John encourages us to see it as a sign of grace and to say with Galileo that in spite of everything we know that our faith is true. When we are amazed to find a love in our hearts that can only come from God's Spirit, John tells us to embrace it as one of his three signs that we are truly saved.

I find this so refreshing. I might have expected the apostle

"Greater love has no one than this: to lay down one's life for one's friends."
[5] John's reference to *"brothers and sisters"* particularly stresses our commitment to Christian community. If we do not commit to a church family, it suggests we do not know God as our Father (2:19 and John 21:15–17).
[6] This also has to be our inescapable conclusion from Romans 5:5 and 8:9.

to echo John 13:35 by telling us to love others like Jesus so that they will respond to the Gospel. Instead, he tells us to love others like Jesus so that we will know for sure we have responded to the Gospel ourselves! Sacrificial love never leaves us in the red. It brings with it its own reward.[7]

In 3:23–24, John therefore ends by repeating his three signs of true spiritual life so that we will grow in our assurance of salvation. He emphasizes that those who accept Jesus as God's Son and Christ have undergone a Copernican revolution in their thinking. Human teaching could never have altered the orbit of their lives so radically. Only the Spirit of God could have put to death their desire for the world to revolve around them and have brought to life in its place an eager desire for their lives to revolve around Jesus. John also emphasizes that only God's Spirit at work in us could ever have motivated us to love others and to make our lives revolve around their needs too.

When we find ourselves loving one another like Jesus and gladly submitting to God's commands like Jesus, John says we can only come to one natural conclusion. *"This is how we know that he lives in us: we know it by the Spirit he gave us."*

---

[7] John also links it to answered prayer, echoing John 14:13, 14:14, 15:7, 15:16, 16:23, 16:24 and 16:26.

No Match (4:1-6)

The one who is in you is greater than the one who is in the world.

(1 John 4:4)

God wants you to doubt everything you hear about Jesus. He really does. Such doubt does not dishonour Jesus. It honours him because there are a lot of false Jesuses around. As John repeats his third sign of true spiritual life, he asks us to run a test. Does our Jesus match up with the one who is described in the four gospels?

Christians are not always very good at this. We often take the lazy road of assuming that if so-and-so says it, it must be true. We forget that Acts 17 commends the Bereans because they *"examined the Scriptures every day to see if what Paul said was true"*. If the Bible commends people for doubting even the words of the apostle Paul until they had checked them against Scripture, how much more do we need to test the preaching we hear on a Sunday, the books we read, the ideas we access online and the prophecies we hear! Despising preaching and prophecy does not just mean forbidding them. It also means listening to them uncritically. A. W. Tozer warns that

> *Many tender-minded Christians fear to sin against love by daring to inquire into anything that comes wearing the cloak of Christianity and breathing the name of Jesus. They dare not examine the credentials of the latest prophet to hit their town lest they be guilty of rejecting something which may be of God. They timidly remember*

how the Pharisees refused to accept Christ when He came, and they do not want to be caught in the same snare, so they either reserve judgment or shut their eyes and accept everything without question. This is supposed to indicate a high degree of spirituality. But in sober fact it indicates no such thing. It may indeed be evidence of the absence of the Holy Spirit. Gullibility is not synonymous with spirituality... We may sin as certainly by approving the spurious as by rejecting the genuine.[1]

In 4:1–3, John tells us how to weigh what we are told about Jesus. He repeats what he told us in 2:18–28, that there are two spirits at work in the world: the Spirit of God who opens the eyes of the spiritually blind to the real Jesus and the spirit of the Antichrist that blinds eyes so that people fall for a fake Messiah. John tells us frankly that anyone who casts doubt on the full humanity of Jesus is inspired by a powerful demon.[2] Since he warns that *"The spirit of the antichrist... is coming and even now is already in the world,"* he clearly expects people to preach a plethora of false Jesuses. Cerinthus and his friends are simply the first line of soldiers in a battle for the truth, a battle that will rage throughout Church history.

How did Arius manage to convince so many thousands of fourth-century churchgoers that Jesus was a created being, not the Creator? Because he was so handsome, so charming and so gifted as a worship leader that they simply assumed his lyrics must be true.[3] How did Bernard of Clairvaux manage to convince so many thousands of Europeans to travel to Jerusalem

---

[1] Tozer said this in a sermon on 1 John 4:1 entitled "Testing the Spirits" (first published in 1978).

[2] The Gnostic preachers denied that Jesus had truly *"come in the flesh"*. Since Cerinthus taught about a separate "Jesus" and "Christ", John may have him particularly in mind when he refers in 4:2 to "Jesus Christ".

[3] Epiphanius of Salamis describes these charms of Arius in c.375 AD, writing in his *Panarion* (69.3).

to murder Muslims? Because his distinguished record as a Bible teacher up until that moment meant that nobody stopped to question his judgment when he launched the Second Crusade.

How did President John Quincy Adams convince his nation that Jesus was the greatest advocate of the American Dream and that *"The birthday of this nation... forms a leading event in the progress of the Gospel"*? Because it was a message that his countrymen were only too happy to hear.[4] How did Adolf Hitler convince the people of Germany that Jesus was a Nazi and that he wanted them to persecute the Jews? Because he seemed so sincere when he told them that *"My feeling as a Christian points me to my Lord and Saviour as a fighter... How terrific was His fight for the world against the Jewish poison!... It was for this that He had to shed His blood upon the Cross."*[5] People judged his message by passing it through the filter of their culture's values instead of through the filter of the four gospels.

In 4:4–6, John warns us not to get discouraged that so much of what passes for Christian preaching bears little resemblance to the gospels. He gives us good news: If it doesn't match up to the real Jesus, it is no match for the real Jesus! He assures us that *"the one who is in you is greater than the one who is in the world."* We must not lose perspective in this Maze of Mirrors. We must remember that the Gospel triumphs in the end.

It should not surprise us that people readily accept false versions of Jesus. That's simply because what the false teachers say matches up with the muddled thinking of the world. It does not mean that the spirit of the Antichrist is somehow stronger than the Holy Spirit. It simply means that people have not yet been born again. The moment that the resurrection power of God brings their dead spirits to life, they are able to smell a rat

---

[4] John Quincy Adams in a speech at Newburyport, Massachusetts, on 4th July 1837.

[5] Hitler said this in a speech delivered in Munich on 12th April 1922. We can easily forget that even Hitler was a preacher of Jesus, who tried to pass himself off as a Christian.

and make a beeline for the real Son of God. John contrasts *"the Spirit of Truth"* with *"the spirit of falsehood"*. There is no match between them. When we have the Holy Spirit inside us, we have the mind of Christ and we can never be fooled for long if we prayerfully test everything we hear against the pages of the Bible.[6]

One day the real Jesus will return from heaven. We will witness a great showdown between the one who lives inside us and the one who lives in the world. Paul predicts the outcome in 2 Thessalonians 2:8: *"The lawless one will be revealed, whom the Lord Jesus will overthrow with the breath of his mouth and destroy by the splendour of his coming."* Read that verse again slowly. Notice how little match there is between the two spirits that are at work in the world. Jesus will not have to lift a finger to defeat the spirit of the Antichrist. He will simply have to blow. He will not debate with it. He will destroy all its lies in a moment by revealing his true splendour to the world.

So let's be on our guard. Let's be aware that many of the Jesuses being preached in our churches and in our culture fail to match up to the real one. But let's be confident too. Let's remember that none of those fake messiahs is a match for the true Son of God whenever he works in power. Let's proclaim the real Jesus in this world's Maze of Mirrors, and let's be confident that as we do so the Gospel will triumph in the end.

---

[6] See 1 Corinthians 2:10–16; John 6:45; 14:26; 16:12–15.

He Lives in You (4:7–5:12)

No one has ever seen God; but if we love one another, God lives in us.

(1 John 4:12)

Near the end of the Disney movie *The Lion King*, the young lion Simba loses confidence that what he has believed for so long can actually be true. Having sung with such assurance at the start of the film about the day when he will finally become king, Simba now doubts he has his father's gifting in him. The baboon Rafiki has to come alongside him and point out reasons to feel confident of his calling by reminding Simba who he is. As Simba stares into a pool, Rafiki points out that just as Simba can see his father in himself when he looks at his reflection, there is something of his father living on in him.

It's a very moving scene despite the fact that we know it is just a piece of Disney fantasy, so let's not be less moved when John says something similar that is actually true. The first time John told us to look inside ourselves for assurance that we are saved, in 1:5–2:28, he told us that these three signs of life are proof that we are now "in Christ". The second time he listed them, in 2:29–4:6, he told us they are proof that we have become *"children of God"*. Now as he lists them a third time, in 4:7–5:12, he says that they are proof that *"God lives in us"*. So don't be more moved by a made-up conversation between a lion and a monkey than you are by John's passionate appeal. He lists these three signs of life one more time because they prove to us that God lives in us.

In 4:7–21, John says that only the fact that God lives inside us could ever make us *love like Jesus*. Note the different order here. The first two times round this was John's second sign. Now it is his first. What is more, the first two times round these three signs were very distinct, whereas this time he blurs them together by treating obedience to God's commands and faith in God's Son as part and parcel of receiving God's love. John wants us to grasp that these three signs are not abstract items in and of themselves. They all point to the one fact that God must have made his home within us. The only way that all these three things could be found in our hearts is if he now lives in us.

In 5:1–5, John says that only the fact that God lives inside us could ever make us *live like Jesus*. Note John's different approach here from ours. When we try to give people assurance that they are saved, we tend to ask them creedal questions. Can they tick all the boxes on a statement of faith? Have they prayed the right kind of salvation prayer? Do they subscribe to five-point Calvinism or five-point Arminianism or the fifty-two points of our catechism? John does not downplay the importance of what we believe (our belief about Jesus is the third of his three signs), but he points out that creed can only take us so far. True assurance does not come from checking our notebooks, but by checking our hearts to see if our thoughts and actions prove that the Miracle Maker lives inside us.

In 5:6–12, John says that only the fact that God lives inside us could ever make us *believe in the real Jesus*. Unlike the first two times round, he does not use the word "antichrist" in these verses, but he is just as clear as ever that it requires a divine miracle to open our eyes to the real Jesus. These verses echo more loudly than ever the teaching that Jesus gave to Nicodemus in John 3:1–8: *"Very truly I tell you, no one can see the kingdom of God unless they are born again... No one can enter the kingdom of God unless they are born of water and the Spirit. Flesh gives birth to flesh, but the Spirit gives birth to spirit."* When we look inside ourselves and find faith in the real Jesus, we know that his Spirit must live in us.

We are about to look at these three signs again in greater detail, but before we do so let's note how vital John's emphasis is to our view of what it means to be a Christian. Martyn Lloyd-Jones was right to observe that *"The essence of the Christian position is experience – experience of God! It is not a mere intellectual awareness or apprehension of truth... If it is not through the Holy Spirit, it is not a true Christian experience."*[1] The big question is therefore not whether our particular brand of Christianity tells us that we were filled with the Spirit at conversion or that we needed to seek it sometime later. The big question is whether we see the Holy Spirit at work in our hearts right now. If not, John says it is not a brand of Christianity at all! We need to take the New Testament seriously when it dates the moment of our conversion, not back to the moment when we prayed a particular prayer, but back to the moment when we began to experience the Holy Spirit.[2] True assurance can never simply come through reciting biblical proof texts, but only through experiencing them in action as we sense God making his home in our hearts.

Let's also note how vital John's emphasis is to our view of what it means to make more Christians. Our biggest need is not a more effective evangelistic technique, but a deeper personal experience of God. Evangelistic fruitfulness comes through our cooperation with the Holy Spirit who has come to live inside us. John Stott explains:

> *The invisibility of God is a great problem. It was already a problem to God's people in Old Testament days. Their pagan neighbours would taunt them, saying, "Where is*

---

[1] He says this in his commentary on Ephesians 6 entitled *The Christian Warfare* (1976).

[2] For example, Romans 8:9–16; 1 Corinthians 3:16; 12:3, 13; Ephesians 1:13–14; Titus 3:5–7.

now your God?" Their gods were visible and tangible, but Israel's God was neither. Today in our scientific culture young people are taught not to believe anything which is not open to empirical investigation. How then has God solved the problem of his invisibility? The first answer is of course "in Christ". Jesus Christ is the visible image of the invisible God. John 1:18: "No one has ever seen God, but God the only Son has made him known."

"That's wonderful," people say, "but it was 2,000 years ago. Is there no way by which the invisible God makes himself visible today?" There is. We return to 1 John 4:12: "No one has ever seen God." It is precisely the same introductory statement. But instead of continuing with reference to the Son of God, it continues: "If we love one another, God dwells in us." In other words, the invisible God, who once made Himself visible in Christ, now makes Himself visible in Christians, if we love one another. It is a breathtaking claim.[3]

It is indeed. It is far more breathtaking than any Disney fantasy because it's true. These three signs are proof that God now lives inside us. So let's read them carefully, as the very heart of Christianity. In the words of Rafiki: *"Look harder. You see? He lives in you."*

[3] John Stott in an interview with *Christianity Today* magazine entitled "Why Don't They Listen?" (September 2003).

God is Love (4:7–21)

God is love. Whoever lives in love lives in God, and
God in them.

(1 John 4:16)

"*God is love.*" That has got to be one of the most quoted and least understood phrases in the entire Bible. Over the past 2,000 years it has been used to defend just about everything: keeping false teachers in church pulpits, covering up child abuse in church youth groups, affirming sexual sin in church members – you name it. John's words have been misquoted to mean that God is willing to tolerate almost anything. But if we read these verses slowly we see that this is the exact opposite of what John is actually saying here. God wants to redefine our understanding of what love really means.

In 4:7, John tells us that he is not talking about the kind of love that exists naturally in the world. The Greeks used the word *eros* to describe the sexual love of a man for a woman. There is plenty of that in the world but it isn't the word John uses. The Greeks used the word *storgē* to describe the family love of a man for his child or mother. There is quite a bit of that kind of love in the world too, but it is not the word John uses here. The Greeks used the word *philia* to describe the love that exists between a man and his friends, but nor is this the word that John chooses to use. He is not talking about the love of sweethearts or families or friends, but about something infinitely better. He is talking about a different kind of love that is literally out of this world.

When the leaders of the early Church looked for a way to describe the love of God, they rejected all three of these Greek words. They felt that none of them did justice to the unique kind of love that only the Holy Spirit brings. Since the Greek Old Testament used the relatively obscure word *agapē* to describe God's love, they latched on to this and made it one of the primary words in their new Christian vocabulary.[1] When John says that *"God is agapē"*, he is therefore not saying that God embodies all the best in human love. He is saying that God redefines love and that, by coming to live inside us, he wants to enable us to love one another with a new kind of love that only he can bring.

In 4:8, John tells us that *agapē* love finds its perfect expression in the character of God.[2] This is utterly radical. The Greeks could claim that Aphrodite was the goddess of love but they could never claim that she *was* love. In the same way, a Muslim can claim that Allah displays love, but not that he is love at the very heart of who he is. No monotheist or polytheist can ever make such a claim, but only a Trinitarian, since this means that a loving community of three-in-one lies at the very heart of who God is. John told us in 1:3 that God has invited us to become part of this community through fellowship with his Holy Spirit, so whether or not our hearts reflect his *agapē* is one of the clearest signs of whether or not we are truly saved. Those who are not born of God simply cannot possess *agapē*. Those who are born of God simply cannot fail to display it.[3]

In 4:9–12, John tells us that the hallmark of this otherworldly love is always self-sacrifice. The Father's *agapē* motivated him to send his Son to earth to be our Saviour. The Son's *agapē* motivated him to lay down his life as an atoning sacrifice for our sins. That same *agapē* motivates us to lay down

---

[1] C. S. Lewis offers a great analysis of these four different Greek words in his book *The Four Loves* (1960). 1 John uses the noun *agapē* 18 times, the adjective *agapētos* 5 times and the verb *agapaō* 28 times.

[2] John never says that *"love is God"* (that our view of love defines God's character), but only ever that *"God is love"* (that God redefines our view of love). Paul gives God's true definition of *agapē* in 1 Corinthians 13:4–8.

[3] This is why Jesus is able to tell people in John 5:42 that he knows they are not saved because there is no sign of the *agapē* love of God in their hearts.

our lives for one another with that same sacrificial love. When John tells us in 4:12 that God becomes visible to the world through our love, he is not saying that people will be impressed when we display a better version of their own affection. He is saying that their chins will hit the floor when they see the Church displaying a love that they have heard about in Jesus but have never seen. When they discover a community of people who love one another sacrificially, they will believe that Jesus truly laid down his life to save us. Love is the ultimate Gospel visual aid.[4]

We therefore need to be very careful about allowing the world to tell us what *"God is love"* ought to mean. It is a rare conversation with an unbeliever about sin, about hell, about sexuality, about other religions or about church discipline when the unbeliever does not shoot back that such things are incompatible with the idea of a loving God. But hold on a minute. John tells us here that *agapē* love means facing up to the reality of sin. Love did not make God close his eyes to our lawless actions. It made him send his Son to earth to die in agony on the cross so that he could atone for our sins and bring us back into fellowship with him.[5] I find C. S. Lewis very helpful here:

> *If God is Love, He is, by definition, something more than mere kindness.... When we fall in love with a woman, do we cease to care whether she is clean or dirty, fair or foul? Do we not rather then first begin to care?... You asked for a loving God: you have one... Not a senile benevolence that drowsily wishes you to be happy in your own way... but the consuming fire Himself, the Love that made the*

---

[4] John 13:34–35; 17:20–21. John says in 4:11 that we *opheilō*, or *owe*, this love to people, just as he did in 3:16.

[5] The Greek word *hilasmos* in 4:10 and in 2:2 means *propitiation* or *appeasement of anger*. It is a word from the Jewish Temple which refers to blood being shed to satisfy God's unbending justice towards sin.

worlds... jealous, inexorable, exacting as love between the sexes.[6]

In 4:13–21, John tells us that if God lives in us, we will begin to see this otherworldly love flowing out of our hearts through the Holy Spirit. Someone who has not been born again can say they love their wife, their children and their friends, because none of those affections require *agapē*, but only a person who has experienced the new life of heaven can ever say with Paul to an entire churchful of people, *"I dote upon all of you with the deep compassion of Christ Jesus."*[7] That kind of utterly selfless love is only ever the fruit of the Holy Spirit. That's why John says it should give us assurance that we are truly saved. We need not fear the verdict on Judgment Day because, unless God had saved us, we would never find ourselves loving other people as we do. That's why *"perfect love drives out fear"* for true believers. It's why *"the one who fears is not made perfect in love."*[8]

So do you see clear signs of God's *agapē* love in your own heart? Is John right to assume it is there? He says that your love or your lack of love is the ultimate sign of whether or not the living God lives inside you.

---

[6] C. S. Lewis in *The Problem of Pain* (1940).

[7] This is a literal translation of Philippians 1:8. See also Romans 5:5 and Galatians 5:22.

[8] The verb *teleioō* in 4:17–18 means *made perfect* in the sense of *brought to completion*. When we see our hearts increasing in their expression of a love that can only come from God's Spirit, we know that we are saved.

Louder Than Words (5:1–5)

This is how we know that we love the children of God:
by loving God and carrying out his commands.

(1 John 5:2)

Reading John's letters, it is hard to believe that the Church was heading into the early heyday of its history. On the surface, it seemed to be on the brink of disaster. False teachers were in its pulpits and a giant wave of persecution lay just around the corner.[1] By rights we might have expected the Church that John addressed to roll over and die. But it didn't. Instead, over the next 200 years it conquered the world.

Origen marvelled in 230 AD at this miraculous turnaround:

> *If we consider how powerful the Gospel has become in just*
> *a few short years, making progress through persecution*
> *and torture, through death and confiscation – a fact*
> *made all the more surprising by the small number of*
> *Gospel preachers and their lack of skill – and if we*
> *consider that the Gospel has been preached throughout*
> *the earth so that Greeks and barbarians, the wise and*
> *foolish, surrender to worship Jesus, then there can be no*
> *doubt that it is not human might and power that have*

---

[1] This broke out under Emperor Domitian in c.93 AD. Since it is not mentioned in any of John's letters but it is in Revelation 1:9, he must have written his letters before receiving his Revelation.

caused the words of Jesus Christ to conquer the minds
and souls of all men with faith and power.[2]

In 5:1, John tells us how it happened. Ordinary men and women were born again through the inner working of the Spirit of God. They weren't persuaded to pray a prayer of salvation through clever sermons or through the promise of material gain. The Holy Spirit simply raised their dead spirits to life and opened their eyes to see the real Jesus, just as John had promised the beleaguered believers that he would. We need to remember this if we want to see a similar Gospel breakthrough in our own day. It isn't about gimmicks or methods. It is simply about partnering with the Spirit of God.

In 5:2–3, John tells us how this small group of born-again believers multiplied so rapidly throughout the world. Very few of them were rich or educated or influential. Celsus, one of the most vocal early opponents of Christianity, dismissed them as a bunch of *"laundry-workers and the most illiterate and rustic yokels"*. He sneered that the Christians were *"only able to convince the foolish, the dishonourable, the stupid, the women and the children"*.[3] But these simple believers put John's instructions into practice. They believed that they had truly become children of God and that the Spirit who now lived inside them would bring out their new family likeness. They began to love God and one another with *agapē* love – the kind that is not measured by what we claim to feel but by what we are impelled to do.[4] They preached no better than us, but their actions spoke louder than

---

[2] Origen wrote this in *On First Principles* (4.2). This translation comes from Rufinus's Latin paraphrase.

[3] Celsus said this in c.175 AD. It is recorded in Origen's response, *Against Celsus* (3.44 and 55).

[4] James 2:14–26 tells us that faith without action is dead. 1 John 5:2–3 tells us that love without action is dead. John also says that true love for God always results in obedience in John 14:15, 14:21–24, 15:10 and 15:14.

their words. Soon the entire Roman Empire began to sit up and listen.

A hundred years after John wrote this letter, Athenagoras of Athens attempted to explain to the Roman emperors why nothing that they did seemed able to prevent the rapid growth of Christianity. He explained disarmingly that

> *Among us you will find uneducated people and manual labourers and old women who, though unable to prove the benefit of our teaching with their words, are able to exhibit by their deeds the benefit which comes from their belief that it is true. They do not rehearse speeches; they exhibit good works. When they are struck they do not strike back. When they are robbed they do not go to law. They give to those who ask them for things. In short, they love their neighbours as themselves.*[5]

That's how the Gospel triumphed in the Church's early days. It is also how the Gospel will triumph in our own day. These three signs of life are not just key to our individual assurance. They are also key to convincing unbelievers that our message of salvation is true. Our world is tired of hearing Christian talk, but it is always surprised to encounter true Christian walk. When people witness the Holy Spirit living inside us, we never fail to find that our actions speak louder than our words.

In 5:4–5, John tells us that this is always how the Church overcomes the evil one. Our belief in the real Jesus unleashes the eternal life of heaven upon the world. The first two times that John listed his three signs of life, they were very tidy. He talked about living like Jesus, then about loving like Jesus, then about believing in the real Jesus, as if they were three separate things. This third time round he deliberately blurs the edges to emphasize that they are all part of a single package. They all

---

[5] He said this in his *Plea for the Christians* (chapter 11), addressed to the emperors Marcus Aurelius and Commodus in c.180 AD.

stem from the fact that God now lives inside us. When the Holy Spirit brought us to new birth, it resulted in true faith in God's Son, which led us into a true experience of God's love, which led us into true obedience to God's commands, which in turn leads us into true fruitfulness.

One of the most striking things about eavesdropping on the way that these early Christians shared the Gospel with unbelievers is just how unafraid they were about presenting the real Jesus as he is described in the gospels. Whereas a lot of our preaching today seeks to make him more palatable to modern ears – *please don't be offended; he didn't really mean what he said about hell or other religions or divorce or giving away our possessions; it's simply metaphor and hyperbole* – the early Christians did not play down the radical change that was required of those who accepted Jesus as the Son of God. It's as if they wanted to ensure that people were either converted by the Holy Spirit's work in their hearts or not converted at all.

Listen to Clement of Alexandria, for example, at the end of a sermon to a group of sophisticated Greek pagans, who believed that the material world was evil and that the gods would never take on mortal human flesh, let alone be willing to die:

> *You people, believe in Him who is both God and man! You people, believe in the one who is both worshipped and who suffered! You slaves, believe in the one who died. People from every race, believe in the one who is the only God of all mankind... Have you found God? Then you shall have life... Become a noble hymn of God, an immortal who is established in righteousness and who has the oracles of truth engraved on the inside... The Divine Power, casting his radiance on the earth, has filled the world with the seed of his salvation!*[6]

---

[6] Clement of Alexandria, speaking in c.195 AD in his *Exhortation to the Heathen* (chapter 10).

Do you want to see a similar Gospel breakthrough as the early Christians did? Then do as John says. Partner with God as he lives inside you, empowering you to love and live and speak boldly like Jesus. Ask him to make your actions speak louder than words.

Water and Blood (5:6–12)

He did not come by water only, but by water and blood. And it is the Spirit who testifies, because the Spirit is the truth.

(1 John 5:6)

I have a lot of sympathy for Nicodemus in the third chapter of John's gospel when he is confused about how Jesus says God saves people. Their conversation is hard to follow and Nicodemus did not even have the benefit of John's extra commentary on it in these verses. Even with the extra commentary, the nineteenth-century Bible teacher Alfred Plummer despaired that *"This is the most perplexing passage in the Epistle, and one of the most perplexing in the New Testament."*[1] But don't give up. The Holy Spirit really wants to teach you how he saves people so that you can partner with him.

John says that Jesus *"came by water and blood"*. He is very insistent about this, adding firmly that *"he did not come by water only, but by water and blood."* It echoes the warning that Jesus gave to Nicodemus that *"no one can enter the kingdom of God unless they are born of water and the Spirit"* and the detail that John gives us about the death of Jesus: *"One of the soldiers pierced Jesus' side with a spear, bringing a sudden flow of blood and water."* This combination of water and blood is clearly of great

---

[1] Alfred Plummer in *The Epistles of St John* (1890). The confusion is worsened by the fact that older translations include a few extra words in 5:7–8, even though they are not in Greek manuscripts prior to 1400.

significance to John, even if its significance is not immediately obvious to us. So what is John trying to say here?[2]

On one level Alfred Plummer is right: we do not know for sure. "Water" may represent the fact that Mary's waters broke when Jesus was born as a human baby in Bethlehem (since Jesus tells Nicodemus that being *"born of water and the Spirit"* means that *"flesh gives birth to flesh, but the Spirit gives birth to spirit"*). Alternatively, it may represent the fact that Jesus was baptized in the River Jordan as a model of perfect obedience (telling John the Baptist that *"it is proper for us to do this to fulfil all righteousness"*). Whichever one it is, we can at least be sure that "water" somehow talks about the early life and humanity of Jesus, whereas "blood" talks about his death on the cross to atone for our sin.

John is therefore making a massive statement in the context of the Gnostic false teachers. He is saying that the third sign that we are truly saved is that we believe Jesus is both fully God and fully human. When the Docetists taught that Jesus merely seemed to become a man, and when Cerinthus taught that "Christ" joined "Jesus" at his baptism and left him before his crucifixion, they were not merely in error. They betrayed the fact that they did not truly know God. Anyone who denies the full humanity of Jesus – either the water or the blood – cannot have God's Spirit living inside them.

John is also making a more general point here that extends beyond the false teachers of his own day. He is pointing out that faith in the real Jesus always requires an inner miracle from God. It was the Holy Spirit who revealed the true identity of Jesus to John the Baptist by descending on him like a dove at

---

[2] The verses quoted in this chapter can be found in John 3:1–8 and 19:34–35, and in Matthew 3:13–17. The solemn oath of testimony in 19:35 shows that John attached enormous significance to the fact that both water and blood flowed out of the side of the dead body of Jesus.

his baptism.[3] It was the Spirit who revealed the true identity of Jesus to the world by raising him from the dead. It is still the Spirit who reveals the true identity of Jesus to the world by performing miracles in his name today. He is *"the Spirit who testifies, because the Spirit is the truth… Whoever does not believe God has made him out to be a liar."*[4] In the midst of this world's Maze of Mirrors, John says it is always the Holy Spirit's work whenever people find the real Jesus.

John waits until the end of his third list to talk about the water and the blood because it is the most obscure element of his argument so far, but the essence of what he is saying is not obscure at all. Just as Jesus told Nicodemus, he means that any genuine response to the Gospel is never man-made. It is always the result of a miraculous work of the Holy Spirit bringing a person to new birth deep in their hearts. That's why John expects us to be very confident about our salvation in 5:13. It did not originate with us, so we can trust the Lord to carry on his work to completion. Understanding what John is saying revolutionizes our own assurance of salvation and it also revolutionizes the way that we share the Gospel to pass that same assurance on to others.

For a start, it transforms *when we share the Gospel*. The truth is that we seldom share because we seldom feel that we are likely to be fruitful. Because our eyes are focused on our own powers of persuasion, we find a thousand reasons why it is not worth sharing. But what John says shifts our focus away from ourselves and onto God. It stops us from viewing ourselves

---

[3] The Father also boomed out a testimony but note that John 1:32–34 places a far bigger emphasis on the testimony of the Spirit. John sees the triple testimony of the Spirit, the water and the blood as the three witnesses required to establish a matter beyond reasonable doubt in a court of law (Deuteronomy 19:15).

[4] This is what Jesus means by "blasphemy against the Holy Spirit" in Matthew 12:25–32. If we treat his testimony as that of a deceiving spirit, we miss out on forgiveness through the real Jesus. All genuine salvation begins with believing the testimony of the Spirit of Truth. See 4:6 and John 14:17; 15:26; 16:13.

like subterranean potholers, frantically trying to manufacture enough light in people's hearts to guide them out of the dark cave of this world's thinking. It helps us to see that we are far more like people in a room on a sunny day with the shutters drawn. The Holy Spirit has all the light we need and he is poised to shine into people's hearts whenever we rattle the shutters through a simple word of Gospel truth.

It also transforms *what Gospel we share*. Because our eyes are focused on our own powers of persuasion we tend to take a "Romans" approach to salvation. We assume that people need to understand the whole landscape of God's plan of salvation in order to respond to his offer of mercy. We forget that Paul wrote Romans to inform Christians about how Jesus had already saved them, not as a tract for unbelievers. His initial message was always a whole lot simpler. In due course we need to explain to them how God's offer of forgiveness works, but they don't need to understand that straightaway. They simply need to understand that Jesus is God, that he is somehow Saviour and that he is calling them to follow him. John says in 5:13 that this makes our task very easy. Evangelism is describing the real Jesus and calling people to *"believe in the name of the Son of God"*.

Finally, it transforms *whom we share the Gospel for*. Instead of focusing primarily on our hearers and therefore looking for ways to make our message more palatable to their ears, John's teaching shifts our focus primarily onto the Holy Spirit. Our fishing partner is the Spirit of Truth, and he refuses to partner with anybody who treats him as a liar by doctoring his testimony. He is listening to what we say, seeing if we honour him with what we share and delighting to partner with anyone who proclaims the real Jesus.

These verses are complicated but their message isn't. God is reminding us that conversion is a miracle. He is inviting us to go fishing with the Holy Spirit as our partner.

Do Ya? (5:13–15)

*I write these things to you who believe in the name of
the Son of God so that you may know that you have
eternal life.*

(1 John 5:13)

I love the famous scene in the first *Dirty Harry* movie, where
Clint Eastwood's detective aims his gun at a criminal who has
dropped his rifle and asks him if he thinks he can reach out to it
in time. He warns, *"I know what you're thinking: did he just fire
six shots or only five?... You've gotta ask yourself one question: 'Do
I feel lucky?' Well – do ya?"*

John has just taken us through three long lists of signs
that help us know for sure if we are saved. When we look inside
our hearts, do we see evidence of the Holy Spirit doing things
that we could never do ourselves? Do we find ourselves living
like Jesus, loving like Jesus and believing in the real Jesus? John
ends by telling us that *"I write these things to you who believe in
the name of the Son of God so that you may know that you have
eternal life."* He is asking us the same blunt question as Clint
Eastwood: Well – do ya?

John asks us: *Do you believe?* He wants to know whether
we have found clear evidence of these three signs of true faith
in our hearts as we have read his letter.[1] One sign focused
on our theology, but two signs focused on how we put it into
practice, because true Christian faith is not seen by what we say

---

[1] John assumes in 5:13 that the majority of his readers are genuine believers,
but the whole thrust of his letter is that we need to apply these three signs to
our hearts to gauge whether that assumption is true.

we believe but by what we do about it. *"Faith by itself, if it is not accompanied by action, is dead,"* we are warned in James 2:17, and John has a quirky way of reinforcing this in the language that he uses here.

Ancient Greek, like English, talked about believing *in* a concept or a person. Men like Homer and Plato and Aristotle, as well as the translators of the Greek Old Testament, all used the little Greek word *en* to describe people placing faith *in* what they saw. John deliberately breaks the rules of Greek grammar throughout his gospel and here in 5:10 and 13 by using the little word *eis* to communicate that true Christian faith always means believing **into** a person.[2] It may not be good Greek and it is pretty clumsy English, but it is a clever way of contrasting the faith that saves with the faith that doesn't. Greek expert Marvin Vincent explains that it means

> *more than mere acceptance of a statement. It is so to accept a statement or a person as to rest upon them, to trust them practically... Hence to believe on the Lord Jesus Christ is not merely to believe the facts of His historic life or of His saving energy as facts, but to accept Him as Saviour, Teacher, Sympathiser, Judge; to rest the soul upon Him for present and future salvation, and to accept and adopt His precepts and example as binding upon the life.*[3]

Well, John asks, do ya? Do you see signs of the faith that impels people to love and live like Jesus? Can you say that you believe *into* Jesus?

John asks us: *Do you believe in the name of the Son of God?* He wants to know whether we find in our hearts faith in the

---

[2] John's friends Luke, Paul and Peter also pick up on this, talking occasionally about believing into Jesus, but John uses this quirky phrase five times as often as all the other New Testament writers put together.

[3] Marvin Vincent in *Word Studies in the New Testament*, Vol. 2 (1904).

real Jesus, who calls us daily to die to ourselves, or whether we are following a cheaper, less demanding, man-made messiah. John wants to know whether the Jesus that we follow puts us in conflict with the values of our fallen world. If he doesn't cause us trouble daily, he isn't the real Jesus.

John asks us: *Do you know that you have eternal life?* He is not just asking if we see evidence to convince us that we are going to heaven when we die. He does not talk about assurance that we *will have* eternal life or anything else. He uses the present tense to tell us that these three signs should make us certain that we *have* eternal life right here and right now. When Jesus took on human flesh, it meant that the life of the eternal age had broken into our dying world (1 John 1:2). When he invited us to know him and allow him to dwell in our hearts, it meant that the life of the eternal age had broken out in us (John 17:3). John is therefore not just asking us here whether we know for sure that we are going to heaven when our earthly life is over. He is asking whether we know for sure that heaven is breaking out in our hearts while we are still alive. Well – do ya?

If our answer to these three questions is yes, then John tells us we can have complete confidence that we are genuinely saved. There is nothing virtuous and humble about a Christian expressing uncertainty about their salvation. Unbelievers insult God and call him a liar when they deny the seriousness of their sin (1:10), but believers insult the Holy Spirit and call him a liar when they deny the certainty of their Saviour (5:10). Neither is good. God wants us to have complete confidence that we are saved, since it is all about his work and not ours. If we can see God's Spirit at work in our hearts to help us live like Jesus, love like Jesus and believe in Jesus, we can *know* that we are saved.

If our answer to these three questions is yes, then John adds that we can have complete confidence that our prayers will be answered. Jesus promises us seven times in three chapters in John's gospel that those who are saved can approach the Father in prayer and be certain that their requests will be treated just as if they were prayed by the Son.[4] A few verses ago, in 1 John 3:22, John repeated it an eighth time and now he says it for a ninth time here. His only caveat is that our requests need to be *"according to his will"* – in other words, they need to be affirmed by the Spirit he has given us to guide us. You have been granted divine power to shape world history through your prayers. John's question is simple: Well – do ya?

If you do, then John tells you to have complete confidence that the Gospel will triumph in the end. How could it not? You have threefold proof that God lives in your heart, and a promise in 4:4 that *"The one who is in you is greater than the one who is in the world."* You have God's pledge that he will unleash the eternal life of heaven on earth through your prayers.

So don't rush on from these verses without responding to John's urgent question. Do you know for sure that you see these signs of the Spirit's life within your heart? Do you let them shape the way you live? John asks: Well – do ya?

---

[4] John 14:13, 14; 15:7, 16; 16:23, 24, 26.

No Nonsense (5:16–21)

He is the true God and eternal life. Dear children,
keep yourselves from idols.

(1 John 5:20–21)

One of my close friends has never learned the art of finishing a phone conversation. To say that his approach is no-nonsense would be a colossal understatement. One minute you are in the full flow of conversation. The next he has panicked about what to say next and hung up the phone without observing any of the customs of a polite goodbye. I find the end of John's first letter a bit like that. There is no list of personal greetings to warn us that it is nearly over. John just does the equivalent of hanging up the phone.

Actually, John did know how to end a letter very gracefully. We can tell that from his second and third letters, where he displays all the social niceties expected in a normal first-century letter. They are probably missing from his first letter because he sent it to several churches, adding different personal greetings to each, and they were left out when the generic template became part of the New Testament. Nevertheless, there is something intentionally abrupt about the sudden ending of 1 John. These final six verses offer us a no-nonsense summary of the message of the letter.

In 5:16–17, John reminds us that he wrote this letter to confront the work of false teachers. He tells his readers to look out for genuine believers – "brothers and sisters" – who have fallen into error and to draw them back to true faith in Jesus. Don't misunderstand him when he contrasts "sins which lead to death" with "sins which do not lead to death". John is clear throughout the rest of his letter that all unconfessed sin bars us from eternal life and that all confessed sin is forgiven.[1] He is distinguishing here between "believers who have fallen into error" and "unbelievers who are spouting error", warning his readers not to be naïve and hesitate in dealing with Cerinthus and his friends in the hope of winning them over.[2] Instead, they must be diligent in prayer that true believers will be rescued from their clutches and brought back to the assurance of 5:13.[3]

In 5:18, John reminds us that he wrote this letter to give assurance to true believers. There is a spiritual war raging in the world between *"the evil one"* and *"the One who was born of God"*, and it is not a war of equals. The spirit of the Antichrist is no match for the Spirit of Christ. John therefore reminds us one final time to look inside ourselves for evidence that we too are *"born of God"*. Do we live like Jesus? Do we love like Jesus? Do we believe in the real Jesus? If we see progress in these three areas, we can know for sure that God has initiated a work in us that he will bring to completion.[4] He will keep us safe from the evil one, fulfilling the promise of Jesus in John 10:28–29: *"I give them eternal life, and they shall never perish; no one will snatch them out of my hand. My Father, who has given them to me, is greater than all; no one can snatch them out of my Father's hand."*

In 5:19–20, John reminds us that he wrote this letter to call us onto the spiritual offensive. Two of his recurring phrases in

---

[1] See 1:7–2:2; 2:12; 3:4–5; 5:12. In context, John cannot be teaching us to categorize wrongdoing into "venial" and "mortal" sins. All sin leads to death and all confession of sin leads to life (James 2:10).

[2] As we will see, the message of 2 John and 3 John is that false teachers should be chased out of the churches.

[3] Note what John says. When we detect sin in the life of a Christian brother or sister, our first reaction ought not to be anger, criticism, complaining, gossip, blogging or rejoicing, but loving prayer.

[4] We saw in 2:29–3:10 that John does not mean that believers achieve sinless perfection in this life. This verse is best translated as *"Anyone who is born of God does not persist in sin."*

the letter are *"eternal life"* and *"the world"*. He ends his letter by telling us that we are on the winning side.

John is not being unrealistic about the challenge that lies before us. He freely confesses that *"the whole world is under the control of the evil one."* He is not fazed by the fact that the Church is hard pressed by false teachers and phoney believers and hostile persecutors. He simply tells us that it is not hard pressed like the British troops on the beaches of Dunkirk in 1940, desperate to get away from the world before it succumbs to its overwhelming power. It is hard pressed like the Allied troops in the fields of Normandy in 1944. Our commander has already succeeded in landing on enemy-held territory and he is leading us on inexorably to victory. It is only a matter of time.

John has taught us this throughout his letter. He has told us that Jesus has landed on the Devil's beaches to become the flesh-and-blood embodiment of heaven (1:2), to destroy the Devil's work and to replace *"the world"* with *"eternal life"* wherever he goes (3:8). The Devil is no match for him (4:4), nor is he any match for us when we partner with God's Spirit (1:3). If we believe that Jesus is the Son of God and keep advancing in faith, our final victory is guaranteed (5:4–5). If John appears a bit too no-nonsense for you in these final verses, try to imagine him as an old colonel drilling his troops for a fight. He does not want anything to get in the way of our clear understanding that Jesus *"is the true God and eternal life"*, or that he lives in us and we live in him. See these as the tersely barked instructions of John's final drill before he sends us out to war.

In 5:21, John reminds us one last time that he wrote this letter to warn us against counterfeit Jesuses. If we take this verse in isolation, it feels like an abrupt change of subject, since John has not mentioned the Temple of Artemis or any of the Greek gods up until now. We therefore need to see this verse in its proper context, as a follow-on from the previous verse. John has just told us that Jesus is the only true God, the only true

Messiah and the only true source of eternal life. His mention of idolatry is therefore a challenge that the trinkets of Artemis are not the only false images being peddled for them to worship. Cerinthus and the Docetists have any number of false images of Jesus on sale to any believer who is gullible enough to fall for their man-made modifications.

John is reminding us of the warning in Ezekiel 14:3 that idolatry means more than worshipping a golden image or a statue of a monkey: *"These men have set up idols **in their hearts**."* The sixteenth-century reformer John Calvin comments on this verse that *"The human mind is, so to speak, a perpetual idol factory... The human mind, stuffed as it is with presumptuous rashness, dares to imagine a god suited to its own capacity... It substitutes vanity and an empty phantom in the place of God."*[5]

John's letter ends with a final appeal for us to worship the real Jesus. It ends with a final reminder that we are in Christ, we are born again, we are home to God, we live in the world but we belong to heaven. Ours is a Gospel that will triumph in the end.

---

[5] John Calvin wrote this in 1536 in his *Institutes of the Christian Religion* (1.11.8).

Part Five:

True Love

(2 John and 3 John)

The Love Doctor
(2 John 1–3)

The elder, to the lady chosen by God and to her
children, whom I love in the truth.

(2 John 1)

I don't know why they call them Saint Valentine's Day cards. If they were looking for a patron saint of love, surely the obvious candidate would have been John? He uses the word "love" two and a half times for every chapter in his gospel and ten times for every chapter in his first letter. Jerome's story about the aged John preaching about love every Sunday is very easy to believe. He is the love doctor of the New Testament.

That's why I find his second and third letters so hugely helpful. Anyone can talk about love but it takes an expert like John to describe what it actually looks like in action. He states his credentials to do so at the start of 2 John and 3 John. He writes one letter *"to the lady chosen by God and to her children, **whom I love in the truth**"*, and the other letter *"to my dear friend Gaius, **whom I love in the truth**"*. He blesses his readers *"**in truth and love**"*.[1] In other words, although we do not know all the background to these two letters, we know that they were included in the New Testament to explain to us what true love means.

We need to do some detective work to identify the recipients of John's second letter. His personal greetings are still intact, but readers take different views on the identity of

---

[1] This blessing comes at the start of 2 John but not of 3 John. It is similar to Paul's opening greetings.

"the lady chosen by God". Some readers see her as a real-life lady, even claiming that her name was *Kyria*, since the Greek word for lady was occasionally used as a girl's name. This might make sense when John addresses her a second time as *"dear lady"* in verse 5, but the rest of the letter points to a better explanation.[2] John doesn't just address his letter to one *"lady chosen by God and to her children"*. He also signs it off with greetings from another one. *"The children of your sister, who is chosen by God"* appears to refer to the members of the church in the city from which John is writing, so the lady and her children must be the church in another city. Again, it makes me marvel that Saint Valentine ever managed to become the patron saint of love. John, who talks more about the Church as the Bride of Christ than any other writer in the Bible, can't even address a letter without referring to Jesus' love for each local expression of his Bride!

John wrote his third letter to one of the leading men in the church that received his second letter. Again, some detective work is needed here because John does not state this explicitly, but the two letters are so similar in their content and style that they must have both been written at the same time. John is evidently so respected as the last surviving disciple that he can simply introduce himself in both letters as *"the elder"*, before describing what true Christian love looks like in action.[3]

John writes these two letters because false teachers have infiltrated this particular local church and as a result the congregation is in two minds over what to do. Its dilemma is captured by the two words that dominate these letters. In 2

---

[2] For example, it makes little sense for John to tell an individual lady in verse 5 to *"love one another"*.

[3] The Greek word *presbuteros* can simply mean *old man*, but in the New Testament it normally means *elder*. Technically anonymous, the early Church always attributed these two letters to John. As an elder of the large church in Ephesus, John probably writes to one of the many churches planted out of it – hence *"what we have worked for"* in many manuscripts of verse 8.

John the words *love* and *truth* are both used five times in just thirteen verses. In 3 John the word *love* is used three times and the words *truth* and *true* are used seven times in thirteen verses. John often uses the two words together in the same phrase – for example, *"love in the truth"* and *"truth in love"* – because he wants the church to see that truth and love are not polar opposites. How can they be, when he has taught us that God is love and God is truth?[4]

John explains to the church that they do not need to choose between dealing with the false teachers in love and dealing with them in truth. If they love with God's *agapē* love, their reaction will be both completely loving and completely true. Love that requires pretence is not God's true love, nor is truth that lacks love. Learning this lesson is so vital for our own day that I wish the history books told us how this church responded to John's letters. The history books are silent, but we have something far better. A few years after he wrote 2 John and 3 John, the apostle wrote down seven letters to the churches of Asia Minor, dictated by the ascended Lord Jesus himself.[5]

In the seven letters of Revelation 2–3, Jesus demonstrates the practical outworking of John's instructions in this letter. They are very challenging, since most of us tend to err on the side of tolerating too much evil in the name of love. Jesus emphasizes that this is not true love when he commends the church in Ephesus because *"you cannot tolerate wicked people"* and because *"you hate the practices of the Nicolaitans, which I also hate."*[6] In contrast, he rebukes the church in Pergamum because they have failed to expel members of their congregation

---

[4] God is love (1 John 4:8, 16) and God is truth (John 14:6, 17; 15:26; 16:13; 1 John 4:6; 5:6).

[5] Since these letters are not dated, we do not know precisely when they were written. Their content suggests that it was at a similar time to 1 John. Their failure to mention any persecution points to before 93 AD.

[6] Revelation 2:2, 6. Refusal to tolerate wicked people does not mean that we cease loving them. Jesus says that he hates the practices of the Nicolaitans, not the Nicolaitans themselves.

who are influenced by the Nicolaitans, and he warns the church in Thyatira, *"I have this against you: you tolerate that woman Jezebel, who calls herself a prophet."*[7]

John's second and third letters are therefore going to be full of surprises. We need to listen very carefully to what they say. John was the love doctor. He couldn't stop writing about it. People complained that he couldn't stop preaching about it. Yet he knew that, in God, love and truth always go hand in hand. Irenaeus was trained by one of John's students, so he gives us many anecdotes about the apostle's final years in Ephesus. He tells us that *"John, the disciple of the Lord, went into the public baths at Ephesus and, spotting Cerinthus inside, he ran out of the baths without bathing, crying out: Let us run away in case the public baths fall down on us, because Cerinthus the enemy of truth is within!"*[8]

That story reminds us that dealing with false teaching is dirty work. True love often is. Parents love their babies through changing nappies as well as through giving cuddles. So let's read these two letters and let's allow John to reshape our view of what true love really means.

[7] Revelation 2:14–16, 20–25. These false teachers were among those addressed by 1 John.

[8] Irenaeus of Lyons wrote this in c.180 AD in *Against Heresies* (3.3.4).

Taken (2 John 4–11)

Anyone who welcomes them shares in their wicked work.

(2 John 11)

It is easy to see why the Liam Neeson *Taken* trilogy was so successful at the box office. There is something thrilling about watching a father take up arms against a team of kidnappers to rescue his wife and child. Romcoms are enjoyable, but they are also two-a-penny. Once in a while most of us like to watch a film where love is expressed, not just with flowers and chocolates, but with the gritty determination of true love.

Maybe that's why John describes these two churches as ladies. He is aware of the Lord's gritty love towards them. When Paul rolls up his sleeves to deal with false teachers in 2 Corinthians 11:2–4, he says something similar:

> *I am jealous for you with a godly jealousy. I promised you to one husband, to Christ, so that I might present you as a pure virgin to him. But I am afraid that just as Eve was deceived by the snake's cunning, your minds may somehow be led astray from your sincere and pure devotion to Christ. For if someone comes to you and preaches a Jesus other than the Jesus we preached, or if you receive a different spirit from the Spirit you received, or a different gospel from the one you accepted, you put up with it easily enough.*

This is what the apostles teach us true love looks like. It is jealous and feisty. Let John explain.

In verses 4–6, John teaches that true love is never anything less than love itself. He tells the church how delighted he is to hear that they are *"walking in the truth"*, but he warns that this must always be twinned with the great command of Jesus to *"walk in love"*. Jesus called this a *"new command"* in John 13:34, and John reflects over fifty years later that such a founding statement of Christianity is still as relevant as ever.[1] John says that only when we walk before the Lord in both love and truth, in both truth and love, can we ever *"walk in obedience to his commands"*.[2]

We need to remember this if we are ever tempted to use this letter to justify lashing out at error in the Church. Some Christians have a tendency to be over-tolerant of false teaching. Other Christians have a tendency to be over-harsh in their pursuit of theological purity. Know which kind of Christian you are. If you are more likely to fall into the second trap than the first, take Francis Schaeffer's warning to heart: *"What divides and severs true Christian groups and Christians, what leaves bitterness that can last twenty, thirty, forty years... is not the issue of doctrine or belief that causes the differences in the first place. Invariably it's lack of love and the bitter things that are said."*[3]

In verse 7, John teaches that true love is never anything less than truth itself. He reminds us that the Devil hates the truth. John 8:44 says that *"He was a murderer from the beginning, not holding to the truth, for there is no truth in him. When he lies, he speaks his native language, for he is a liar and the father of lies."*

---

[1] Even when Jesus gave it as a new command to his disciples, it was really the Christian restatement of Leviticus 19:18. The command for us to love with God's love is as ancient as God's people.

[2] One of John's recurring themes is that true love is always proven by our obedient commitment to God's truth. See John 14:15, 21–24; 15:10, 14; 1 John 5:2–3.

[3] Francis Schaeffer in *The Mark of the Christian* (1970).

When people claim that Jesus is less than fully God or less than fully human or less than anything that he really is, they are not merely deluded individuals. They are so inspired by the father of lies that they embody *"the deceiver and the antichrist"*. John's choice of words here could hardly be more serious! Allowing false teachers to go unchallenged is never the path of God's true love. They must be expelled from the Church for their own sake and for the sake of others.[4]

In verses 8–11, John warns us that failure to do so means participating in their sin. When I conduct a wedding, I usually see the bride at the door of the church before she enters. Imagine the horrified look on her face if I tripped over as I greeted her and spilled the red wine and canapés down the front of her white dress. You know as well as I do that it would be a total disaster – so why are we less concerned when it comes to the Bride of Christ? That's what Paul is trying to express when he tells the Corinthians, *"I am jealous for you with a godly jealousy. I promised you to one husband, to Christ, so that I might present you as a pure virgin to him."* It is a terrible thing when Christians are so desperate not to be judgmental or to offend that they allow the Devil to pour filth all over Jesus' Bride. That isn't true love and it isn't a smart move. Get this: John says that it is partnering with the Antichrist. He warns us that *"Anyone who welcomes them shares in their wicked work."*[5]

One of the most painful decisions I have ever had to make with my fellow church leaders in London was over a good friend of mine. He had come to faith out of a lifestyle of cocaine and gross immorality, but he hadn't really changed. Every few months he would slip back into his old ways, disappear for a few weeks and then resurface, ashamed. He was not a false

---

[4] Jesus laid down this principle in Matthew 18:15–17, and Paul outlines the process in 1 Corinthians 5. The fact that we tend to dismiss such passages as over-harsh accounts for a lot of the mess in the Church today.

[5] The Greek verb *koinōneō* in verse 11 is linked to the noun used for *partnering* with God's Spirit in 1 John 1:3.

teacher, so in a way his conduct was far less serious than what John is describing here, but after three years we could see no sign of God's miraculous work inside him. With heavy hearts, we decided that we needed to expel him from the church.

Our problem was that we really loved the man. He was our friend. We did not feel angry with him, just disappointed and desperate for him to stop polluting Christ's Bride with his seedy sexual encounters and cocaine. The next eleven months were painful for us and even more painful for him, but we can trust what John teaches us here. After almost a year, our friend's repentance was so obvious from his changed lifestyle that we were able to bring him back into the church body as a transformed man. Here is part of what he shared with the congregation as part of an amazing worship celebration:

> *Experiencing God's discipline is a tough and lonely place,*
> *but it's discipline borne out of love for a son... It has been*
> *a long time since I've done drugs or had sex. You have an*
> *idea of my past, so you'll know what an incredible miracle*
> *that is... But the very issue that used to keep me away*
> *from Him now brings me close to Him... I have given up*
> *everything, but I have gained everything too. I have my*
> *life back, I have my mind back, my past is forgiven, I am*
> *clean. I am loved and I have an incredible life – an eternal*
> *life – ahead of me.*

I will never forget watching my friend stand at the front of the church and proclaim the freedom that he found on the receiving end of true love. The grand finale of one of Liam Neeson's *Taken* movies could not compare with the joy of seeing my once-hoodwinked friend now walking free. So let's take John's teaching seriously. God wants the Church to walk in both love and truth as a pure and spotless Bride worthy of his Son.

Backward (2 John 9–13)

Anyone who runs ahead and does not continue in the teaching of Christ does not have God; whoever continues in the teaching has both the Father and the Son.

(2 John 9)

It is hard to believe now that there was once a time when liberal Christianity was seen as the future and when those who believed in historic Christianity were viewed as the dying remnants of a backward breed. We almost have to pinch ourselves to remember that in the late nineteenth century, after Charles Darwin published his seminal book on evolution and the rate of scientific discovery began to rocket, most people believed that it was game over for historic Christianity and that liberal theology presented the Church with its only realistic chance of survival.

Over a century later it is easy to forget this because we have the benefit of hindsight. We now know what happened to most of the churches that dropped all talk of miracles, of virgin birth, of creation, of the Holy Spirit's inner working and of many other aspects of the Christian faith that were deemed too superstitious for the modern mind. We now know that, for every hundred people who were in the liberal churches of Europe and America in 1900, there were fewer than ten in the year 2000. During the same period the historical Gospel advanced with astonishing speed all across the developing world.

It helps, however, to remind ourselves of the situation in the late nineteenth century if we want to understand John's second letter. The apostle was addressing a similar situation. Many of the Church's greatest thinkers were complaining that talk of God taking on human flesh was all very well for a bunch of backwater Jews, but if the Church wanted its message to take root across the Roman Empire, it had to face up to some unpalatable truths. The backward ideas of Galilee would never gain traction with the sophisticated thinkers of the Greek- and Latin-speaking world.[1]

In verse 9, John responds by telling believers that the only way forward with the Gospel is to go backwards. He urges his readers, whenever they are dismissed as backward, to wear the insult as a badge of honour: *"Anyone who runs ahead and does not continue in the teaching of Christ does not have God; whoever continues in the teaching has both the Father and the Son."* John warns that those who seek to advance beyond apostolic Christianity make a terrible mistake.[2] Our calling is to remain in the truth that God revealed to the first apostles, not to rack our brains as to how best to modify it.[3] John warns us that those who think the words of Scripture are backward don't go forward: they only go astray. Those who seek to broker a compromise between the Gospel and their culture always end up losing both. They fail to experience God as the apostles did and they fail to pass on their powerless faith to others.

When Charles Spurgeon tried to put John's teaching into practice, he was despised and hated by the great thinkers of Victorian Britain for warning that

> *A new religion has been initiated, which is no more Christianity than chalk is cheese; and this religion, being destitute of moral honesty, palms itself off as the old faith*

---

[1] John 10:30–33 tells us that the idea of God taking on human flesh was actually equally offensive to Jews, but such is the nature of false teaching. It always assumes the Gospel was easier to believe in another time.

[2] Although the verb in a few manuscripts of verse 9 is *parabainō*, or *to transgress*, in the most reliable texts it is *proagō*, meaning *to advance* or *progress*. John says true progress is keeping firm hold of apostolic Christianity.

[3] Ephesians 3:2–5; 2 Thessalonians 2:14–15; 1 Timothy 6:20–21; 2 Timothy 1:13–14.

with slight improvements... The atonement is rejected, the inspiration of Scripture is derided, the Holy Spirit is degraded into an influence, the punishment of sin is turned into fiction, and the resurrection into a myth, and yet these enemies of our faith expect us to call them brethren, and maintain a confederacy with them![4]

Eventually, Charles Spurgeon led a group of churches out of his denomination. It was the most painful experience of his entire ministry but he explained:

A chasm is opening between the men who believe their Bibles and the men who are prepared for an advance upon Scripture... We cannot hold the inspiration of the Word, and yet reject it; we cannot believe in the atonement and deny it; we cannot hold the doctrine of the fall and yet talk of the evolution of spiritual life from human nature; we cannot recognise the punishment of the impenitent and yet indulge the "larger hope". One way or other we must go... With steadfast faith let us take our places; not in anger, not in the spirit of suspicion or division, but in watchfulness and resolve. Let us not pretend to a fellowship which we do not feel.[5]

In verses 10–11, John explains that there does indeed come a time when true love demands that churches call false teachers what they are and go their separate ways – either by expelling preachers from their church or by withdrawing their church from a denomination. There comes a time when the leading Christian voices in a nation need to warn people not to listen any longer to a particular teacher. Everything within us wants to avoid doing this. It seems unloving, intolerant, divisive, closed-minded and backward. That's why we tend to do the exact

---

[4] Charles Spurgeon in *The Sword and Trowel* magazine (August 1887).

[5] Spurgeon in *The Sword and Trowel* magazine (September 1887).

opposite. The more controversial a gifted communicator, the more we rush to buy their books and to hear their interviews. John says this is madness. We must not even allow their teaching into our houses, because *"Anyone who welcomes them shares in their wicked work."* The Greek word here for *sharing* is *koinōnia*, the same word that 1 John 1:3 used to describe our partnership with the Holy Spirit. John warns that we can only choose one type of partner. We need to choose well.

John knows that this is never easy. He knows that he is writing to believers who think that Matthew 10:40–42 promises them a reward from God for giving lodgings to the Gnostic travelling preachers. He has to warn them that they are in danger of losing the far bigger reward of letting the true Gospel lodge within their hearts. He has to threaten them that the reward for lodging false teachers is far more than they have bargained for! They will reap the same reward as King Jehoshaphat in 2 Chronicles 19:2, when he made an alliance with King Ahab of Israel on the basis that their two kingdoms were both nominally part of God's people. He was rebuked by the Lord's prophet: *"Should you help the wicked and love those who hate the Lord? Because of this, the wrath of the Lord is on you."*

Charles Spurgeon paid a heavy price for his actions. He died five years later aged only fifty-seven, his health shattered by the conflict. However, many historians believe that his firm stand prevented liberal Christianity from overrunning the Western Church entirely. Spurgeon had no regrets and insisted that true love always means such sacrifice:

> *The New Theology can do no good towards God or man... If it were preached for a thousand years by all the most earnest men of the school, it would never renew a soul.... [But,] where the gospel is fully and powerfully preached, with the Holy Ghost sent down from heaven, our churches not only hold their own, but win converts.*[6]

---

[6] Spurgeon in *The Sword and the Trowel Annual: 1887*.

Name Your Fuel
(3 John 1–13)

It was for the sake of the Name that they went out,
receiving no help from the pagans.

(3 John 7)

John's third letter carries on directly from his second one. I know that sounds a bit obvious, but make sure you don't miss it. John's second letter brought us to the question that Charles Spurgeon asked us at the end of the last chapter. What fuel are we relying on as we seek to advance God's Kingdom in the world? Are we looking to the man-made fuels that drove the false teachers – fuels such as logic, charm and popularity – or are we looking to God's Spirit alone? The style and content of 3 John are so similar to those of 2 John that it seems the apostle wrote both of them in one sitting for the same messenger to deliver.[1] Having posed a general question to the church as a whole, John now asks for a personal response. He wants this letter to help us clearly name our fuel.

Gaius was a good friend of John who possessed the commonest name in the Roman world.[2] It was so common that in the Roman wedding ceremony every bride told her husband that *"ubi tu Gaius, ibi Gaia"* – *"Wherever you are Gaius, I am Gaia."* His name is so common that we do not know whether this was the Gaius that Paul baptized in Corinth, the Gaius who joined

---

[1] Both letters are short – the two shortest books in the Bible – as if written rapidly, with a messenger waiting.

[2] Since John calls Gaius his "child" in verse 4, but not the other believers, he may have led him to salvation. However, we saw in 1 John that the elderly apostle very readily called younger people "my children".

Paul's team for some of his missionary journeys or another Gaius altogether.[3] All we know is that his parents gave him a name which spoke of his being fuelled by earthly delights. Gaius meant *Happy* or *Joyful* in the sense of delighting in the best food, wine and friendship that the Roman Empire had to offer.[4]

John holds him up as an example of somebody who has learned to drink deeply from the Holy Spirit as his fuel supply, rather than from the world. Despite his name and despite the fact that he was wealthy enough to be able to lodge travelling preachers in his home, he refused to draw his joy from his earthly possessions. John commends him in verse 2 for allowing the Holy Spirit to fuel the growth of his soul, and he tells him that he is praying for his body to become as healthy as his soul.[5] In other words, Gaius had chosen faithfulness over food, truth over treats and love over luxurious living.

John also commends the personal response of the travelling teachers who stayed at the home of Gaius. Most of us have no idea how perilous it was to become an itinerant preacher in the ancient world. If a person ran out of money in a foreign city, there was no local charity or government embassy to assist them. People who became penniless became beggars and the victims of unscrupulous innkeepers. As a result, travelling philosophers and religious teachers sought wealthy patrons to finance and protect them.

The travelling preachers who stayed at the house of Gaius must have been sorely tempted to do this, but they refused *"for the sake of the Name"*. They knew that pagan patronage would inevitably come with strings attached so they resolved

---

[3] See Acts 19:29; 20:4; Romans 16:23; 1 Corinthians 1:14.

[4] For Latin geeks, the name Gaius comes from the verb *gaudere*, meaning *to rejoice*. John rejoices with great joy over the fact that Gaius chose heavenly rather than earthly fuel.

[5] The Greek word translated as *spiritually* in verse 2 is *psychē* and not *pneuma*. It is therefore talking about the flourishing of Gaius's *soul* through the Holy Spirit's deep work within him.

to glorify Jesus by preaching for an audience of One. That meant arriving in the city where Gaius lived with nothing but a letter of commendation from the elders of the church that had sent them.[6] God faithfully honoured their reliance on his Spirit. Gaius not only gave them food and lodgings, but he also sent them on their way with funding for the next stage of their journey. When we rely on the Holy Spirit for our fuel, our tanks never run empty.

The third personal response was far less positive. The parents of Diotrephes had given their son a name that meant *Nourished by Zeus*, and he had lived up to the name they had given him. Whereas John's second letter warned the church that they were too quick to open the door to travelling preachers, Diotrephes was too quick to slam it on them. He saw every new arrival as a potential rival, and he expelled good people from the church for threatening his position within it. He was a self-promoter, a gossip, a slanderer and a bully, who even had the audacity to say no when John wrote to tell him he was coming.[7] John therefore warns Gaius that he is about to come and deal with Diotrephes for choosing to rely on the same type of fuel as the pagans around him.

The fourth personal response in this short letter comes from a man named Demetrius.[8] If you don't know much about Greek mythology, you might miss his significance here. Like Diotrephes, his parents had given him a name which spoke of his being fuelled by the best resources of the pagan world. Demetrius means *Dedicated to Demeter*, the Greek harvest goddess, who was petitioned by pagans wanting success on their farms or in conceiving a child.[9] He was therefore very

[6] Such letters of commendation are mentioned in Acts 18:27, 1 Corinthians 16:3 and 2 Corinthians 3:1–3.

[7] 1, 2 and 3 John are clearly just a selection of John's letters. We do not have his earlier letter to Diotrephes.

[8] Some readers conjecture that this was the Demetrius of Acts 19:24, now converted, but it is mere conjecture.

[9] Demeter was known to the Romans as *Ceres*. You recall her name whenever you eat *cereal* for breakfast.

similar to Diotrephes in his background and his name, but he chose a very different destiny. John commends him for choosing the path of true love over self-promotion and the Holy Spirit over the spirit of the world.

The fifth personal response in this short letter has to be our own. John mentions the wider church community in the final verse of the letter because we all need to make an active choice of fuel. The seventeenth-century Puritan John Flavel reminds us:

> *Ecstasy and delight are essential to the believer's soul and they promote sanctification. We were not meant to live without spiritual exhilaration, and the Christian who goes for a long time without the experience of heart-warming will soon find himself tempted to have his emotions satisfied from earthly things and not, as he ought, from the Spirit of God. The soul is so constituted that it craves fulfilment from things outside itself and will embrace earthly joys for satisfaction when it cannot reach spiritual ones. The believer is in spiritual danger if he allows himself to go for any length of time without tasting the love of Christ and the felt comforts of a Saviour's presence. When Christ ceases to fill the heart with satisfaction our souls will go in silent search of other lovers. By the enjoyment of the love of Christ in the heart of a believer, we mean an experience of the "love of God shed abroad in our hearts by the Holy Ghost which is given to us" (Romans 5:5). Because the Lord has made himself accessible to us in the means of grace, it is our duty and privilege to seek this experience from Him.*[10]

Make no mistake. Your heart is fuelled by something. John wants to make sure that we choose to satisfy ourselves in God and that we operate on the right fuel.

---

[10] John Flavel in *The Method of Grace in the Gospel Redemption* (1680).

Prosperity (3 John 2)

Beloved, I wish above all things that thou mayest prosper and be in health, even as thy soul prospereth.

(3 John 2, King James Version)

John wrote this letter to help deal with false teaching. That makes it pretty ironic that the second verse of the letter has so often been used to promote some terrible teaching.

The argument is most readily made from the King James Version of the Bible. Since there the verse reads *"Beloved, I wish above all things that thou mayest prosper and be in health, even as thy soul prospereth,"* some preachers argue that God is just as interested in prospering our finances and our physical health as he is in prospering our inner beings.[1] In fact, he may even be more interested in those things, since John prays for God to prosper those things in the life of Gaius *"above all things"*. I'm sure that you have heard that type of preaching. I hope that you have also seen the flaws in it.

John Piper points them out for us in the most explosive of terms:

> *The prosperity gospel is no gospel because what it does is offer to people what they want as natural people. You don't have to be born again to want to be wealthy, and therefore you don't have to be converted to be saved by*

---

[1] This is actually a poor translation. The Greek word *euodoō* means *to have a good journey*. It comes from *hodos*, meaning *the Way*, and is less about prospering than about *progressing*. See Acts 9:2; 18:25–26; 19:9, 23.

the prosperity gospel. When you appeal to people to come to Christ on the basis of what they already want (First Corinthians 2) it makes no sense. "The natural man does not receive the things of the Spirit; they are foolishness to him." Therefore if you offer to people what they do not consider foolishness in the natural man, you are not preaching the Gospel. And the prosperity gospel offers people what they desperately want as long as people get to do things and grow churches. And we export it to Africa and the Philippines, flying in with our jets, milking up their money and going back to our condos, worth $3 million. It is horrific what we export as Americans! I can't believe what we tolerate in the church! So I'm on a crusade to crucify the prosperity gospel. I hate the prosperity gospel because I love the glory of God.[2]

The fact that people preach a false gospel from a letter that was written to counter false teaching ought to teach us that the Devil is determined to stop people from relying on the Holy Spirit's fuel. The spirit of the Antichrist is just as active in the world today as it was when John wrote his letters, persuading people to worship Jesus as a get-rich-quick scheme. We need to be very sobered by the misuse of this verse, of all verses, and to remind ourselves why the prosperity gospel is so dangerously misleading.

First, preaching Jesus as a way to earthly prosperity peddles people a lie.[3] Jesus was not a rich man. He was born in a borrowed stable, he preached from a borrowed boat, he entered Jerusalem on a borrowed donkey, he ate the Passover in a borrowed room and he was buried in a borrowed tomb.

---

[2] John Piper said this in a sermon at the *"Resolved"* conference in Palm Springs, California, in June 2008. Although he is quoting from 1 Corinthians 2:14, he could just as easily be quoting from 1 John 4:5–6.

[3] This is the very opposite of the Gospel, since John's shorthand name for the Gospel in verse 8 is *"the truth"*.

To promise people that walking in the footsteps of Jesus will guarantee them health and wealth is a barefaced lie. For Peter it meant poverty and crucifixion. For John it meant exile to Patmos. The fact that the footsteps of Jesus have nail-marks in them is a clue that stepping into them is never going to be a walk in the park. If we pretend it is, we are not preaching the real Jesus.

Second, preaching Jesus as a way to earthly prosperity simply confirms people in their idolatry. Jesus was very clear with his disciples that our allegiance to money has to die for us to be able to follow him. That's what it means for us to own him as Lord. Jesus called Peter and John to leave their fishing business behind. He called Matthew to leave a table piled high with Roman coins. He explained why in Matthew 6:24: *"No one can serve two masters. Either you will hate the one and love the other, or you will be devoted to the one and despise the other. You cannot serve both God and Money."* The Gospel calls people to turn their back on money as a master that can never satisfy, while the prosperity gospel affirms money as a master and says that Jesus will help us to serve it even better.

Third, and as a result of this, preaching Jesus as a way to earthly prosperity actually leaves people worse off than they were before they met us. Paul addresses this in 1 Timothy 6:5–10, talking about those *"who have been robbed of the truth and who think that godliness is a means to financial gain"*. He warns that *"Those who want to get rich fall into temptation and a trap and into many foolish and harmful desires that plunge people into ruin and destruction. For the love of money is a root of all kinds of evil. Some people, eager for money, have wandered from the faith and pierced themselves with many griefs."* Persuading people to follow Jesus for the sake of money is therefore luring them onto a sure-fire pathway to pain in the short term and to eternal destruction in the long term. It is the spiritual equivalent of a

Ponzi scheme, hoodwinking gullible people into destroying their lives so that a preacher can feel his ministry is successful.

Fourth, preaching Jesus as a way to earthly prosperity fills churches with people who will never become disciples. The reason why so many church leaders look tired and discouraged is that they are worn out trying to disciple non-disciples. As we have already seen, Jesus warned Nicodemus in John 3:6 that *"Flesh gives birth to flesh, but the Spirit gives birth to spirit."* If we fill our churches with crowds of people through appeals to their flesh, we also have to bring those crowds to maturity through appeals to their flesh. It never works. Only the Holy Spirit can produce in people's hearts the three signs which John repeated throughout his first letter. We cannot teach people to live like Jesus, love like Jesus and believe in the real Jesus by selling them a false Jesus.

Fifth, preaching Jesus as a way to earthly prosperity creates churches that will never know the advance of the Kingdom of God in their generation. That's the irony when well-meaning preachers use dishonest means to advance the Christian cause. They actually undermine it. Look at those who have responded to the prosperity gospel. Which one of them is willing to suffer? Who is willing to renounce everything for Jesus? Who is willing to go to the ends of the earth and to live among the poor in order to pass on the knowledge of Jesus to an unreached nation? Nobody. The prosperity gospel creates people who are turned in on themselves. It is infertile and ultimately suicidal.[4]

So let's learn from this verse and resolve before God that we will preach the real Jesus by the power of the Holy Spirit. This is true love for people and for God. It is the only way to see the Gospel triumph in the end.

---

[4] John emphasizes in verse 8 that the real Gospel is about giving, not grabbing. He tells Gaius that we *opheilō*, or *owe it*, to people to become *sunergoi*, or *co-workers*, for the salvation of the world.

Spoiling the View
(3 John 9–13)

I wrote to the church, but Diotrephes, who loves to be first, will not welcome us.

(3 John 9)

The Eiffel Tower is a magnificent sight. Once the tallest man-made structure in the world, it still dominates the Paris skyline. It therefore isn't strange that more people visit it than any other paid tourist attraction in the world. What is strange, however, is what those people choose to do in front of it. More selfies are taken in front of the Eiffel Tower than in front of any other object on the face of the earth. Hordes of people gaze at the tower's iconic beauty and decide that it would look a whole lot better with their grinning face in front of it. It's enough to make even Edith Piaf regret what's happening in her city.

Diotrephes never went to Paris and he never saw the Eiffel Tower. He never owned a camera or a selfie-stick. Nevertheless, he was gripped by the same spirit that possesses tourists to plant their own sweet features in front of objects of great beauty. Whenever he pictured the church in his city, he always saw his own face right in front of it. John had to warn him firmly that his attitude was nothing like the true love of Jesus.

Each first-century church was led by a team of elders and overseen by apostles.[1] The elders of one church would often

---

[1] We find eldership teams in Acts 11:30, 14:23, 15:4, 20:17 and 21:18, in 1 Timothy 4:14 and 5:17, in Titus 1:5 and in James 5:14. We find them overseen by apostles in Acts 15:1–31, 1 Corinthians 1:1, 9:1–5 and 12:28–29 and in Galatians 1:1, 1:17, 1:19 and 2:8.

try to bless the elders of the other churches by sending some of their most gifted prophets, evangelists and teachers to help them bring their churches to maturity.[2] The system worked well whenever church leaders remembered that God's Kingdom is all about the glory of Jesus and the beauty of his Bride, but it fell apart whenever they forgot and started to put their own faces in the foreground of what God had pictured for their city.

F. F. Bruce argues that verse 9 ought to be translated as, *"I wrote to the church but Diotrephes, their would-be leader, refused to accept our authority."* He argues that *"the language suggests a self-promoted demagogue rather than a constitutional presbyteros or episkopos,"* although he concedes that *"It is conceivable, of course, that even a constitutional leader might have been regarded by the Elder as no better than a trumped-up dictator if he behaved in the way described here."*[3] Even if it is unclear whether Diotrephes was one of the church's elders or simply a thorn in the side of the elders, it is clear he was an egotistical and insecure attention-seeker. He saw the church as a stage for his own self-promotion, and he sent visiting preachers packing rather than allowing them to steal the limelight from him. He even resisted John's right to speak into the church as an apostle, and he bullied people out of the church if they allowed outsiders to threaten his monopoly on ministry.

John warns Gaius not to listen to Diotrephes. He tells him in verse 11 that the man's lack of *agapē* love for others proves that he is not truly a child of God. We should find this sobering, given how many church leaders and church members seem to be governed by their insecurities and by a spirit of command-

---

[2] Ephesians 4:11–13. We find references to such travelling teams in Acts 11:27–30, 13:1–3, 15:24, 18:27 and 20:2–4, in 1 Corinthians 9:1–6 and elsewhere throughout Paul's letters.

[3] F. F. Bruce in his commentary on *The Epistles of John* (1970). The two Greek words he uses are the normal New Testament words for a local church elder. Although John says literally in verse 9 that *"he does not receive us"*, many English translations take this to mean *"he does not acknowledge our authority"*.

and-control. John says that true believers act like Jesus. They display his sacrificial love and his servant-hearted lifestyle.[4]

John does more than criticize this lack of true love. He also demonstrates what true love looks like by sacrificing his own fame for the sake of the churches. He does not assert the fact that he is an apostle at the start of his letters. He introduces himself as a simple elder and does not even state his name. He is happy to be lost among the crowd of faceless elders who have served Christ faithfully throughout Church history. He does the same in his gospel, referring to himself obliquely as *"the disciple Jesus loved"*.[5] Instead of revelling in his status as the last survivor of the Twelve, he revels in his service to others. That's what the true love of Jesus looks like. It never grabs the limelight. John says in verse 4, *"I have no greater joy than to hear that my children are walking in the truth."*[6]

Gaius also demonstrates for us what true love looks like by sacrificing his own comfort for the sake of the churches. It cannot have been easy for him to receive strangers into his home just because they were travelling Christian preachers. John wants us to copy his selfless love through the same Holy Spirit who lives inside us. The travelling preachers demonstrate for us in turn what true love looks like by accepting the charity of a stranger in order to minister God's grace to people they have never met before. We should find this challenging, if we agree with Eugene Peterson's assessment of the Western Church: *"Most religion is not gospel. Most religion is idolatry. Most religion is self-aggrandisement... Religion has never been so taken up with public relations, image building, salesmanship, marketing*

---

[4] John does not accuse Diotrephes of being a false teacher, but of having a lifestyle that denies the truth. Nobody can love being first and follow Jesus at the same time (Matthew 6:33; Philippians 2:5–11).

[5] John's is the only gospel not to name him frequently. See John 13:23; 18:15; 19:26; 20:2; 21:7, 20, 24.

[6] This is not a one-off turn of phrase. John says something very similar in 2 John 4.

techniques, and the competitive spirit... We live in golden calf country. Religious feeling runs high but in ways far removed from what was said on Sinai and done on Calvary."[7] Church leaders who promote themselves are simply spoiling the view.

Demetrius also demonstrates for us what true love looks like by sacrificing his own safety for the sake of the churches, since it appears he was the delivery boy for 2 John and 3 John. No postman can ever have feared a dog as he walked up a pathway as much as Demetrius feared delivering these two letters to a church that had Diotrephes as guard dog at its front door. The willingness of Demetrius to take risks for the sake of his Christian brothers and sisters inspires John to commend him as a faithful witness in the same wholehearted manner that the elders of his own church commend him at the end of his gospel.[8] Our confession of faith in Jesus is not proved by the volume with which we express it, but by the virtue that accompanies it. True faith in Jesus always unleashes the fruit of the Holy Spirit in our lives: true selflessness, true sacrifice and true love.

As if to emphasize this, John signs off his letter without even stating his name. His focus is on how he can best serve the needs of *"the friends here"* and *"the friends there"*. His sign-off demonstrates what true love really means. He refuses to spoil the view with his own grinning face. He lives out the words of 1 John 3:16:

> This is how we know what love is: Jesus Christ laid down his life for us. And we ought to lay down our lives for our brothers and sisters.

---

[7] Eugene Peterson in *Under the Unpredictable Plant: An Exploration in Vocational Holiness* (1992).

[8] Compare 3 John 12 with John 21:24.

Conclusion: The Gospel Triumphs in the End

Everyone born of God overcomes the world. This is the victory that has overcome the world, even our faith.

(1 John 5:4)

Everybody loves a comeback story. There is Ulysses S. Grant, the army dropout and alcoholic, who overcame his drinking problem to re-enlist and lead the North to victory in the American Civil War before being elected president of the nation he had saved. There are the people of Texas, who were heavily outnumbered by the Mexicans and defeated at the Alamo, but who overcame the odds to secure independence. There is Steve Jobs, whose friends found him sobbing in his unfurnished house after being fired by the board of Apple in 1985, but who later returned to make the company that fired him one of the greatest success stories in corporate history. The list goes on. But all those comeback stories put together cannot compare with the history of the Church that the Lord founded through Peter, John and Jude and their friends. Time and time again the message of these letters has been proven true: The Gospel triumphs in the end.

Peter, John and Jude wrote these six letters at a time when the Church's enemies were convinced that it was weak enough to be defeated through threats and persecution, or through false teaching and moral compromise. One Roman governor assured his emperor that *"It seems possible to check and cure it... It is easy to imagine what numbers might be reclaimed.*"[1] Nevertheless, for all the weaknesses and struggles revealed in these letters, within 250 years the Gospel had conquered the Roman world.

Even after the Roman emperors made Christianity their state religion in the fourth century, many critics still believed the Church was in unstoppable decline. Its advance in temporal power had been accompanied by spiritual compromise and canker. They felt vindicated when Islam began its swift advance through North Africa and Southern Europe from the seventh century onwards. The Church's conquest of the world appeared, on reflection, to have been the world's conquest of the Church.

Once again the critics were proved wrong. Those devout believers who had withdrawn from the corrupted Church to pursue partnership with God in the monasteries burst back into the world with the Gospel. The monk Patrick saw Ireland converted. The monk Bede wrote such a great history of English Christianity that most medieval Englishmen assumed that loving Jesus was simply part and parcel of what it meant to be English. The monk Boniface saw large parts of Germany and Holland converted. The Spanish Franciscan Ramón Lull led the first concerted mission to the Muslims of North Africa, telling them before they killed him that *"My religion has its root and increase not, like yours, in force and warfare, but in preaching and in the shedding of blood."*[2]

When the influence of monks and devout missionaries faded in the fourteenth century, many people assumed that the power of the Gospel was spent. Then a lecturer at Oxford University named John Wycliffe translated the Bible into English and provoked the Lollard revival. One contemporary exclaimed that *"You cannot travel anywhere in England but of every two men you meet one will be a Lollard."* We need to remember this. Peter,

---

[1] We studied this letter from Pliny to Emperor Trajan in the chapter "No Surprises".

[2] He says this in his book *The Disputation of Ramón the Christian and Omar the Saracen* (1308).

John and Jude are telling the truth in their letters. No matter what the state of the Church in your nation, God wants you to trust him that the Gospel will triumph in the end.

Corruption reasserted itself in the fifteenth and sixteenth centuries. The papacy fell into the hands of the Borgias, and the Church became far more corrupt than it had ever been in the days of Peter, John and Jude. Many people assumed that it was finally game over for Christianity. Then Erasmus published the first printed Greek New Testament, aiming to undermine the clerics who had kept its message concealed from the world for so long, and *"who destroy the Gospel itself, make laws at their will, tyrannise the ordinary people, and measure right and wrong with rules constructed by themselves... who sit not in the seat of the Gospel, but in the seat of Caiaphas and Simon Magus, prelates of evil."*[3] The following year a German monk named Martin Luther echoed Erasmus when he nailed ninety-five Gospel challenges to a church door. Suddenly revival swept through Europe. The Reformation saw millions of people saved.

When the Reformation ran out of steam, the English writer Thomas Woolston looked at the sorry state of the Church in 1710 and predicted that Christianity would be wiped out by 1900. Less than thirty years later, God used John Wesley and George Whitefield to unleash another great revival across the English-speaking world – not just in Europe, but now also in America. When the French thinker Voltaire mocked them and predicted that Christianity would be destroyed within fifty years, God turned a shoemaker named William Carey into "the father of modern missions". Through his influence, the European Church took the Gospel to the unreached nations of Africa, South America, the Pacific, India, China and the rest of Asia. Instead of dying, the Church began the greatest two centuries of growth that it had ever seen. Between 1800 and 2013, the number of

---

[3] Erasmus says this in his comments on Matthew 23 in his Greek New Testament, first published in 1516.

people in Africa calling themselves Christians increased from fewer than 5 million to well over 500 million.[4] Despite the fears of eighteenth-century Christian leaders and the premature rejoicing of Voltaire, the world saw more converts to Christ in the nineteenth and twentieth centuries than in the previous eighteen centuries combined.

We need to remember this when we read surveys like the one with which we started this study of the six letters written by Peter, John and Jude. Many people will tell you that the Church is finished, that it is too weak to stand up under persecution and that it needs to chop and change the message of the Bible if it ever hopes to make Gospel inroads into the modern world. Don't listen to them. Listen instead to the three apostles who wrote these letters. They tell us that if the Spirit of God lives inside us, we have all we need to take part in the greatest comeback story of them all. They tell us that the one who came back from the dead and who will one day come back from heaven wants to launch the Church's comeback through people like you and me today.

Peter, John and Jude tell you that if Jesus dwells inside you through his Spirit, *"the one who is in you is greater than the one who is in the world."* They tell you that *"This is the victory that has overcome the world, even our faith. Who is it that overcomes the world? Only the one who believes that Jesus is the Son of God."*[5] Against a backdrop of persecution and false teaching, these apostles assure you that the Father will not allow the Son to fail in his mission, that the Son will not allow the Spirit to fail in his mission, and that the Spirit will not allow you to fail in yours. They assure you that if you hold firm to your faith in Jesus, you will see the Gospel triumph in the end.

---

[4] Data taken from a report by Gordon Conwell Theological Seminary entitled *Status of Global Mission, 2014.*

[5] 1 John 4:4; 5:4–5.

STRAIGHT TO THE HEART SERIES

TITLES AVAILABLE: OLD TESTAMENT

ISBN 978 0 85721 001 2

ISBN 978 0 85721 056 2

ISBN 978 0 85721 252 8

ISBN 978 0 85721 428 7

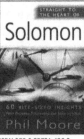

ISBN 978 0 85721 426 3

ISBN 978 0 85721 754 7

STRAIGHT TO THE HEART SERIES

TITLES AVAILABLE: NEW TESTAMENT

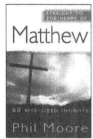

STRAIGHT TO THE HEART OF
Matthew
60 BITE-SIZED INSIGHTS
Phil Moore

ISBN 978 1 85424 988 3

STRAIGHT TO THE HEART OF
Mark
60 BITE-SIZED INSIGHTS
Phil Moore

ISBN 978 0 85721 642 7

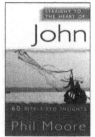

STRAIGHT TO THE HEART OF
John
60 BITE-SIZED INSIGHTS
Phil Moore

ISBN 978 0 85721 253 5

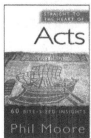

STRAIGHT TO THE HEART OF
Acts
60 BITE-SIZED INSIGHTS
Phil Moore

ISBN 978 1 85424 989 0

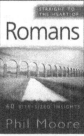

STRAIGHT TO THE HEART OF
Romans
60 BITE-SIZED INSIGHTS
Phil Moore

ISBN 978 0 85721 057 9

STRAIGHT TO THE HEART OF
1&2 Corinthians
60 BITE-SIZED INSIGHTS
Phil Moore

ISBN 978 0 85721 002 9

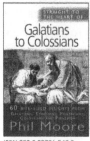

STRAIGHT TO THE HEART OF
Galatians
to Colossians
60 BITE-SIZED INSIGHTS FROM
GALATIANS, EPHESIANS, PHILIPPIANS,
COLOSSIANS AND PHILEMON
Phil Moore

ISBN 978 0 85721 546 8

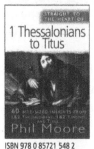

STRAIGHT TO THE HEART OF
1 Thessalonians
to Titus
60 BITE-SIZED INSIGHTS FROM
1&2 THESSALONIANS, 1&2 TIMOTHY,
AND TITUS
Phil Moore

ISBN 978 0 85721 548 2

STRAIGHT TO THE HEART OF
Hebrews
& James
60 BITE-SIZED INSIGHTS
Phil Moore

ISBN 978 0 85721 668 7

STRAIGHT TO THE HEART OF
Peter, John & Jude
60 BITE-SIZED INSIGHTS
Phil Moore

ISBN 978 0 85721 756 1

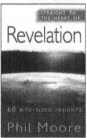

STRAIGHT TO THE HEART OF
Revelation
60 BITE-SIZED INSIGHTS
Phil Moore

ISBN 978 1 85424 990 6

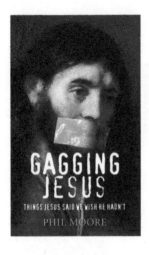

GAGGING JESUS
Things Jesus Said We Wish He Hadn't
Phil Moore

"Whether you are a believer or merely a curious sceptic, this book will help you to discover Jesus as he really is."
Sandy Millar, co-founder of the Alpha Course

Jesus of Nazareth wasn't afraid to tell it like it is. Those who claim to follow him, on the other hand, often are.

It's easy to settle for a tamed and domesticated Jesus. A bound-and-gagged Jesus. A Jesus of our own thinking. That's why this book focuses on the fifteen most outrageous things Jesus said: the fifteen things you are least likely to hear preached about in church.

If you ever suspected that Jesus wasn't crucified for acting like a polite vicar in a pair of socks and sandals, then this book is for you. Fasten your seatbelt and get ready to discover the real Jesus in all his outrageous, ungagged glory.

"Downright dangerous! It demands attention. Prepare to be shocked, undone, and put back together again."
Greg Haslam, Senior Pastor, Westminster Chapel, London, UK

ISBN: 978 0 85721 453 9

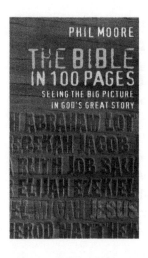

THE BIBLE IN 100 PAGES
Seeing the Big Picture in God's Great Story
Phil Moore

"If you want to get a grip on the Bible, this is a great place to start."
R. T. Kendall, theologian and author of *Sermon on the Mount*

Most people want to discover the message of the Bible. The problem is simply that they are too busy. It just looks far too long. When they do read it, they often find it hard to see the wood for the trees amongst its 66 books, 1,189 chapters and 31,102 verses. That's why *The Bible in 100 Pages* is so important. It will help you to see the big picture in God's great story. It will help you to read the Bible with fresh eyes.

"Bold, fresh, fast-moving, relevant and often controversial, The Bible in 100 Pages *gives you the best of Phil Moore, and the best of the Bible. An excellent resource for anyone wanting to get their heads round the biblical story."*
Andrew Wilson, author of *If God, Then What?*

ISBN 978 0 85721 551 2

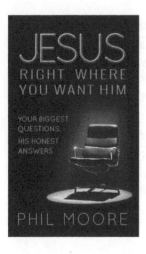

JESUS RIGHT WHERE YOU WANT HIM
**Your Biggest Questions.
His Honest Answers.**
Phil Moore

*"I enjoy Phil Moore's books. He writes
about Jesus and the Christian life
with perception, wisdom and wit."*
**Nicky Gumbel, co-founder of the
Alpha Course**

We all have tough questions we would like to ask Jesus. Most of
us assume we will never get an answer.

But Jesus welcomes people's questions. This book takes
your fifteen toughest questions and sees what happens when
Jesus places himself right where we want him to answer them.
There are no excuses and no evasiveness. Just honest answers.

*"Jesus loved responding to confrontation. Phil Moore has
provided you with an excellent resource to help you grill Jesus
with your toughest questions and to hear him respond from the
pages of the Bible."*
Terry Virgo, founder of Newfrontiers

ISBN: 978 0 85721 677 9